Cyberkids

Children are at the heart of contemporary debates about the possibilities and dangers that new Information and Communication Technologies might bring.

Cyberkids: Children in the Information Age draws upon extensive research with teenagers at school and home to explore children's on-line and off-line identities, communities and sense of place in the world.

Stimulating and insightful, the book addresses key policy debates about social inclusion and exclusion, as well as academic debates about embodiment/disembodiment and 'real'/'virtual' worlds. It counters contemporary moral panics about the risk from dangerous strangers on-line, the corruption of innocence by adult-oriented material on the web and the addiction to life on the screen. Instead, *Cyberkids* shows how children use ICT in balanced and sophisticated ways and, in doing so, draws out the importance of everyday uses of technology.

Sarah L. Holloway is a lecturer in Geography at the University of Loughborough. **Gill Valentine** is Professor of Geography at the University of Sheffield.

Cyberkids

Children in the Information Age

Sarah L. Holloway and
Gill Valentine

RoutledgeFalmer
Taylor & Francis Group

LONDON AND NEW YORK

First published 2003
by RoutledgeFalmer
11 New Fetter Lane, London EC4P 4EE

Simultaneously published in the USA and Canada
by RoutledgeFalmer
29 West 35th Street, New York, NY 10001

RoutledgeFalmer is an imprint of the Taylor & Francis Group

© 2003 Sarah L. Holloway and Gill Valentine

Typeset in Sabon by
M Rules
Printed and bound in Great Britain by
St Edmundsbury Press, Bury St Edmunds, Suffolk

British Library Cataloguing in Publication Data
A catalogue record for this book is available from the
British Library

Library of Congress Cataloging in Publication Data
A catalog record for this book has been requested

ISBN 0–415–23058–6 (hbk)
ISBN 0–415–23059–4 (pbk)

Contents

List of figures   vii
Acknowledgements   ix

1   Cyberworlds: children in the Information Age   1

2   The digital divide? Children, ICT and social exclusion   20

3   Peer pressure: ICT in the classroom   42

4   On-line dangers: questions of competence and risk   72

5   Life around the screen: the place of ICT in the
    'family' home   99

6   Cybergeographies: children's on-line worlds   127

7   Bringing children and technology together   153

    Notes   160
    References   162
    Index   177

Figures

3.1	Surfing for pornography on-line reinforces boys' understandings of themselves as heterosexual young men	56
4.1	Parents need guidelines to help them raise children in the digital age	86
4.2	'Net nanny' filter systems provide one curb on children's on-line excesses	89
5.1	The computer is implicated in the development of children's bedroom culture	111
5.2	The location of the PC in a shared space can provide a gathering point for members of the family	111
5.3	How the PC 'fits' into children's everyday lives: a Westport after-school time-budget diary	120
6. 1	The Internet provides children with a window on the wider world	151

Acknowledgements

We are grateful to the ESRC for funding the research *Cyberkids: children's social networks, 'virtual communities' and on-line spaces* on which this book is based (award number L129 25 1055). Gill Valentine wishes to acknowledge the support of the Philip Leverhulme Prize in enabling her to work on this manuscript.

Thanks are also due to Nick Bingham who was employed as a research assistant on this project. Charlotte Kenten provided an invaluable service tracking down references, statistics and websites. We are indebted to the children, parents and teachers from our three case-study schools who allowed us into their homes and classrooms and gave up their time to talk to us about the role of information and communication technologies in their lives.

The 'Cyberkids' project that this book draws upon was part of the ESRC Children's 5–16 Programme. We wish to acknowledge our appreciation of the guidance we received from its director Professor Alan Prout, the intellectual and social exchanges we enjoyed with the other award holders at programme meetings, but most particularly all the encouragement and support we received from Professor Chris Philo of our steering committee.

Chris Durbin played a key role in helping us to get the research off the ground. Chapter 6 includes material produced as part of the involvement of one of our case-study schools, Westport, with the *Interlink* initiative. This was commissioned by the British Council in New Zealand as part of their 50th year celebrations. *Interlink* was developed and managed by Copeland Wilson and Associates (CWA) Ltd, New Zealand. CWA is a specialist producer of education learning materials across all media (www.cwa.co.nz).

Deborah Sporton and Charles Pattie have provided Gill with occasional, much needed technical support not to mention numerous cups of coffee and a welcome social diversion from work. Sarah O'Hara has put up with endless discussions about the Cyberkids project, and provided both Gill and Sarah with food and liquid sustenance at key moments during the project.

This book was commissioned by Anna Clarkson. We are very grateful to her, and her editorial assistants, for the support they have shown for this proposal and for waiting so patiently for the final manuscript to be delivered.

The quality of the final product is largely due to the hard work of Susan Dunsmore, the copyeditor, Sonia Pati, the production editor, and M Rules for the project management.

We are grateful to Jacky Fleming for permission to reproduce Figure 3.1 (page 56) and to *The Sheffield Telegraph* for permission to reproduce Figures 4.1 (page 86) and 6.1 (page 149). Every attempt has been made to obtain permission to reproduce copyright material. If any proper acknowledgement has not been made, we would invite copyright holders to inform us of the oversight.

Chapter 1

Cyberworlds
Children in the Information Age

Cyberspace is one of 'the zones that scripts the future' (Haraway 1997: 100). Just as industrial technology was seen to transform Western society in the nineteenth century, so many contemporary academic and popular commentators argue that Information and Communication Technologies (ICT) are about to inflict far-reaching economic, social, cultural, and political changes upon the twenty-first century (for an overview see Kitchin 1998a, 1998b). Most notably, ICT are popularly understood to be about, if they have not already led to, the transformation of work and the production of value, as manufacturing is substituted by information as the dominant form of employment (Marshall 1997). The opportunities that ICT offer users to access information and communicate with whom they want, freed from the material and social constraints of their bodies, identities, communities and geographies mean that these technologies are regarded as potentially liberating for those who are socially, materially or physically disadvantaged (Turkle 1995). Likewise, the speed and connectivity of the Internet offer scope to facilitate greater participation in the political process, to re-scale politics from the local or nation to the global, and to produce more informed democracy. However, these opportunities also bring new risks. Most notably that those who lack technological skills to participate in the Information Age will be excluded from these activities and, unable to exercise their rights and responsibilities, will consequently be denied full citizenship.

Children, as symbols of the future themselves, are at the heart of debates both about how the possibilities that ICT afford should be realised, and about the 'new' dangers that these technologies might also bring for the Net generation. The British Prime Minister's statement that 'Children cannot be effective in tomorrow's world if they are trained in yesterday's skills' echoes a similar point made in a Labour Party document *Communicating Britain's Future*.[1] This claims that:

> We stand on the threshold of a revolution as profound as that brought by the invention of the printing press. New technologies, which enable rapid communication to take place in a myriad of different ways around

the globe, and permit information to be provided, sought and received on a scale so far unimaginable, will bring fundamental changes to our lives . . . In many ways it will be in education that the greatest potential use for the new networks will emerge.

(The Labour Party 1995: 3, 18)

While supporting such political aims to advance children's technological literacy, popular commentaries have also highlighted the fact that children may be at risk of corruption from material that they can find on the Internet, and abuse at the hands of strangers whom they might encounter in on-line spaces (Wilkinson 1995; McMurdo 1997; Evans and Butkus 1997). These fears are exacerbated by the fact that parents and teachers – particularly those who are less technologically literate than the young people in their care – have a limited ability to control or filter what children might see and learn on the World-Wide-Web (henceforth WWW). The Internet-connected PC, as the latest form of media (following on from television, stereos, console games, etc.) to play an important role in children's peer group relationships (Suss et al. 2001), is also imagined to threaten children's off-line activities. Popular concerns have been expressed that using a computer is a solitary and potentially addictive activity, provoking fears that some children might become so obsessed with the technology that they will socially withdraw from the off-line world of family and friends (Hapnes 1996). In doing so it is suggested that they will also miss out on the imaginative opportunities for outdoor play that public space is perceived to offer, putting not only their social, but also their physical well-being at risk (Gumpert and Drucker 1998; McCellan 1994). In such ways, ICT are regarded by some as a potential threat, not only to individual children, but also to childhood as an institution because of their potential to threaten childhood 'innocence' and blur the differentiation which is commonly made between the states of childhood and adulthood.

Despite these fears in the popular imagination, little is known about how children actually employ ICT within the context of their everyday lives. We suggest that two key factors contribute to this oversight. First, children and young people are a social group that has been relatively neglected by academic research. Sociology has been criticised as an adultist discipline (see the following section), prompting a new theoretical turn in the study of children and childhood (James et al. 1998). A similar accusation has also been levelled at Geography (see also the following section). While there is a small but significant literature about children's geographies that dates back to the 1970s (Bunge 1973; Hart 1979), it is only recently that research in this sub-field of the discipline has reached a critical mass (Holloway and Valentine 2000a). As such, it is widely acknowledged in the social sciences that as adults we still know relatively little about children's own social worlds.

Second, despite the growing importance of ICT in the contemporary

Western world, there are surprisingly few empirical studies of how people actually use these technologies in an everyday context. Much of the contemporary writing about cyberspace in the social sciences is theoretical rather than empirically informed. Where research has focused on actual practices, this has tended to concentrate on the growth of on-line cultures through Multi User Domain (MUD) environments (textual virtual environments created by a programmer or participants) (see, for example, Turkle 1995). In other words, it has primarily focused on extreme users and utopian visions of virtual life rather than looking at the complex ways that ICT is used, and made sense of, in everyday worlds (Kitchin 1998a, 1998b).

This book is important because in it we address the issues raised above through an empirical investigation of the ways that ICT are used in practice by British children aged 11 to 16. The material we present, from children's own accounts of their on-line and off-line worlds, not only advances our theoretical understanding of children as social actors, it also has the potential to inform public policy initiatives designed to promote children's technological literacy, and to contribute to the popular debates about the threats ICT may pose to children and childhood.

In this chapter we first introduce the understanding of children and childhood that underpins the way the research upon which this book is based was conducted. Then we introduce our understanding of technology by outlining some of the theoretical debates about ICT, drawn from the social studies of technology and geographies of cyberspace. Finally, we introduce the empirical research upon which this book is based and outline the structure of the six chapters that follow.

Introducing children

'Child' appears at face value to be a biologically defined category determined by chronological age. Children are assumed by the nature of their youth to be not only biologically, but also socially less developed than adults. The notion of immaturity, for example, is used not only to refer to children's physical bodies but also to their presumed lack of social, intellectual, emotional and practical knowledge and competencies. This less-than-adult status means that childhood is understood as a period in which children have to be schooled in their future adult roles. The process of learning to become an adult takes place not only through the educational system, but also the everyday processes of socialisation that children undergo as part of family and wider civic life. The flipside of being treated as less-than-adults is that children in the West are assumed to have the right to a childhood of innocence and freedom from the responsibilities of the adult world (though in practice poverty, ill-health and so on rob many children of the right to enjoy such a childhood). As such, we, as adults, are charged with the duty to both provide for children in the widest sense (materially, emotionally, etc.), and to protect them from dangerous information, situations and people that might pose a threat to their 'innocence' and 'freedoms' (Holloway and Valentine, 2000a).

This essentialist understanding of children as a homogeneous social group defined by their biology, that in turn positions them as 'other' in relation to adults, has been critiqued by academics from across the social sciences. Rather, like many other social identities, 'child' has been demonstrated to be a socially constructed identity. Cultural historians, for example, have shown that the contemporary understanding of children in the West as less developed, less able and less competent than adults (Waksler 1991) is historically specific (see, for example, Ariès 1962; Hendrick 1990; Steedman 1990; Stainton-Rogers and Stainton-Rogers 1992). The work of Ariès (1962), whose study of mainly French cultural artefacts has been generalised to the rest of the Western world (Jenks 1996), is commonly used as evidence of the socially constructed nature of childhood. He demonstrated that in the Middle Ages young people, rather than being imagined as a distinct social category, were actually regarded as miniature adults. It was only in the sixteenth century, when children began to emerge as playthings for adults from privileged backgrounds, that they started to be defined in opposition to adults. It is from the Enlightenment onwards that this understanding of the category 'child', as inherently different from 'adult', has gone on to dominate our social imagination (Jenks 1996).

Within this understanding of childhood, Jenks points to two different ways of thinking and talking about children. He labels these Dionysian and Apollonian. Dionysian understandings of childhood view children as 'little devils', who are inherently naughty, unruly, and must be disciplined and socialised into adult ways in order to become fully human. In contrast, Apollonian views of childhood which emerged later, conceptualise children as born inherently 'good', only for the 'natural' virtue and innocence of these 'little angels' to be corrupted by adults as they are socialised into adulthood. These ideas underpin the emergence in the nineteenth century of a concern for the education and welfare of children, which is evidenced in the contemporary provision and/or regulation of much childcare, education, and interventionist welfare services. Although notions of the Apollonian child emerged after that of the Dionysian child, the former did not supplant the latter. Rather, both apparently contradictory understandings of the child continue to be mobilised in contemporary Western societies (Stainton-Rogers and Stainton-Rogers 1992; Jenks 1996; Valentine 1996a).

Even though these conceptualisations of childhood draw on essentialist understandings of children as inherently good, or bad, by demonstrating the historical specificity of childhood in the Western world, they prove that far from being a biological category, childhood is a socially constructed identity. Yet, the boundaries that mark the divide between child and adult are not clearly defined. James (1986) cites a number of legal classifications, such as the age at which young people can consume alcohol, earn money, join the armed forces, and consent to sexual intercourse, to show how the definitions of where childhood ends and adulthood begins in the UK are variable, context-specific and gendered. Such variations are equally evident between countries, and are also contested by different groups of children and adults, providing further proof of the social nature of childhood.

One 'academic' consequence of the social construction of child as less than adult, and childhood as a phase of socialisation, is that research on children has been less valued than that on other topics (Holloway and Valentine 2000b). In the mid- to late-1980s a variety of authors began to bemoan the lack of research on young people. Ambert (1986), for example, identified the invisibility of children in North American sociological research, claiming that this reflected the continuing influence of founding theorists whose preoccupations were shaped by the patriarchal values of the societies in which they lived. She also argued that the system of rewards within the discipline that favours research on the 'big issues' such as class, bureaucracies or the political system contributes to the devaluation and marginalisation of children as a legitimate research subject. Brannen and O'Brien (1995) point out that the position is little different in British sociology where children and childhood have tended to be ignored, with children only being studied indirectly in sub-disciplinary areas such as the family or education. Here, children tended to be regarded as human becomings rather than human beings, who through the process of socialisation are to be shaped into adults. This understanding of children as incompetent and incomplete 'adults in the making rather than children in the state of being' (ibid.: 70) means that it is the forces of socialisation – the family, the school – that have tended to receive attention rather than children themselves (James *et al.* 1998: 25).

This relative absence of children from the sociological research agenda is increasingly being challenged. A number of key texts (e.g. James and Prout 1990; Qvortrup *et al.* 1994; Mayall 1994; James *et al.* 1998) are beginning to define a new paradigm in the sociology of childhood. This recognises children as competent social actors in their own right (beings rather than becomings) and acknowledges children's understandings and experiences of their own childhoods. A growing body of work within the sociology of education is also beginning to draw attention to children's agency in relation to questions of identity and difference in the school setting (e.g. Skeggs 1991; Dixon 1997; Epstein 1997). In making the claim that such work marks an epistemological break with earlier studies, James *et al.* (1998) identify this approach to the study of children as 'the new social studies of childhood'. This name reflects a growing cross-fertilisation of ideas between researchers in a variety of social science disciplines, linkages that have contributed (among other things) to a renewal of interest within Geography in children as social actors (Holloway and Valentine 2000a).

Like Sociology, and for much the same reasons, children have not been a traditional focus of concern in geography (see James 1990). Though as we suggested earlier, there is a small but significant literature about children's environments that dates back to the 1970s (Blaut and Stea 1971; Bunge 1973). This work was marked by two discernible differences in approach that persist today. One, informed by psychology, has focused on children's spatial cognition and mapping abilities (e.g. Blaut and Stea 1971; Matthews 1987; Blaut 1991). The other, inspired by Bunge's (1973) pioneering work on children's spatial oppression (through which he sought to give children, as a minority group, a voice in an adultist world) but more recently informed by new social studies of childhood, addresses children's access to, use and attachment to space (Hart 1979).

Geographical research contributes to social studies of childhood by providing evidence for the ways that childhood is constructed differently, not only in different times but also in different places (Holloway and Valentine 2000b). In this book, for example, we show in Chapter 2 how place matters by demonstrating the wide variations that exist in children's access to ICT at global, national and local scales. At the same time, however, we also seek to illustrate the connections between these global and local processes (see Chapter 6). In classifying work within the new social studies of childhood, James *et al.* (1998) identify an irreconcilable split between research which is global in its focus (e.g. by examining the importance of global processes in shaping children's position in different societies of the world) and that which has more local concerns (e.g. work showing how children are important in creating their own cultures and lifeworlds). By employing an alternative, and more thoroughly spatial understanding of global/local, geographical work transcends this dichotomy to reveal a more complex picture. For example, in a study of New York and a village in Sudan, Katz (1993) has demonstrated that local manifestations of global restructuring have had serious, and negative, consequences for children in both locations. At the same time her study illustrates how these 'global processes' are worked out in 'local' places through 'local' cultures. In doing so, Katz shows that the global and local are not irreconcilably split, but rather are mutually constituted. It is an approach that we also adopt in this book, most notably in Chapter 6 where we consider how children's use of the WWW is at one and the same time both global and local.

A second, and related, way that geographers have examined the spatiality of childhood is by focusing on the everyday spaces in, and through which, children's identities and lives are produced and reproduced (Holloway and Valentine 2000b). The street, and 'public' space in general, have been key sites of concern in geographical studies of children's access to, use of, and attachment to, space. Most recently work has centred on contemporary concerns in North America and Europe about children's presence in 'public' spaces. These are characterised by twin fears, on the one hand, that some (Apollonian) children are vulnerable to dangers in 'public' places, and on the other hand that the unruly behaviour of other (Dionysian) children can threaten adult hegemony in 'public' space (Valentine 1996a, 1996b). As we explain in Chapter 4, these same fears are also apparent in debates about children in cyberspace. Indeed, Jackson and Scott (1999) argue that notions of risk and safety are increasingly central to the construction of childhood. They write:

> Because children are . . . constituted as a protected species and childhood as a protected state, both become loci of risk and anxiety: safeguarding children entails keeping danger at bay; preserving childhood entails guarding against anything which threatens it. Conversely, risk anxiety helps construct childhood and maintain its boundaries – the specific risks from which children must be protected serve to define the characteristics of childhood and the 'nature' of children themselves.
> (Jackson and Scott 1999: 86–87)

Schools are one particular institutional space through which adults attempt to control and discipline children. In doing so, Aitken (1994) argues that they serve wider stratified society, preparing young people to assume roles considered appropriate to their race, class and gender identities. A number of geographical studies have been concerned with these moral landscapes, including both the historical context of Victorian reformatory schools (Ploszajska 1994) and the contemporary context of primary schools (Fielding 2000). Contemporary geographical research also illustrates the importance of schools as sites through which gender and sexual identities are made and remade. Hyams (2000) has examined discourses of femininity among Latina girls in Los Angeles, showing how ideas about appropriate femininities both structure, and are contested through, the girls' everyday practices. In Chapter 3, we focus not only on the production of femininities, but also on masculinities, within the context of the heterosexual economy of the classroom. This chapter builds on our consideration of children's access to ICT within the institutional context of the school outlined in the previous chapter. Here, we consider how national discourses about children and the Information Age are (re)negotiated by schools through their specific policies on information technology according to the schools' assessments of the needs of the local communities that they serve.

The home is a space that has been of particular relevance to feminist geographers who have been concerned with gender relations within households headed by heterosexual couples (see, for example, England 1996). As such, other members of these families, mainly children but also elders, have often been constructed in terms of the time/care demands they place upon the household rather in terms of their role as social actors in their own right. Recent work on children and parenting, however, has identified the home as an important site for the negotiation of adult–child power relations (e.g.

Aitken 1994; Sibley 1995; Valentine 1999a, 1999b). Indeed, the home itself is a space that is constituted through familial rules that demarcate appropriate ways for children to behave (Wood and Beck 1990). Some of this research has drawn attention to the power of children's voices within the household. This is not only in terms of their ability to articulate their own identities and desires, but also in terms of their ability to shape the identity and practices of the household as a whole (Valentine 1999a).

In part, the willingness of parents to acknowledge children as social actors in their own right is a reflection of the value of their offspring to them. Within the context of individualisation Beck and Beck-Gernsheim (1995) suggest that parents feel increasingly responsible for their children and under pressure to invest in their childhoods in order to maximise the children's opportunities and chances of success in adulthood. In doing so parents are not only thinking of their offspring but also of themselves. This is not only because young people can be a conduit for parents to live out their own hopes and ambitions (Beck and Beck-Gernsheim 1995; Jackson and Scott 1999) but also because being a 'good' parent is a rewarding identity in its own right. Geographical research has had an important role to play in exploring the connections between childhood and adulthood as discursive constructions and in examining a variety of spatial discourses. A number of studies have identified local communities as important sites through which understandings of what it means to be a 'good' mother or father and specific parenting cultures are developed (Dyck 1990; Holloway 1998; Valentine 1997a). In a less predictable world these definitions are increasingly structured around the ability of parents to protect their children from social and physical risks.

In the case of children's use of ICT adult anxieties about children's use of the Internet are heightened by the discursive construction of children's safety on-line as the responsibility of their parents, yet young people's technical competencies often exceed those who are charged with protecting them. While some parents regard children's skills as a threat to their status as adults, others embrace the opportunities ICT offers to renegotiate their relationships with young people. Debates about children's safety and competence are also negotiated through spatial discourses about the spaces of the home and the Internet. We explore these issues in Chapter 4. The importance we identify here, of children and parents to each other's social identities, highlights the need to look at children's accounts of their lifeworlds within the context of their 'family' relationships. As such, in Chapter 5 we focus on the role that the home PC plays in the constitution of 'the family' and in the production of domestic time-spaces. Here we use the term 'family' not just to describe traditional nuclear families but to cover the diverse, fluid and complex living arrangements of modern households (Stacey 1990).

To summarise, therefore, in this book we understand children to be social actors within their own right. We recognise, however, that children's identities are constituted in and through particular places, spaces and spatial discourses (Holloway and Valentine, 2000b). Here we focus on the sites of school, home and cyberspace. At the same time we acknowledge the ways that understandings of childhood can also shape the meaning of these spaces and places. Throughout the book we challenge the split between global and local approaches to childhood by showing how children's everyday use of ICT is situated within the context of shifts in the global economy, and national educational policies and by examining how children's on-line activities are constituted and interpreted within the context of local cultures. In doing so, this book contributes to interdisciplinary work on children and parenting in four significant ways. First, we advance the notion that children's identities and relationships are constituted not only through their relations with other people, but also through their relationships with 'things' that we share our world with, in this case, the Internet-connected PC. Second, we redress the paucity of studies that examine children's ICT usage in different socio-spatial environments. This relative lack of attention to the ways in which children use ICT in different off-line spaces is important because, as James and Prout (1995) suggest in a different context, certain styles of agency are foregrounded in some social environments, with other styles being more appropriate elsewhere. In so doing, our aim is also to learn more about the ways in which these off-line environments are geographically constituted through their links with other places and spaces, by the actions of individuals within those spaces, and through ideas about appropriate childhood spaces. Third, through our focus on questions of risk and competence in this book we explore the possibilities that exist for children to renegotiate the flexible boundaries of adulthood and childhood. Finally, we do not treat children as a homogeneous category but rather focus on questions of difference, not only between traditional social categories such as gender, but also within them.

Introducing technology

In the initial flood of academic and popular commentaries on cyberspace a clear opposition has often been drawn between off-line and on-line worlds, or the 'real' and the 'virtual' (Laurel 1990; Heim 1991; Springer 1991). In such representations the two worlds are viewed as distinct or unconnected from each other and as possessing different, usually oppositional (see Doel and Clarke 1999), qualities. For some commentators (e.g. Heim 1991; Thu Nguyen and Alexander 1996), whom we have termed 'boosters' (Bingham *et al.* 1999), 'virtual' space is understood to be an advance on the 'real' world, an opportunity to overcome its limitations. For others (e.g. McLaughlin *et al.* 1995), whom we label 'debunkers', the 'virtual' is regarded as inauthentic, a poor imitation of the 'real'.

Notably, on-line worlds have been uncritically celebrated by boosters as disembodied spaces in contrast to the materiality of 'real-world' environments. As such, this technology has been heralded for the possibilities it is perceived to offer its users to escape the constraints of their material surroundings and bodies by enabling them to create and play with on-line identities (Springer 1991, Plant 1996). In these terms the human body is regarded not only as invisible on-line but also as temporarily suspended such that it becomes a complete irrelevance (Thu Nguyen and Alexander 1996). In this way, cyberspace is claimed to offer its users an escape from social inequalities – such as racism or gender discrimination – that relate to their embodiment (Turkle 1995). In a similar vein boosters have also claimed that ICT create new forms of social relationships in which participants are no longer bound by the need to meet others face-to-face but rather can expand their social terrain by meeting others located around the globe on-line, mind-to-mind. This is a privileging of mind over body that characterises masculinist rationality. Some observers even claim that 'virtual' relationships are more intimate, richer and liberating than off-line friendships because they are based on genuine mutual interest rather than the coincidence of off-line proximity. In all these representations 'virtual' space is characterised as a space that is not just set apart from everyday life, but also one that offers the possibility to transcend everyday life. It is a zone of freedom, fluidity and experimentation that is insulated from the mundane realities of the material world (Springer 1991; Laurel 1990). In Doel and Clarke's (1999) terms it provides a hyper-realisation of the real.

Like the boosters, debunkers also view the 'real' and the 'virtual' as both different and separate worlds. However, for these commentators on-line worlds are viewed as unambiguously bad. The 'virtual' is conceptualised as a poor substitute for the 'real world'. Disembodied identities are viewed as superficial and inauthentic compared with embodied identities. Likewise, on-line forms of communication are regarded as fleeting, individualised and one-dimensional exchanges in contrast to the more permanent and complex nature of human engagements in the off-line world (McLaughlin et al. 1995). ICT users are often characterised as so immersed in on-line culture that they become detached from their off-line social and physical surroundings and consequently their responsibilities in the 'real' world (Willson 1997). For example, as we argue above, some commentaries paint a picture of children as so absorbed in their on-line worlds that they reject 'the real', becoming detached from off-line social and familial relationships and withdrawing from public outdoor space into on-line fantasy spaces (see Chapter 5). In these understandings the 'real' is represented as a fragile world under threat from the seductive lure of the 'virtual' (Doel and Clarke 1999).

While boosters and debunkers differ about whether the development of on-line worlds are positive or negative, what they share is a tendency to regard the 'real' and the 'virtual' as not only different, but also as discrete. Research on cybercultures has commonly focused on users' on-line activities, ignoring the way that these activities remain embedded within the context of the off-line spaces, and the social relations of everyday life. Such understandings of the relationship between on-line and off-line worlds are now increasingly subject to critique (see, for example, essays in Crang *et al.* 1999). For example, the ability to access on-line space presupposes certain off-line material resources, not least access to a computer and the electricity to run it. Given the digital divide in terms of access to ICT both between countries/parts of the world and within them (a point we focus on in Chapter 2), not everyone is equally positioned to take advantage of on-line opportunities (Kitchin 1998a). The importance of the off-line spaces in which technologies are accessed has also been highlighted by Wakeford (1999). She refers to cyber cafés as 'translation landscape[s]', off-line spaces through which on-line spaces are produced, mediated and consumed. The 'translation landscapes' we focus on in this book are the school (Chapters 2 and 3) and the home (Chapters 4 and 5).

Other writers have disputed imaginings of the 'real' and the 'virtual' in opposition to each other arguing that 'virtual geography is no more or less "real"' (Wark 1994: vii). In a study of the use of the Internet by community organisations in Chicago, Light (1997) criticises the way that ICT are perceived to threaten the vitality of 'real' cities. Her observations suggest that on-line activities, rather than being set in opposition to the off-line world, provide new ways to revitalise people's engagement with the urban environment. Other authors have also begun to question the discourse of disembodiment. Sobchack's (1995) account of experiencing post-operative pain while on-line, exposes the error of the boosters' claims that ICT enable users to transcend their physical bodies. Green (1997: 63) observes that:

> Attending only to digital spaces ignores the physicality of technological production and consumption in everyday processes of interaction and the negotiation of meaning that occurs during such encounters. Disregarding this is precisely what has allowed the discourse of disembodiment to become so prevelant in both popular and academic discussions of cyberspace.

Critiques are also emerging of the debunkers' claims that on-line interactions and relationships are not only distinct from, but also less authentic than, off-line encounters. As Smith (1992) comments:

> Despite the unique qualities of the social spaces to be found in virtual worlds, people do not enter new terrains empty-handed. We carry with us the sum-total of our experiences and expectations generated in more familiar social spaces.

Yet, despite the growing unease with the ways that on-line and off-line spaces are often dichotomised, research has so far failed to map the complex ways that on-line activities are embedded within 'real-world' lives (Kitchin 1998a). In this book we reject any suggestion that on-line and off-line worlds are oppositionally different or unconnected. Rather, by focusing on children's situated consumption of ICT, our aim is to provide primary empirical material which demonstrates *how* on-line spaces are used, encountered and interpreted within the context of young people's off-line everyday lives. In doing so we consider the mutual constitution of the 'real' and the 'virtual'.

By examining how children and technology come together, however, we want to reject any simple technological determinism. By technological determinism we mean narratives in which a 'new' technology is presumed to *impact* (either positively or negatively) on society, replacing what has gone before, and producing a predictable set of effects which are presumed to be more or less the same everywhere (Bingham *et al.* 2001). Technologically determinist accounts are commonly apocolyptical in that they usually draw on metaphors of inevitable change in which people are seen as under threat from techno-'shocks' or 'waves' (Thrift 1996; Bingham 1996). As such, they ignore the way that the impact of any technology varies according to specificities of time and place, who is using it and their intentions, and the other agendas to which technology may become attached (Thrift 1996; Bingham *et al.* 2001). It is what Bryson and de Castell (1994) term an 'artifactual' view, where technology is severed from the normative social context. As Thrift explains:

> What is missing from technologically deterministic accounts . . . is any concerted sense of new electronic communication technologies as part of a long history of rich and often wayward social *practices* (including the interpretation of those practices) through which we have become *socially acquainted* with these technologies.
>
> (1996: 1472)

Despite such criticisms, Winston (1995) observes that technological determinism is still popularly employed to explain material–social change. This is perhaps most apparent in the theorisations of ICT.

Bromley (1997) cautions, however, against adopting the polar position, viewing technology as a 'neutral tool' whose impact is entirely determined by the intentions of its users. Authors who take this approach commonly fall into the trap of assuming that the meanings of technology are stable and unproblematic. This is because they do not acknowledge the interpretive processes that are part of all of the practices through which we become socially acquainted with technologies, from their design manufacturer and marketing, through to their domestication (see Chapter 5) in the home or workplace (Thrift 1996; Bingham 1996). In other words, they substitute a technological determinism with a social determinism in which the assumption is that only people have the status of actors (Ackrich 1992).

Wajcman (1991) labels these two positions use/abuse and social shaping models. Both are based on setting up false and unproductive oppositions between 'technology' and 'society' in which either strong technology impacts on weak society or strong society shapes weak technology (Bingham 1996). As such, they ignore the mutual implication and complication of bodies and objects.

An alternative approach is offered by scholars from the social studies of technology such as Michel Callon (1991), Bruno Latour (1993) and John Law (1994). These writers argue that we always live amongst, and are surrounded by, objects, and that these bits and pieces that we enter into assemblage with matter. As such, we need to recast the social to include non-humans. Callon and Latour (1981), for example, point out that it is our use of objects that is one of the things that differentiates us from animals such as baboons. Whereas baboons only form associations and order their social worlds through actions between one body and another, as humans we use a range of objects or 'props' to mobilise, stabilise and order our society. In these terms, agency is not something possessed by humans but rather is an effect generated by a 'network of heterogenous, interacting materials' (Law 1994: 383). It is therefore both precarious and contingent. Callon and Law (1995: 484) further demonstrate this point with what they call a thought experiment. Referring to the example of an imaginary office manager called Andrew they write:

> [J]ust imagine what would happen if they took away Andrew's telephone and his fax machine. If they blocked the flow of papers and reports. Imagine what would happen if they shut down the railway line to London and stopped him from using his car . . . Then imagine, also, that his secretary were to disappear. And his room, with its conference table, its PC and electronic mail were to vanish.

In other words, the world cannot be unproblematically divided up into 'things' (on the one hand) and 'the social' (on the other) (Bingham 1996). Rather, in order to understand human activity and society we need 'to take full account of those crowds of non-humans mingled with humans' (Latour 1988: 16).

For these advocates of what has become known as Actor Network Theory (ANT), society is produced in and through patterned networks of heterogeneous materials in which the properties of humans and non-humans are not self-evident but rather emerge in practice. In other words, the social and the technical always co-develop. As Nigel Thrift explains:

> the actors in these actor networks redefine each other *in action* in ways which mean that there are no simple one-to-one relationships from technology to people but rather a constantly on-going, constantly

> inventive and constantly reciprocal process of social acquaintance and re-acquaintance.
>
> (1996: 1485)

This study of children's use of the Internet is informed by these ideas. We do not view computers as things 'with pre-given attributes frozen in time' (Star and Ruhleder 1996: 112), nor as objects which impact on social relations in fixed ways producing a predictable set of effects (either as positive like the boosters or negative like the debunkers). Nor do we understand computers to mirror the logic of their designers and manufacturers. Rather, we understand them to be 'things' that materialise for children as diverse social practices and which may thus have as many everyday translations as the contexts in which they are used (Bingham *et al.* 2001). In other words, we understand computers and their users to be in a relational process of coming into being, in which each is transforming and transformative of the other (Ackrich 1992). In this way, our account in this book moves beyond technological determinism by demonstrating some of the ways in which computers and children co-develop in ways that cannot be read off from presumed states of the computers or children individually (Bingham *et al.* 2001).

Notably, we recognise that computers may play a diverse range of roles within children's different 'communities of practice' and thus emerge as very different tools. Here we draw on Eckert *et al.*'s (1996, 4–5) definition of communities of practice. They write:

> united by a common enterprise, people come to develop and share ways of doing things, ways of talking, beliefs, values – in short practices – as a function of their joint involvement in mutual activity. Social relations form around the activities, the activities form around relationships, and particular kinds of knowledge and expertise become parts of individuals identities and places in the community.

Learning new knowledge and competencies that open up fresh strands of involvement in the world (Horning *et al.* 1999) is one of the ways that people come to participate in, and become members of such communities. In this book we focus on the different communities of practices that emerge in the off-line spaces of schools (Chapters 2 and 3), and homes (Chapters 4 and 5), and the on-line spaces of the Internet (Chapter 6). In doing so, following Horning *et al.* (1999: 296) we think of practices both as the application of already existing possibilities – 'as repetitive, unfoldings' – and as new creative 'enactments' or 'novel appropriations'. In other words, as both 'repetition and invention' (ibid.).

By adopting the approach to technology outlined in this section, in this book we contribute to geographies of cyberspace and social studies of technology by providing empirical evidence of how ICT is embedded within everyday life. In other words, we clearly demonstrate the mutual constitution of on- and off-line worlds. In doing so we also emphasise the mutual constitution, not only of the social and technical but also of the spatial and temporal, by showing how each is transformed and transformative of the other. The different 'communities of practice' that we identify and the diverse ways that ICT emerge for them also challenge popular commentaries on children's use of cyberspace (outlined above), by providing a foil for the claims of both the 'debunkers' and 'boosters'.

Introducing the research

The findings presented in this book are based on material collected as part of a two-year study of children's use of ICT at school and home that was funded by the Economic and Social Research Council.

The first stage of the research was based in three secondary schools. Two of the schools, Highfields and Station Road, are located in a major urban area in Yorkshire; the third, Westport, is in an isolated small rural town in Cornwall.[2] Highfields is a mixed comprehensive school for pupils aged 11 to 18 located on the residential edge of a major city. The area is dominated by private housing and is relatively advantaged, with unemployment being well below local and national averages. The majority of the pupils are 'white', though at 7 per cent, British Pakistanis form a significant minority of the school population. The school has benefited from some investment since its designation as a technology college, and exam results compare favourably with the national average. Station Road is a mixed comprehensive for pupils aged 11 to 16 located in a much less well-off part of the same city, where the percentage of children eligible for school meals is higher than the national average. The school has a much greater percentage of pupils scoring below the national average on examinations. However, given that 8 per cent of the children are from homes where English is not the first language, the school is seen by authorities to be performing relatively well. Westport is a mixed comprehensive school for pupils aged 11 to 18, and is located in one of the most isolated rural coastal towns in the UK. The school serves a large, mainly rural catchment area, with some pupils travelling considerable distances to attend. While there is a variation in the pupils' socio-economic backgrounds, the school catchment area as a whole is less disadvantaged than the national average. The number of children with statements of Special Educational Needs is relatively high, though exam results for the school as a whole are close to the national average. In all three schools pupils are taught in nationally recognised age-groups. The youngest, those aged 11 to 12, are in what is known as year seven (or Y7), those aged 12 to 13 are in year eight (Y8) and so on up to 15 to 16 year olds who are in what is known as year 11 (Y11).

Within the case-study schools, we undertook a questionnaire survey of

753 children aged 11 to 16 asking about their use of computers and the Internet in both school and home environments. This was followed by observation work in a number of case-study classes and focus group discussions – based mainly on existing friendship groups – which covered children's experiences of Information Technology (IT) within the school environment. All the pupils in selected case-study classes were asked to fill out a time–space diary designed to help us find out how important ICT was relative to other activities (such as school work, sport, etc.). Semi-structured interviews with the IT and Head teachers from these schools were also carried out.[3]

On the basis of this stage of data collection, ten children from each school and their families were asked to participate in a further stage of the research (along with another ten households where children were deemed to be 'high-end' users). These forty households included not only traditional nuclear families, but also lone parent households and reconstituted families. This work involved separate in-depth interviews with the parent(s)/carers and the children in the household. These focused on: the purchase of home PCs and Internet connection, use of computers and the Internet by different household members, different competence levels, issues of unity and/or conflict around shared use, ownership, location, and control of the domestic PC, as well as whether being on-line had affected household relations.

The conduct of our research was informed by our understandings of young people as competent agents in their own lives. As such, during the course of the fieldwork we sought to engage directly with the children and to treat them as independent actors, listening to their accounts of their own lives rather than just relying on the accounts of adult proxies such as teachers and parents. In doing so our research relationships were also guided by sociological codes of ethics which have attempted to identify ways that as academics we might work *with*, not on or for children (Alderson 1995). This approach is discussed in more detail in Valentine (1999b).

The structure and content of this book

In Chapter 2 we look at the development of the Information Society, particularly the way that this is leading to many 'normal' activities – from shopping and banking to political participation – being transferred on-line. We argue that the potential impact of these changes is such that at scales from the global to the local there is concern that technologically disenfranchised nations and individuals, who do not have the equipment or skills to participate in this new world, will be excluded from the information-led global economy. We go on to examine patterns of global inequalities in terms of access to ICT. Then, we focus on the national scale of the UK. Here, policies to develop children's technological competencies through the education system have formed a key plank in the Government's drive to promote IT for all. Through our empirical material we show that, contrary to the

Government's rhetoric, the provision of ICT (in terms of hardware/software and access to use this equipment) in UK schools varies widely. Some children have better access to computers and the Internet than others. We argue that these differences in terms of our three case-study schools relate to the ways that these technologies emerge differently in these different communities of practice according to their individual visions of ICT, and their attitudes towards the Government's aim of using technology to counter social inequalities. In the final section of this chapter we evaluate what this means for our understanding of social exclusion.

In Chapter 3 we develop this understanding further, and also maintain our focus on the school, by examining the ways that boys and girls form markedly different relationships with ICT in the classroom. We begin the first section with an overview of research in critical educational studies. This body of work highlights the fact that differences between pupils can be reproduced through the schooling process, a fact clearly in evidence in relation to the gendered nature of children's ICT usage in our three case-study schools. Conventional explanations for these differences between children, that are evident in our own findings, suggest that they are likely to result from a mixture of factors including school policy, teacher practice and pupils' cultures. We argue that this theorisation of the multi-faceted nature of institutional culture is attractive, not least because it rests implicitly on the conceptualisation of the school as a spatial project, and on children as active social agents. However, as we show, there is a lack of ethnographic work to date which assesses the validity of these proposed explanations, or which considers exactly how these processes might work in practice.

In the second section of this chapter we draw on this theorisation of institutional cultures in a consideration of the different ways that children's relationships with ICT are shaped, played out and (re)produced within the classroom environment of our case-study schools. We begin this section by analysing how teachers' classroom practices can mean diverse pupil cultures come to dominate in the classroom. We then move on to examine how the relationships of four different groups of children – the techno boys, the lads, the luddettes and the computer-competent girls – emerge within these institutional cultures. In the process we pay special attention to gender differences between pupils, both in terms of the relations between boys and girls, and differences within these groups. Nevertheless, we also draw out differences in pupils' class and ethnic backgrounds where appropriate, and identify the ways in which the heterosexual economy of the classroom shapes the ICT usage of different groups. This analysis demonstrates that despite the much hailed revolutionary potential of ICT, the consequences of introducing such technologies into education are neither simple nor obvious, as the ways they are understood and consequently taken up or rejected by different children are mediated through the institutional cultures. In the conclusion to this chapter we relate this material back to the question of social exclusion that we introduced in Chapter 2. Here, we demonstrate the need to think about social exclusion from the Information Age in terms of questions of everyday access to ICT, rather than merely focusing on the broad-scale distribution of resources. We suggest that this understanding of ICT within a school context exposes the need for the UK Government to pay more attention to what happens when children and technology come together by listening to children's accounts of how ICT emerge for them in practice.

In Chapters 4 and 5 we switch from our emphasis on the school to the home. In Chapter 4, first we examine the wider contemporary discourses about children's use of ICT in contemporary debates. Current public and policy understandings of children's use of ICT, we suggest, contain paradoxical ideas about childhood and technology. On the one hand 'boosters' celebrate children's command of a technology which is assumed to be our future; on the other hand, 'debunkers' raise fears that this technology is putting children's emotional well-being at risk. In examining these discourses we consider how ideas about childhood in these debates resonate with notions of the Apollonian and Dionysian child (outlined above), and the ways that ICT are constructed in a technologically determinist framework (i.e. as impacting either positively or negatively on society). We then go on to argue that these discourses are problematic both because they essentialise the category 'child', denying children's diversity and their status as social actors, and because of their techno-determinism. Drawing instead on research in the new social studies of childhood, and the sociology of science and technology (outlined above), we suggest an alternative agenda. This highlights the need to trace the different understandings of childhood and technology that emerge for parents and their offspring as they negotiate and make sense of children's technical and emotional competence in the domestic setting.

In Chapter 5 we retain our interest both in the home and in moral panics surrounding children's use of ICT. Here, we address popular fears about children's potential addiction to computers, and the consequences that this addiction might have for family time and unity, and for children's use of outdoor public space. By looking at the location of the PC within different domestic communities of practice we begin to unravel the complex ways that PCs are domesticated, and the processes through which they transform, and are transformed by, the time–spaces of the home. In doing so we refute many of the debunkers' fears about the consequences of ICT for family life. This chapter also links the home to the wider space of the local neighbourhood. Again, we use our empirical material to challenge popular concerns about the impact the home PC is imagined to be having on children's use of local, outdoor space. Just as we show in Chapters 2 and 3 how ICT emerges as a different tool within different educational communities of practice, here we also identify the way that these technologies emerges as different tools within different domestic communities of practice.

Chapter 6 marks a clear departure from those that have gone before by taking on-line rather than off-line spaces as its focus. In this chapter we consider both the information and communication aspects of children's use of Internet-connected PCs. First, we examine the ways that young people use the WWW to access information from around the globe and explore what this means for the local cultures in which their lives are embedded. Second, we look at some of the many ways that different children use ICT to communicate with both off-line and on-line friends and acquaintances. In doing so we think about how they represent the bodies and places that they inhabit to their 'virtual' friends. In the final section of this chapter we look at the role of the Internet in contributing to children's sense of place in the world. In doing so we question popular representations of cyberspace as a placeless social space, and evaluate the extent to which the WWW might be considered an Americanised landscape. The conclusion to this chapter emphasises the extent to which children's on-line and off-line worlds are mutually constituted.

In the final chapter of this book we bring children and technology together. Here, we return to think about the popular commentaries on ICT outlined at the beginning of this chapter (and which are also referred to throughout the subsequent chapters). Drawing together insights from across the five substantive empirical chapters (2 to 6) that make up this book, we show how children use ICT in balanced and sophisticated ways. We then outline how this understanding of children's use of ICT, which is primarily derived from their own accounts (as well as those of their carers, siblings, teachers and peers) rather than just adult narratives of young people's activities, should inform Government policy. In particular, we observe the different temporal and spatial frameworks within which adults and children operate. While adults tend to be future-oriented and to think globally as well as locally, children's approaches to ICT are more strongly focused on the present and the everyday, local context of their own peer group worlds. This has obvious consequences for the ways that adults (in terms of parents, schools and governments) should introduce children to ICT if they want their own agendas about the importance of computer literacy to prevail. We then return to the academic debates, introduced in this chapter, which frame the whole book, to show how our empirical work informs research within the social studies of childhood, children's geographies, the sociology of science and technology, and geographies of cyberspace.

Chapter 2

The digital divide?

Children, ICT and social exclusion

In this chapter we begin by thinking about the importance of the changes that are being wrought by the Information Age and identify why many nations of the world are trying to get onto the technology bandwagon. Here we view discourses about ICT and social, economic and political inclusion within the framework of pre-existing global inequalities. In the second section we adjust our focus to the national scale of the UK. Here we again explore the contrast between Government rhetoric about the inclusive possibilities of ICT and evidence for the existence of a digital divide. We then go on in the third section of this chapter to examine the potential role of schools as a bridge over this divide. Drawing on our empirical evidence we show how the provision of ICT in UK schools varies widely, and explore not only the differential levels of hardware and software available to individual schools, but also the diverse ways that ICT is made available to pupils both inside and outside of formal lesson times. In doing so, we also reflect on the way that individual schools accept or ignore the UK Government's vision of using technology to address social inequalities. In the final section of this chapter we evaluate what all of this means for our understanding of social exclusion.

The Information Age

It is popularly acknowledged that the industrial age of the nineteenth and twentieth centuries is coming to a close and that a profound shift is taking place in the global economy. Manufacturing is being replaced by information as the dominant form of employment and investment in the contemporary West. ICT are being hailed as the harbingers of widespread social transformation which will leave no aspect of our lives untouched: from the way we live, work and socialise, to the form of politics, education, leisure and relationships we engage in (Loader 1998).

The potential of ICT to improve industrial and commercial competitiveness and productivity, and as a resource in itself, means that many countries are striving to jump on the new technologies bandwagon. Whereas Western nations are motivated by a fear of losing their economic dominance and influence on the world stage, other countries see it as an opportunity for accelerated growth which might enable them to close the development gap (Abiodun 1994). Baranshamaje *et al.* (1995: 2) argue that:

> In an increasingly knowledge-based economy, information is becoming at least as important as land and physical capital. In the future, the distinction between developed and non-developed countries will be joined by distinctions between fast countries and slow countries, networked nations and isolated ones.

As a result, almost all nations, from those in the developed West to newly industrialised countries like South Africa, and developing countries such as Thailand, are pursuing policies to extend the reach of their telecommunications networks to provide universal access to ICT (Moore 1998).

At the national scale ICT are often tied to political visions of social inclusion and cohesiveness because they are seen as potentially facilitating higher participation levels in the political process and as producing more informed democracy (Moore 1998). Many governments around the world now use the Internet to communicate with at least some of their citizens. In 1998 over forty countries had websites for 70 per cent or more of their agencies (URL 1). In the USA various experiments have been carried out using public electronic networks (PENS) to enable citizens to access local politicians and to take part in on-line debates about local issues (Schuler 1995). Non-governmental organisations, and social and political groups, such as PeaceNet, widely use the Internet to publicise political and human rights abuses and social actions for change (Doheny-Farina 1996). Supporters of the Zapatista movement in Mexico are just one example of a group who have used the speed and connectivity of the Internet to mobilise international support for a local struggle (Froehling 1999). By facilitating information acquisition, and direct involvement in the political process, some commentators suggest that ICT will change the nature of politics. In particular, these technologies have the potential to decentralise power bases, and re-scale individuals' political horizons, as we are increasingly able to recognise and take on responsibilities at the global as well as at local and national political scales.

At the scale of the individual, ICT are promoted as empowering or liberating, particularly for disadvantaged groups. This is because of the freedom that they offer users to access information and communicate with whom they want, freed from the material and social constraints of their bodies, identities, communities and geographies (Plant 1996; Springer 1991; Stone 1992).

However, the potential for promoting social inclusion that ICT are understood to offer needs to be viewed within the framework of existing global inequalities. There is a digital divide in terms of access to ICT both between countries/parts of the world, and within them (Dodge and Kitchen 2001). Not everyone is equally equipped to take advantage of the opportunities which the Information Age is seen to offer. Figures from the ITU World Telecommunications Indicators Database for the number of PCs per 100 inhabitants in 1994 revealed a very diverse pattern: USA 29.7, Germany 14.4, UK 15.1, Hungary 3.4, Israel 2.2, Argentina 1.7, Brazil 0.9, and India 0.1 (Holderness 1998). Similar geographical disparities are evident in terms of access to the Internet. Figures for those on-line in January 2000 showed a world-wide total of 242 million connections. Here, Canada and the USA led the way with over 120 million Internet connections, followed by Europe with 70 million, Asia/Pacific with 40 million (the majority of which were in Japan), South America with 8 million, Africa with 2.1 million (of which 1.6 million were in South Africa), and finally the Middle East with 1.9 million users on-line (URL 2). Even within the nation–states of Europe further inequalities of access are evident. NetValue, a panel-based service that measures levels of Internet activity in Europe, found that 50 per cent of Danish households, and 30 per cent of British households were on-line in the year 2000. Yet, the figures for France and Spain showed that only 17.5 and 12.7 per cent of households respectively were connected to the Internet (URL 3). As Haywood points out:

> There may be eight million documents available on the World Wide Web, but 70 per cent of the host computers are in the US and fewer than ten African countries are connected to the Internet. A modem in India costs about four times as much as it does in the US, and Internet access can be twelve times more expensive in Indonesia than the US.
>
> (1998: 24)

Within most developing countries there are also significant disparities between the levels of access to ICT in rural and urban areas. In particular, use of the Internet tends to be centred on major cities, and in the hands of the privileged urban elite. As Kitchin (1998a) points out, cyberspace is the domain of young, white, educated, middle-class, males from the West. There is also increasing recognition that the global village promoted by ICT enthusiasts is Western-oriented, and in particular US-led in terms of innovation, use and culture (a theme we return to in Chapter 6). The dominant language on the Internet is English and most emails are sent from the US (Holderness 1993). Sardar goes so far as to claim that: '[c]yberspace . . . is the "American dream" writ large; it marks the dawn of a new "American civilization" . . . Cyberspace is particularly geared up towards the erasure of all non Western histories' (1995: 780–781). As such the governments of countries such as Singapore, Vietnam, China, and Saudi Arabia, who regard the Americanisation of the Internet as a threat to their social and cultural values

or political system, are trying to expand the use of ICT by the elite, while at the same time attempting to restrict access to the Internet by the rest of the population (Haywood 1998).

Given that to send an email you need not only a computer and a modem, but also a phone line and a reliable electricity supply, 'talk amongst the technologically elite of advanced capitalist societies of joining the Information Superhighway is a discourse which has little meaning in many regions of the globe where even intermediate telecommunications are under-developed' (Loader 1998: 3). As Haywood (1998: 24–25) observes: 'In poorer countries the "superhighway" is more often than not a long and tor-tuous dirt-track miles from a made-up road which itself is miles from the nearest medical centre or school.' Not surprisingly, some commentators argue that money that is being earmarked for ICT within some developing countries might be better invested in housing, infrastructure and stabilising the economy (Dyrkton 1996).

Moving from the global scale to the national scale in the UK it is possible to see similar evidence of discourses of inclusion in government rhetoric, yet digital divides are evident in practice.

Falling through the net: the case of the UK

Personal computers first came on the market in the 1970s, with home Internet access not available for over another twenty years. The take-off in sales of domestic ICT is usually dated to the mid-1990s (URL 1). Despite the continued steep upward trajectory of sales, figures at the turn of the millen-nium showed that only one-third of UK households owned a home PC (URL 4) or had access to the Internet[1] (URL 5). Unsurprisingly, Motorola (1998: 2) defines Britain as 'a nation of technology Haves and Have-Nots'. The 'haves', whether in terms of PC ownership, Internet usage or access to train-ing, are more likely to be young, male, well educated, employed and from the upper and middle classes. Figures from the National Statistics Omnibus Survey,[2] which is based on a random sample of 1800 adults aged 16 and over, living in private UK households, are particularly telling (URL 5). This data shows that at the end of the year 2000 only 27 per cent of those living in households headed by an unskilled person had accessed the Internet, com-pared to 78 per cent of those whose households were headed by a professional. There was a gap of 12 per cent between the number of men (57 per cent) and the number of women (45 per cent) who had been on-line, and a drastic decline in usage of the Internet with age. While 85 per cent of 16–24 year olds had used the Net, the same was true for only 6 per cent of those aged 75 and over. Two-thirds of all of the adults surveyed who had been on-line were aged between 16 and 44 (URL 5).

Other government research has reproduced a similar pattern of techno-logical disadvantage. The report by the National Working Party on Social

Inclusion (a group established by IBM in collaboration with the Community Development Foundation) states that:

> The category of people most likely to be marginalised are people on low incomes. Everyone of course can be categorised in several ways, and many experience multiple disadvantage. Three social groups in particular have frequently been identified as being 'at risk' from exclusion in the Information Society, whether or not they experience poverty: women, ethnic and racial groups [sic], and older people. In addition, people in rural communities may experience particular difficulties, which are related to the adequacy of the infrastructure provided.
>
> (INSINC 1997: 3)

Ironically, then, while in theory cyberspace is often hailed for its potential to liberate disadvantaged groups, in practice these are the very groups that often do not have the skills or financial resources to access these opportunities (Graham and Marvin 1996).

Our own questionnaire survey also identified a familiar pattern of inequality. The proportion of children who claimed to have used a computer at home varied considerably between our three case-study schools. These were reported at 73 per cent for Highfields, which has a predominantly 'middle-class' catchment area; 61 per cent for Westport, which is socially mixed; and 55 per cent for Station Road, which has a largely 'working-class' catchment area. When analysed in terms of parents' occupation, our results show that 87 per cent of children with parents in professional or managerial employment have access to a home computer, compared with 57 per cent of children with parents in skilled non-manual work, and 35 per cent of children with parents in skilled, semi-skilled or unskilled manual work.[3]

This pattern is perhaps not surprising given the gap between rich and poor in the UK. Summarising the results of a UN Human Development Report,[4] Haywood (1998) points out that the poorest 40 per cent of UK citizens now share a lower proportion of the national wealth than any other country. The average income of the richest fifth of the population is over ten times that of the poorest fifth. While access to ICT does not correlate directly with income, it is certainly true as Golding points out that:

> Entrance to the new media playground is relatively cheap for the well to do, a small adjustment in existing spending patterns is simply accommodated. For the poor the price is a sharp calculation of opportunity cost, access to communication goods jostling uncomfortably with the mundane arithmetic of food, housing and clothing.
>
> (1990: 112)

It is a pattern that is not unique to the UK. The National Technologies

Information Administration (NTIA) of the USA (using data from Current Population Survey carried out by the Census Bureau) has identified that the groups with consistently low levels of access to ICT at home are: black, hispanic, Native Americans, the less educated, single female-headed households, and households in the south, rural areas or central cities (URL 6). In 1998 46.6 per cent of white Americans owned a home PC, compared with only 23.2 per cent of black Americans. A persistent difference that the NTIA suggests cannot be explained by level of income and education alone. While excluded groups have significantly increased their levels of access to ICT since 1995, other groups have adopted these technologies at an even faster rate. As such, the digital divide is actually widening rather than closing (URL 6).

Inequalities in access to, and use of, ICT matter because these technologies are popularly understood to be about, if they have not already led to, the transformation of work and the production of value (Marshall 1997). In the USA, for example, it is estimated that 60 per cent of jobs now require technological skills (URL 7). Moreover, the Economic Policy Institute estimate that the gap between wages for skilled workers who can use new technologies and unskilled workers increased by 23 per cent between 1979 and 1995 (URL 1). Kroker and Weinstein (1994: 163) argue that computer literacy will be key to membership of the emerging future 'virtual class' because the technologically competent will be able to convert their intellectual capital into both economic and cultural capital.

Indeed, as the use of ICT becomes more widespread, with more activities such as shopping, banking and even voting on-line, then the disadvantage of lacking technological skills will stretch beyond the labour market. In this way the technological 'have-nots' will suffer wider social exclusion because they will be unable to participate in 'normal' activities. For example, Haywood (1998: 22) observes that 'without institutions to mediate digitised information to economically deprived groups, their access to something that was often relatively easy via a public library, law centre or citizens advice bureau could be severely impaired'. Further, if individuals or groups are unable to exercise their rights and responsibilities, they will also be denied full citizenship (Steele 1998). This point is made particularly clearly in *The Net Result*, a report published by the National Working Party on Social Inclusion:

> Whereas full citizenship hitherto has been associated with having a job and somewhere to live, it may be the case that in the future an additional 'badge of citizenship' will be access to the information highway. Just as in today's society, those who do not have homes and jobs are at risk of social and political exclusion, so in the future those who are unable to make effective use of information resources will also risk exclusion unless social, economic and educational policies are introduced to maximise opportunities for participation and contribution.
>
> (INSINC 1997: 7)

Loader (1998: 9) warns against the consequences of such technological disenfranchisement, arguing that '[w]ithout the resources for access, understanding and knowledge to compete in the information marketplace there is little opportunity or incentive for the underclass in advanced societies to have a stake'.

In the following section we narrow our focus from the national stage to look at how these patterns are played out in the local contexts of our three case-study areas.

'I would sell my soul to get him a PC': the domestic digital divide

Given the importance being placed on computer literacy in the Information Age, it is not surprising that commercial organisations, such as PC manufacturers, retailers and Internet providers, have been quick to emphasise the educational values of ICT in their efforts to promote the domestic purchase of these technologies (see also Chapter 5). Advertisements often target parents by stressing that the sooner a child develops technological skills, the better their educational and subsequent future employment prospects will be (Haddon 1992). As Nixon explains:

> The family is being constructed as an important entry point for the development of new computer-related literacies and social practices in young people . . . what is discursively produced within the global culture economy as digital *fun and games* for young people, is simultaneously constructed as *serious business* for parents.
>
> (1998: 23)

In this discursive climate, the blanket importance parents and the majority of children attach to ICT skills, and consequently to having a home computer, is unsurprising. Paralleling the attitudes of both government and commercial interests, parents regard ICT skills as essential to their children's future job prospects:

MRS PHELPS: They [computers] are a fast growing area. They are becoming a – not becoming, they have become – an essential communication medium, and they also have huge capacity for usage. David, for example, wants to do something like architecture. Most design is on computers, you know, so it won't be an option, it will be a necessity. If you go into something vaguely academic then computers are a necessity . . . We've [society] devoted vast amounts to it (Highfields).

MR THYME: I mean, we're not stupid. I mean, we can see the way the world is going now and computers are a thing of the future, I mean, my personal theory on it is if you can't use a computer you aren't going to go anywhere in this world, you know what I mean, the way it's going at the moment (Westport).

MRS WEBB: They just, it seems to be whatever shop you go in or office they've got one, haven't they, do you know what I mean? Everybody seems to have got them and every job you seem to go into apart from being a cleaner like me, at some stage or another they want, they want you to be able to use a computer (Station Road).

Marshall (1997: 71) labels parental concerns that the absence of a home computer might lead children to become disconnected from the impending information economy as 'technophobia of the projected future'. He identifies the rapid expansion of ICT into the space of the home in the late twentieth and early twenty-first centuries as one of its primary consequences. Surveys on both sides of the Atlantic (URL 1 and URL 4) have shown that families with children are more likely to own a home PC or to be connected to the Internet than single people or couples without children. Marshall (1997), however, suggests that technophobia of the projected future is more or less a middle-class phenomenon, describing the ways that middle-income parents struggle to reproduce their class advantages for their offspring. He writes 'The computer's integration into the home is connected to education desires so that the family's children can maintain their class position through a vague conception of computer literacy' (ibid.: 75).

However, our interviews with working-class parents show that these mothers and fathers are just as fearful as their middle-class counterparts that their children might end up on the wrong side of a technologically polarised world. As a result some go to great lengths borrowing money or selling possessions to purchase a PC, while others, despite their best efforts, are frustrated by their inability to provide their children with the opportunity to develop their technological competence.

MRS READ: I'd give me right arm to get him a PC, I mean, like I say, me husband's unemployed and we've no money what-so-[ever] and I would sell my soul to get him [my son] a PC. If there were any way we could get him one, I would get him one, but there's just . . . no way and it's all he wants. What can we sell, and we ain't got owt to sell to get him one, have we? I've got nothing. Poor sod (Station Road).

Children from across the socio-economic spectrum draw on similar discourses to their parents, claiming that ICT-related skills will be a necessary requirement for their entry into diverse areas of the labour market. However, a minority of technophobic children (see Chapter 3) do refuse to entertain the idea that in the future they might work in occupations that involve using a computer.

MAL HIGGENS: When you get a job all the finances and everything's going to be done on the computer. If you get asked to do something like write a letter to this person because he's complained about a staircase or something [Mal wants to be a joiner] then you've got to write it and be able to use it and if you can't, you'll like, you won't get that job (Highfields).

DARREN BROWN: I think nearly every person is going to need to have some knowledge in using computers because the jobs, most of the jobs are turning towards using computers now, more than, say, not using them, 'cos, even like on farms now, where they've never used computers at all before, they're using them now, for like doing their financial stuff (Westport).

STEPHANIE PRICE: I think it is going to become very important because . . . like every job now you've gotta have like a computer so it's gonna be pretty important. Like, computer is *the* thing now (Station Road).

Technical skills are not only seen as a necessary requirement for children's smooth transition into future labour markets. Parents and children also draw on the educational motifs in both government and commercial discourses. There is a strong sense in which parents understand access to a home computer to be a prerequisite for academic success in the present (itself also a passport into the future labour market). This is a view that is often reinforced by their children:

INTERVIEWER: And why did you kind of think of buying one [a home PC]?
MRS GARDNER: Basically, we needed one, or Alan felt he needed one for school. Because he felt he was missing out. A lot of children had got them. He's in his GCSE year. They're getting all this information off the system and, as good as anyone can be, you can't hold enough books in your house to hold the same information that a child can touch a button and get off the system. So that child is at an advantage. And I felt that my child was at a disadvantage 'cos we hadn't got one. So I've had to go out and buy a second-hand cheapest model I can get hold of just so he could be one step on the ladder if you like (Westport).

MRS WEBB: They were, well, they were blackmailing me really. They said they couldn't do their work at school because they needed a computer to do it on. Homework, they desperately needed one for homework 'cos they couldn't finish their homework, 'cos all their friends had one. (Station Road)

Indeed, as these quotations indicate, some children are feeling the disadvantage of not having a home PC beginning to bite in terms of their academic attainment at school. They use this connection between these two socio-spatial environments to pressurise their parents into purchasing a computer. Indeed, Sefton-Green and Buckingham (1998: 82) claim that 'access to home computers is possibly as important a part of the distribution of cultural capital as access to books'. This is of special concern to those children producing course-work for national examinations. They highlight the use of computers to improve the presentation of work, the amount of information available on-line, and the time to develop understanding of ICT through experimentation as three of the most important advantages which accrue to those who have access to ICT at home. As these children explain:

LOUISE LANGTON: You just see the work what they've [children with computers at home] produced with it, and everything, and you just kind of want to be able to do it. Because in class you don't get to, like, finish everything off what you want to do, and then when they do it at home, they do it up in neat, and it looks right good, but whereas mine were just, like, on paper and pen and it doesn't look as good as it does by computer (Station Road).

JOHN BATTY: Like [if] you learn something in school and didn't really understand it, you can go home and think, now what was it, and you just fiddle about [on the computer] and teachers don't say 'finish that now' (Westport).

However, children's motives for wanting a home PC are not always this virtuous. While most children recognise the importance of ICT to their educational and employment prospects, they also valorise these technologies for the social and leisure opportunities that they offer them in the present. For example, for some children ICT emerge as tools for playing computer games, for others as information sources about sports, pop and film heroes and heroines, while some prefer to use these technologies to communicate with friends and family (see Chapter 6). Some children – demonstrating their competence as social actors – self-consciously manipulate wider discourses about educational success to persuade their parents to buy computers which they primarily want, and intend to use, for fun rather than school-work.

HELEN OATS: Well, we [she and her sister] wanted it but we kind of ... conned him [their father] into getting it because it had, we were there going 'Oh look it's got Encarta [an on-line encyclopedia] on it and we'll use it all the time' and he believed us so we got it (Highfields).

In this sense we can see that all the parents and children we interviewed are part of wider national discourses about the importance of ICT. The assessment of home computers as a crucial advantage to children's educational performance and employment prospects, as well as their potential as play machines, are held regardless of class background, and regardless of whether the family in question actually owns a PC. However, these families are also bound into wider sets of class relations which means that some are able to purchase a home computer for their children and others are not. It is these financial, rather than cultural, differences between middle-class and working-class families that mean some children come to benefit from the perceived advantages home computing can bring while others do not. In the following section we consider the role that schools might play in bridging the digital divides that we have just described.

School as a potential bridge over the digital divide

It is widely recognised that in order to prevent the introduction of ICT reproducing existing social and spatial inequalities, these technologies need to be affordable, and intellectually accessible to everyone (Fernback and Thompson 1995). The UK Government has identified schools as important intervention points to provide access for all to ICT and to challenge any emerging domestic or generational inequalities. Schools are not only places where children as workers of the future are educated, they can also be sites for accessing parents. The technological skills pupils are taught at school are transmitted into the home (see Chapter 4) when children show or teach their parents what they have learned in the classroom (Tang 1998). Schools can also provide adult education courses and distance learning opportunities to benefit the wider community. Kenway (1996: 230) even goes so far as to suggest that because 'technological competence is a new basic for education, equal access and equal competence [to ICT] must be a basic concern for educators'.

In 1997 the UK Government published a White Paper on education stating that:

> In the last twenty years, business has been transformed by new technology, particularly computers and communication networks. But education has been affected only marginally . . . We shall therefore create a new National Grid for Learning for the Millennium, to unlock the potential of these technologies in schools and more widely, and to equip pupils and other learners for this new world.
>
> (Department of Employment and Education 1998: 41)

The following year the National Grid for Learning (hereafter NGfL) was formally launched with a £700m investment earmarked to help use the Internet to construct a network to which all 30,000 UK schools are being connected, and on which every child will have an email address. At this point the UK was fifth among OECD countries in terms of 'school nets' behind the USA, Canada, Australia and Japan (Tang 1998).

The UK Government's vision of the role of technology in education not only imagines that it will reproduce a computer-literate labour force but also that new technologies will raise conventional literacy standards and empower individuals. The Government Minister Kim Howells has claimed, for example that:

> We believe absolutely that new technology in information and communications can actually help to drive up standards in schools. We think it will help people to read and to write and to access information in all kinds of ways and it will also help teachers to monitor more closely the progress of pupils and students.
>
> (URL 8)

Despite such initiatives, and the Government's vision of providing equal access to ICT for all British children, we found wide variations in the technological resources available in different schools. This is because while the UK Government has triggered initiatives to install hardware in schools, many such initiatives involve the allocation of resources through 'beauty competitions' in which schools must compete against one another, and much of the momentum and decision-making to bring this about occurs at the local level. The importance of technology in schools' marketing has been growing for some time because symbolically (if not materially) it enables them to appear to be responding to a more technical world by becoming more technical themselves (Bigum 1997; Nixon 1998). A computer-based curriculum is seen as a symbol of the quality of education (Bromley 1997). However, some local authorities have placed greater emphasis on ICT than others; likewise different schools have also taken different decisions about the amount to invest in hardware, reflecting their individual visions of the role of technology in the school curriculum, budgetary positions and educational priorities (Valentine and Holloway 1999). Don Bains (Deputy Head and IT co-ordinator) describes how Westport's commitment to developing its ICT resources has necessitated making sacrifices in other areas. This prioritisation of technology has not always been universally well received by the other staff.

DON BAINS: It was hard work, last year was a particularly bad financial year, and trying to absorb something like £8,000 worth of on-going costs [of ICT] took a fair bit of creativity. There was a fair bit of opposition as well at the time, from, well you know what it's like on staffs, and you will have found here that there are those who are pro-IT and equally there are those who are anti putting a lot of IT provision in schools. And at a time when we made, I think, one teacher redundant last year there were some staff who couldn't understand why or how we were able at that time to be setting aside something like £25,000 to do what we wanted to support the project [development of ICT] and bring the infrastructure up to scratch. So there are those arguments (Westport).

The choices particular schools such as Westport have made are in turn heavily dependent on the competence and commitment of individual teachers to research and bid for the funding which the Government makes available on a competitive basis for IT provision, and to develop the resources which they have. Bigum (1997) points out that the nature (e.g. keeping track of changes in software and hardware, installing and testing new equipment, technical troubleshooting) and amount of work expected from the designated 'computer teacher' often exceeds the amount of time they are allocated in this role. As a result, the computing facilities of schools are commonly dependent on the enthusiasm and unpaid labour of the teachers concerned.

Thus, a very uneven pattern has been created which reflects the attitudes and priorities of different Local Education Authorities (LEAs), and especially the teachers and governors of particular schools. This is evident both in the results of our questionnaire survey of schools and in the everyday experiences of teachers. As Dave Matthews, the IT Co-ordinator at Highfields explains, his school has been successful at bidding against other schools for IT resources and this has caused some resentment within the LEA:

DAVE MATHEWS: when you look round other schools in [his region] it's just unbelievable the variation of kit . . . I mean, the only people, the only places that have got machines like we have are people who've applied for and made bids. The Head here applied for this bid and got it. I go to meetings and people [teachers from other schools] are looking at you like it's your fault, so like, yeah you've got all this gear and they haven't (Highfields).

However, the hardware and software available in any school alone does not explain children's access to, and use of, the technology. For example, the Government Statistics Service Survey of IT in schools (McKinsey and Company 1998) revealed that while 83 per cent of British secondary schools are connected to the Internet, this does not necessarily mean that the children in these schools have access to it. Rather, many schools severely restrict use of the Internet. This is, first, because of the costs involved, which include access to an Internet provider, routes and servers, upgrading, extending or installing a network at school, and the need for relatively powerful computers. Second, because of parental fears (a theme we return to in Chapter 4) that children might access unsuitable material on-line (Valentine and Holloway 2001a).

While in some schools ICT is employed cross-curricula in lessons such as

English, Geography, and so on, in many cases its use is confined to Information Technology (IT) lessons. This is not necessarily a consequence of the number of computers or Internet connections available. Rather, it more often reflects the number of teachers with the training and motivation to utilise these resources in their lessons, at a time when there are many other competing demands on their energies. Teachers are under pressure to integrate new technologies across the curriculum, yet many of them are reluctant or ambivalent about doing so because they lack training or the hands-on experience of how to use ICT. In a demanding job teachers have little time to spare to adapt their teaching to incorporate new technologies (Bryson and de Castell 1994). With minimal technical or troubleshooting support available, some are fearful of encountering problems using ICT in front of pupils whose technological competence may outstrip their own. Mrs Grayson, a teacher, explains why she avoids using ICT while Tim Simpkin, a very computer-literate pupil at Station Road, describes how his teachers both draw on his knowledge, but also feel threatened by his competence.

MRS GRAYSON: Yeah, well, I don't think, I mean, I mean, when I said to you [the interviewer] I don't use them [computers] at school, if at all possible I will avoid them because they create more hassle for me than they do anything else. [Edit, later she returned to this theme] . . . you don't actually know what's happening in this box, that it's happening and what, and you're getting the result out that you want (Highfields).

TIM SIMPKIN: Usually you're, like, working away at summat and they'll go 'Tim!' [when they need his technical help]. 'What?' You know you've got to go over there and help them [the teacher], like. Sometimes the teachers get irritated because they're there for that, you know. And they take you outside and go, 'Look Tim' [warning him to stop helping other pupils, to which he replies]. 'I'm only trying to help.' [The teachers respond, . . .] 'But I'm the teacher, I'm in control.' You know, they tell you that (Station Road).

Given the potential threat that ICT may pose to some teachers' identities, professional status, day-to-day practices and authority within the classroom, it is not surprising that many are accused of being contemporary Luddites for resisting its wider incorporation within the curriculum.

Our emphasis here on usage rather than provision starts to raise important questions about access to ICT within schools. Different schools structure access to ICT and their use in different ways. These policies and their microgeographies have very important impacts – a point clearly demonstrated by our three case-study schools.

At Highfields, there are 120 PCs or Macs, 28 with full Internet access. The computers are concentrated in IT labs, and access to these is largely limited to lesson times. All pupils receive one lesson per week of IT in years 7, 9, 10 and 11 (which sometimes includes use of the Internet) and follow a National Curriculum Certificate Course in the subject (with most pupils entered for the national GCSE examination). Children are allowed access out of school hours in what is termed 'extended study time'. However, following a complaint from parents about their son and his friends finding unsuitable material on-line, access to ICT must now be under the supervision of a teacher and children are usually expected to do school work. The school has also installed a filter system in order to try to curb children's inappropriate uses of the Internet. An IT teacher does allow keen pupils (a small group of technologically competent boys whom he trusts as technologically competent and enthusiastic) to use the machines in his classroom out of hours if they ask. In this way, children who have access to ICT at home and are already technologically competent are able to maximise their access to school machines which enables them to spend more time developing their technological skills. In contrast, technologically poor or technophobic children who do not have home-based access to ICT are not allowed the same opportunities to explore and develop their confidence with the technology independently of formal IT lessons (see also Chapter 3). The fluency gap between children, which Calvin and Sally describe below, is potentially exacerbated:

CALVIN HIGGENS: I'm not real good at 'em. Those who are really good are the one that have got them at home, 'cos that go on 'em all day and everything . . . if we have computers at home we'd be as good as the Boffins [a technologically competent group of boys] (Highfields).

SALLY STONE: You can tell in our class who's got a computer at home. 'Cos, like, when we have to do something, even like typing a letter, Chlöe will be like la, la, la and it's done. And some people are like a, . . . b, . . . You have more confidence if you know how to use it. The reason we find it easy is that computers are so slow here compared to the computers we have at home. We sit there going, chat, and it's done (Highfields).

Highfields, then, implictly has a vision of ICT as a privileged tool which has potentially harmful consequences and thus needs to be monitored and controlled, rather than as an everyday object which is part and parcel of the school environment. As such despite the UK Government's rhetoric, the way that Highfields implements the use of ICT within the school may actually have the effect of reproducing, rather than challenging differences in levels of home-based access to, and use of, ICT between its pupils. Indeed, the Head Teacher does not believe that it is the school's responsibility to counter such inequalities. He explains:

BILL JONES: You, you can't in a school, schools . . . can't function as, er, sort of social equalisers . . . We can't do all of that, we're here fundamentally as educators and that's what our job is to do . . . I can't make up for the fact that Johnny Bloggs at home has a PC and Christina hasn't. Can't do that. All I can do is to provide what we've got here . . . We give them a taste of something, and that's about as far as I think schools can go. They can't be social engineers beyond all that (Highfields).

This attitude towards the role of schools in tackling social inequalities contrasts strongly with the approach adopted at Station Road. Station Road has 39 PCs or Macs, almost all of which can support the Internet. ICT skills are taught to all pupils on a separate course in year 7 and year 10, and it is used cross-curricula in years 8 and 9. Pupils are allowed to use the computers after school if 'someone is around' and there are two weekly computer clubs. One of these is a girls-only club which was established specifically to counter the exclusion of girls from the original male-dominated club (see Chapter 3). Internet access at these times is restricted; however, pupils may get permission to use the Internet during break/lunch times by booking one of four multi-media PCs that are located in the library.

Consequently, while Station Road has significantly fewer PCs than Highfields, its pupils actually have potentially greater access to the technology because its more formalised system secures more children better access than the dependence on informal requests and 'favours' from the teacher at Highfields. Indeed, Station Road is concerned that its pupils, who live in a socio-economically disadvantaged area, should not be further marginalised because they lack the IT skills that will be required in future labour markets. The school also recognises that its pupils will have broader usage for ICT beyond the labour market, envisaging technological competence as a 'life skill'. Its vision of using ICT to promote social inclusion is also evident in the way that the school uses technology to draw parents back into the education system and to bind the school and local community together. Station Road, for example, currently offers nine ICT evening classes each week for parents. The success of this approach is epitomised by the story of one father who had never read a book and had no examination qualifications. As a result of attending the ICT classes he re-discovered education, developed his literacy skills and is now enrolled on a university course. The school's future vision of ICT also includes providing distance learning for pupils who are unable to attend because of illness, disability or because they are disaffected or excluded. As these initiatives imply, in contrast to the Head Teacher at Highfields, the Head and IT teachers at Station Road believe that their school does have a responsibility to challenge existing social inequalities in access to ICT, and to prevent new social cleavages from opening up:

PETER THOMAS: It's gonna be a life skill, it's not gonna be something that we

develop and it's developed in an academic sphere and never used out in
the larger world . . . it's as much of a life skill as learning to read and
write . . . without that, it's the fastest way to create the two-tier society,
those who have access and those who don't (Station Road).

JAMES FALIGNO: I mean, it's almost inevitably to be the case that some youngsters come here with some understanding of the world of ICT 'cos
they've got them at home or their fathers operate in industry or in com-
merce and they are used to seeing them around and using them. But it's
also true that if you take them through an entitlement programme, I
often find that the youngsters who don't have that access [to ICT] prior
to arrival very quickly pick up the skills and overtake those youngsters.
I think you'd be hard pushed to go into any of the ICT rooms and put
your finger on children who are middle class and advantaged in computer terms as opposed to youngsters who are not . . . [Later he returned
to a similar theme] What we're trying to build here, we're trying to
build Station Road as the centre of a learning community, that's what we
would wish it to be in so far that it's located geographically, conve-
niently for the people who come in and out of the school . . . What we've
actually got is a very firm platform to begin to build not only an improving community in relation to its literacy skills and its numeracy skills and
all the other skills that so many or our, so many members of our community have lost somewhere along the line (Station Road).

Pupils at Westport have significantly more independent access to computers
and the Internet than their counterparts at either Highfields or Station Road.
There are 79 PCs in the school, all with Internet connections. All pupils in
years 7 and 8 are provided with a foundation course in ICT. Learning to use
the Internet forms a key part of this course, which ends with the children creating their own webpage. Cross-curricula use is also made of the technology
in years 10 and 11. The IT teacher describes some of the uses to which on-
line resources are put:

JAMES PUNT: I passed some of the information to our Economics teacher, to
say that did you know, that BT [British Telecom] I think, were doing a
special thing [on-line] on the run up to the budget . . . it's had all sorts of,
you know, good, all the key industrial indicators, people second guess-
ing . . . you could use that, couldn't you? (Westport).

Like Station Road, ICT emerges at Westport school as an important everyday skill rather than merely a passport to educational qualifications.
Westport is spatially isolated, being located in a small rural coastal town. As
such, the school envisages the Internet as an important tool to enable its
pupils to overcome the tyranny of distance (a point we return to in Chapter

6) by accessing information from, and communicating with, those in the wider world (Valentine and Holloway, in press a). The IT teacher observes that:

JAMES PUNT: I mean there's just no other way our children can get access to research facilities at the local library, they might be able to do a 120-mile round trip and go to the University Library, I mean they just can't do it. There is no access here to anything, as you know. I mean, so it is particularly important that they can get on-line and the 6th form can look at the university pages . . . the year 10 and 11 art students can have a look at galleries around the world and see what's going [on] (Westport).

In particular, communication is at the heart of the school's vision of ICT and how it is used in practice. The school has an Intranet and all the children at Westport have email addresses which they use to communicate with each other, their families and people whom they have never met face-to-face. Special projects (see Chapter 6) have also been initiated to allow the pupils to develop on-line links with their peers in a New Zealand school (Holloway and Valentine 2000c). The IT teacher explains his philosophy of using ICT in ways that appeal to, and have relevance for, all children rather than merely employing these technologies for academic purposes:

JAMES PUNT: My own philosophy, which I think is becoming the school's philosophy . . . is that the computers are there, use them . . . We'd started our taught course and it was a very formal course . . . this is a word processor, this is underlining, this is a database, this is a field. And it became obvious the children were bored to tears, just typing stuff in, work wasn't relevant to them . . . So I re-wrote our course, told my colleagues to scrap what they were doing, and give the children a magazine to do. [Later he returned to the same theme] . . . we've always had a school view that we should put the resources into IT for all, rather than focusing on small groups of students, like doing an exam in computer study. We've always shied away from that (Westport).

At break times and lunch times the pupils are allowed to use PCs which are situated in 'clusters' within the school with little restriction. As the Deputy Head Teacher explains below, the school treats children as competent, responsible, independent social actors and as such does not encounter many problems with damage to, or inappropriate use of the machines. This is both a micro-geography and attitude to children that contrast starkly with Highfields' policy of containment and control. While there are fewer PCs at Westport than Highfield and Station Road, the pupils at Westport actually have more access in terms of the quantity and quality (independent rather than regulated use) of time that they have to use the machines than at either of the other two schools. This access is also equitable in that each child has the same level of opportunity.

DON BAINS: When we first got into this, I mean, I remember feeling very fearful, you know, Oh God, we've invested a lot of money in these machines, I couldn't possibly let children loose without supervision, and the funny thing is . . . I think what we found is that if you have a cluster or a room full of these machines and you allow pupils access, they will treat . . . the hardware and software in that situation very respectfully. Very rarely do we get problems in the IT rooms or the clusters. Where we've had problems it's tended to be with the individual machine in the corner of a classroom, which probably doesn't get used very much anyway, and we can only assume it's been targeted by somebody who themselves are not particularly interested in IT. People who go into the IT rooms, in their own time, are by definition converts anyway (Station Road).

Like Station Road, Westport understands itself to have a role to play in bridging the skills gap between those who have home-based access to ICT and those who do not. In contrast to Station Road, however, Westport does not extend this approach to the pupils' parents or the wider community. Indeed, whereas at Highfields it is teachers' fears about the children's immaturity which constrain the way the technology is mobilised, here it is the school's fears about the way adults might corrupt the PCs that shape their use. The IT and Deputy Head Teacher explain the positions that the school has adopted:

JAMES PUNT: [Describing the advantages which accrue to children with a home PC]: Because they can use, like a bit of geography homework, you know, they can go there, cut and paste a picture from the Internet, put it in [their essay]. You know, they do a nice word-processed thing, they spell check it. And of course they get very good marks for doing things like that . . . perhaps a very good reason for having access in school is to counter those advantages . . . to make sure . . . that kids aren't left behind. So I think that the investment we make is partly because, you know there's bound to be a situation, probably when you know, let's say, seven, eight, ten years time when 80 per cent of the population will have this sort of access [at home] but 20 per cent won't . . .

INTERVIEWER: Sure, so you think it's a very important, that school is a place where children . . .

JAMES PUNT: That school is a place where all children can get access and have their own email accounts. You know, and not be like disenfranchised from a technologically literate age (Westport).

DON BAINS: What as a school we struggle with, is getting over the nervousness and allowing the general public to use our facilities . . . I'm a community-school person at heart anyway, so I would like the community to be using our facilities more than they are. I understand the feelings of the two staff whose responsibility it is to ensure that the network is not corrupted and keeps running. I understand their reluctance to allow the community in without a lot of safeguards . . . we have never run . . . an adult continuing-education class using our facilities for Information Technology. And that sort of saddens me (Westport).

The evidence of these three case studies and our survey therefore suggests that contrary to Government rhetoric – which is advancing a policy of universal access to ICT as an antidote to potential future social exclusions – the provision of ICT in UK schools varies widely. Some children have better access to computers and the Internet than others. This disparity is evident in terms of the differential levels of hardware institutions possess, the diverse ways that ICT is employed in the curriculum, and the quantity and quality of access time that children are allowed outside the structure of formal lessons. It is also apparent in the different attitudes of schools towards extending their ICT resources to the wider community. All these differences in turn are at least a partial reflection of the extent to which individual schools embrace or dismiss the Government's vision of using technology to counter social inequalities. In the final section of this chapter we evaluate what this means for our understanding of social exclusion.

Social exclusion as an everyday practice

Social exclusion differs from poverty in that it is, according to Walker and Walker:

> [a] more comprehensive formulation which refers to the dynamic process of being shut out, fully or partially, from any of the social, economic, political or cultural systems which determine the social integration of a person in society. Social exclusion may, therefore be seen as the denial (or non realisation) of the civil, political and social rights of citizenship.
>
> (1997: 8)

The Director of the Centre of Analysis of Social Exclusion, Julian Le Grand, offers a similar definition. He states:

> A (British) individual is socially excluded if (a) he/she if geographically resident in the United Kingdom but (b) for reasons beyond his or her control, he/she cannot participate in the normal activities of United Kingdom citizens, and (c) he/she would like to participate.
>
> (quoted in Barry 1998: 4)

In this chapter we have shown that at the end of the twentieth and beginning of the twenty-first centuries technological developments, and the changes in the global economy that they have wrought, have led to the emergence of what has been dubbed the Information Age. In this process many 'normal' activities – from shopping and banking to political participation – are slowly being transferred on-line. The impact of these changes is such that at scales from the global to the local there is concern that a digital divide is emerging between the technologically rich and the technologically poor. Nation–states that do not have a strong ICT base fear that their ability to participate in the global economy will be eroded. Likewise, there is a fear that those individuals who do not develop technological skills will be unable to participate fully, not only in the workforce, but also in 'normal' activities and as such will be denied full citizenship rights. In order to prevent technologically disenfranchised individuals or groups from becoming socially excluded, and nations as a whole from becoming excluded from an information-led global economy, governments around the world are instigating policies to develop the technological competencies of their citizens. In Britain schools have formed a key component in the Government's drive to promote IT for all.

The UK Government's vision of IT in education emphasises the power of technology and its essential benefits (e.g. economic gains, access to information, lifelong learning, the empowerment of individuals, and so on). The implicit assumption is that putting a computer on a child's desk, and providing IT teaching, will produce a technologically literate adult of tomorrow who will be able to adapt to, and take advantage of, the information society. This vision is technologically determinist (see Chapter 1) in that particular outcomes are attributed to technology which are presumed to be more or less the same everywhere. When in fact the way that ICT emerge in practice varies according to the specificities of time and place, who is using it and their intentions, and the other agendas to which the technology may become attached (Ackrich 1992). In other words, Government policy does not acknowledge the mutual implication of the technical and the social. This is not to suggest that questions about the provision of computer hardware and software are unimportant, far from it. However, understandings of 'information rich' and 'information poor' that focus only on the provision of equipment in the classroom, and ignore wider questions about social practices are, in the words of Knobel and Lankshear (1998: 3), 'radically incomplete'. As Bruce (1998: 12) points out '[t]he more we examine technology, the less we find it useful to focus on its technical attributes per se'. Rather, '[t]o understand what technology means, we must examine how its designed, interpreted, employed, constructed, and reconstructed through value-laden daily practices,' (ibid.: 12).

Our three case studies demonstrate that ICT emerges as a very different tool in different schools, or what we have termed, after Wenger (1998), 'communities of practice'. We can pick out three clear examples of these differences. First, in Westport the town's spatial isolation means that ICT emerges as an important tool for communication (between pupils within the school, between the school and home/local community and between the school and the wider world); whereas at Station Road the socio-economic deprivation of the local community means that ICT emerges as a 'life skill'. Second, while at Highfields ICT is anchored to an agenda of academic attainment for pupils in which social inequalities are overlooked, at Station Road ICT is woven into a much broader community-oriented agenda. Here, some parents have been redefined through their use of ICT (as have their relationships with the school, labour market, and so on) – going on to gain higher education qualifications. In this way, while ICT is mobilised at Highfields in a way that serves to channel or stabilise existing social relations, at Station Road ICT emerges as a tool which has political strength, changing and redefining actors and the relationships between them. Third, while the access policy at Westport means that twice as many children regularly use ICT outside lessons than at Station Road; adults in the community are excluded from using the technology, presenting an obvious contrast with Station Road.

In other words, by thinking about social exclusion from the Information Age in terms of questions of everyday access to ICT, rather than merely focusing on the broad-scale distribution of resources, we have begun to highlight the importance of the way that technologies and people/institutions co-develop. This understanding of ICT within a school context has obvious consequences for government policies aimed at preventing the emergence of a society in which the technologically poor are disenfranchised from 'normal' activities. If the UK Government is to pursue its stated aims of providing IT opportunities for all, it needs to pay more attention to what happens when schools and technology are brought together. Rather than focusing on the provision of hardware and software alone, it needs to recognise the complex ways in which ICT emerge as different tools within different communities of practice (Valentine *et al.* 2002).

We further develop this focus on social exclusion as something produced through everyday practice in the following chapter. Here, in keeping with our understanding of children as social actors in their own right, we move first from considering adult-structured institutional cultures, towards a focus on children's own worlds and their own understandings of technology.

Chapter 3

Peer pressure
ICT in the classroom

In Chapter 2 we began to cut a way through much of the hype about the inclusionary and exclusionary potential of ICT. Looking first at the global level, we showed that the rapid development of ICT may well underpin 'globalising' processes and the creation of a networked society but argued that the results are far from global in their impact. Indeed, most of the world's population do not have access to, or in some cases even live within easy reach of, such technologies (Kitchin, 1998a). We then examined British policy within this context, to show how the Labour Government is attempting to harness the wealth-creating potential of an ICT-skilled workforce in the global economy, at the same time as trying to prevent the technologically poor from becoming socially excluded by providing 'IT for All'. These twin concerns of the need for future workers to develop ICT skills, and fears that some may be left out of these new developments are articulated in relation to children through education policy debates and also, in different ways, within our case-study schools. These different agendas, as we showed in the previous chapter, are not only evident in teacher rhetoric, but also in the ways that the staff organise the physical distribution of, and social access to, on-line computers in their buildings. As a result, computers come to mean different things in the different schools, and some children benefit from greater access to them than others. In sum, the different ways that these schools have incorporated ICT into their institutional agendas and practices demonstrate that technology has no pre-given effects, but that its meanings and implications emerge as computers and social actors come together in different communities of practice (Wenger 1998).

We want to take this argument further in this chapter by exploring in more detail the importance of institutional cultures in shaping the relationships different children form with ICT. So far we have considered the importance of institutional cultures primary in terms of official school policy, and to a lesser extent teacher practice. Here, we broaden this view to consider further the importance of teacher practice, and the crucial influence of children's own cultures. For it is not simply the case that the Government presents technology to teachers in certain ways, and that teachers pick selectively from this in introducing ICT into their school in a particular way. Teachers' everyday practices and differences between children also matter to the ways that pupils understand, value, take up or reject ICT within the school context. Our aim then is to explore how different children's classroom computing cultures are shaped not only by official school policy but also through teachers' classroom practices and pupil cultures. In doing so we highlight the ways that these multi-layered institutional cultures draw on wider repertoires of resources, for example, socially sanctioned ideas about the inherent properties of technology and acceptable modes of masculine behaviour. We also show how they are reproduced within the micro-geographies of the classroom, as this space is shaped by and reshapes regulative codes of behaviour for different social groups. The chapter is organised into two main sections. The first draws on critical studies of education to place the school, as an institution, in a broader social context. The second section develops insights from this literature to examine the ways that different groups of children relate to ICT in our case-study schools.

Computers in the classroom: education, ICT and identity politics

To begin to analyse the importance of inclusionary and exclusionary processes in children's school-based use of ICT we first need to place this institutional space – the school, and more specifically the ICT classroom – in a broader context. Schools, a wide variety of researchers in the social sciences argue, are an arena where children's identities are shaped, often in ways that reproduce inequalities between pupils. In Aitken's words:

> A major purpose of school control is to socialize children with regard to their roles in life and their places in society. It serves the larger stratified society by inculcating compliant citizens and productive workers who will be prepared to assume roles considered appropriate to the pretension of their race, class and gender identities.
>
> (1994: 90)

One of the first concerns to be raised was that working-class pupils were being short-changed by the educational system, and in the terms of Willis's (1977) classic study were 'learning to labour' (see also Corrigan 1979). The class biases that this genre of investigation exposed were of considerable importance, and differences in the quality and form of education available to middle-class and working-class students continue to be a pressing concern for researchers today. Nevertheless, these studies of 'how working-class kids get working-class jobs' were subject to feminist critique for their near universal focus on working-class boys rather than girls (see Acker 1994; Skelton 1998). This neglect of girls was challenged through the 1980s and 1990s. An increasing body of work addressed the ways in which the formal and hidden curriculum in schools can lead to gender inequality and the reproduction of stereotypically masculine and feminine gender identities (Riddell 1989; Shilling 1991; Clark and Millard 1998; Paechter 1998). A similar trend is evident in respect to racial discrimination, as researchers in this field explore the processes that close down the choices and potential of students from ethnic minorities. By the end of the 1990s, however, the debate appeared to have come full circle as girls' increasing success in examination results led to considerable academic and policy concern about the under-achievement of boys (Spender 1997; Skelton 1998).

Such research which examines how differences between children are (re)inscribed in the school context has addressed pupils' experiences in a variety of different subject areas, and ICT lessons are no exceptions to this. Much of the literature produced over the past ten to twenty years has examined gender differences in children's attitudes to, and use of, ICT, although differences in class background have also been considered. Overall, these studies have demonstrated that boys tend to like computers more than girls (Shashaani 1993; Reinen and Plomp, 1997; Brosnan 1998; Opie 1998) and express greater confidence in their ability to use them (Comber *et al.* 1997; Nelson and Cooper 1997; Reinen and Plomp 1997). Although some cyber-feminists have argued that computer-mediated communications may open up potentially liberatory spaces for women (Light 1997; Plant, 1996), girls in school are often a little more wary. In what has become known as the 'we can/I can't' paradox (Collis 1985), they tend to make a general argument for gender equality by insisting that girls as a whole are as good at computing as boys (a view which not all boys share – Shashaani 1993). At the same time, however, they downplay their own confidence and abilities by stating that they personally are not very good at using them (Shashaani 1993; Comber *et al.* 1997; Reinen and Plomp 1997). These differences in attitudes are reflected in usage patterns. These show that boys' greater access to computers in the home (Durndell and Thomson 1997; Reinen and Plomp 1997; Opie 1998) tends to be compounded by their school experiences, where they both use computers more than girls, and for a wider range of activities (Hickling-Hudson 1992; Reinen and Plomp 1997). Such a pattern is also evident where we consider class inequalities. Middle-class students are more likely to have access to a computer in the home than their working-class counterparts (see Chapter 2). This is an advantage compounded in many countries where schools serving a middle-class constituency tend to have better computing provision than schools with fewer financial resources in more deprived areas (Hickling-Hudson 1992).

These variations in the level of provision available in different schools, though significant in Britain, are not the focus of this chapter. Rather, we draw on research in three schools with levels of provision which would be considered good when compared to the national average in order that we might examine how children use ICT when it is available to them. Over 95 per cent of children we surveyed in these schools had used a computer in class, and most enjoyed doing so, reporting that they prefer lessons that involve ICT to those that do not (see Table 3.1). Far fewer children have taken advantage of computer facilities out of class time, but interestingly Westport, which at 52 per cent, already has the highest level of out-of-class usage is also the school where demand for more access is greatest. In all schools, pupils use this out-of-class access for a range of activities. The two most popular at Highfields and Station Road are word-processing and game playing, whereas at Westport email is the most common out-of-class activity, followed by word-processing. However, while differences in the levels of provision between schools are not of central concern here, the gender differences in pupils' attitudes towards ICT that have been highlighted in a number of previous studies are of considerable importance in our case-study schools (see Table 3.1). More boys than girls in these schools said they preferred lessons that utilise computers, and they were also more likely to rate computer skills as very important in their future. Similarly, more boys than girls in all three schools had used computers out of class time, and with the notable exception of Westport, it was boys who were most keen for further out-of-class access.

(Re)producing difference in the classroom

Considerable effort has been made within critical studies of education (see, for example, Riddell 1989; Skeggs 1991; Epstein 1997; Paechter 1998) to identify the mechanisms through which the school system (re)produces differences between children. The hope is that by critiquing current practice, problems might be identified, rectified and a more equitable education system put into place. Perhaps unsurprisingly, what researchers in this field have found is that the processes through which difference is made and remade are complicated, and thus while some simple policy initiatives can represent an important step in the right direction, they are unlikely to solve these enduring problems overnight. Particularly important in this has been the insistence by researchers in this field that the problems identified are not simply the 'top down' creations of school management practices. Rather, these studies explore the importance of different factors, including school policies, teachers' classroom practices and pupils' cultures, and the different time and spaces within the school in which they dominate (e.g. the staffroom, the classroom before and after the teacher arrives, and the playground), in shaping the institutional culture through which difference is (re)produced. In effect, they characterise the school as an institution that is constituted through multiple cultures, and consist of a series of (overlapping) time-spaces (Holloway *et al.* 2000).

Table 3.1 Children's attitudes to and use of computers in the three case-study schools (%)

Questions	Highfields			Station Road			Westport		
	All	Boys	Girls	All	Boys	Girls	All	Boys	Girls
Attitudes									
Prefer lessons with computers	80	85	73	82	87	76	69	74	62
Computers skills very important to my future	43	50	35	53	58	48	43	48	38
Internet very important to my future	28	34	21	33	45	16	33	44	21
Access									
Have used a computer in class	99	99	98	96	96	95	98	99	97
Have used a computer at school out of class	40	45	35	44	47	40	52	57	47
Want more out-of-class access to computers	48	57	37	46	51	40	60	58	61
Out-of-class use									
Word-process	57	60	52	39	39	41	47	53	40
Spreadsheets	22	26	15	16	19	10	20	26	12
Browse WWW	21	24	16	14	16	10	43	53	30
E-mail	4	3	5	2	2	0	51	43	62
Chat on Internet	18	17	18	5	7	2	19	22	13
Play games	30	33	25	51	55	43	30	34	24

This emphasis on the multi-faceted nature of institutional cultures can also be discerned in the range of possible explanations put forward by educational researchers keen to account for children's varied relationships with ICT in the classroom. Some authors suggest that institutional policy might be important in reproducing gender differences and contrast, for example, the different ways in which schools integrate the teaching of ICT into the curriculum (Hickling-Hudson 1992, Reinen and Plomp 1997; Schofield, 1997; Opie 1998). Equally important is the suggestion that the predominance of male teachers and their classroom practices may serve to make computers more interesting to boys than to girls (Hickling-Hudson 1992; Shashaani 1993; Reinen and Plomp 1997; Schofield 1997; Spender 1997; Opie 1998). Finally, a number of authors have pointed out that pupil cultures are likely to be important. Girls and boys not only learn about the gendering of technology within the classroom but also bring gendered attitudes to computers with them to the classroom, attitudes that have been shaped through their experiences in other environments (Hickling-Hudson 1992; Schofield 1997; Spender 1997; Opie 1998).

We find the emphasis in critical education on the different aspects of institutional cultures particularly compelling, and research specifically focused on children's use of ICT would seem to suggest this three-fold approach might have some explanatory power. However, while educationalists have put considerable effort into identifying differences in pupils' attitudes to and use of computers, and into suggesting possible explanations for these patterns, there are few detailed ethnographic studies of computer use in schools that evaluate the verity of these possible explanations, or analyse how the processes might operate in practice. Given our insistence in the previous chapter that the introduction of ICT into a school does not have any inevitable, pre-definable effects, we consider it essential to examine exactly what does happen when children and computers come together in the classroom context. It is only by examining in detail the development and nature of the relationships that different children form with ICT that we can begin to understand why the differences between pupils, such as those highlighted above, are so prevalent.

Before we go on to examine the importance of school policy, teacher practice and pupil cultures in relation to our own research, however, we want to draw out two further elements of these arguments about multi-faceted institutional cultures which have not yet been examined in relation to children's computing practices. First, as geographers, we are interested in the notions of spatiality with which work in the field of critical education is imbued. In arguing that institutional cultures are shaped by a variety of actors, some of whom are more important in some time–spaces than others, researchers in this field implicitly theorise institutional cultures as spatial as well as social projects. A few go further and explicitly theorise the ways in which the school is both embedded within wider socio-spatial relations, and a site through which these socio-spatial relations are reproduced (Shilling 1991; Dixon 1997). Shilling, for example, argues that:

> Schools and areas within them, such as the playground areas and the staffroom, are gendered locales in which boys and male staff draw on patriarchal rules and resources (ranging from violence to sexist humour) in attempting to exert dominance over girls and women teachers. In doing this, they attempt to reproduce locales as areas which both facilitate and symbolise their super-ordinate position.
>
> (ibid.: 39)

In doing so, he simultaneously draws attention to the ways in which the school is embedded within wider structures – the individuals within schools draw upon societal rules and resources in their everyday social interaction –

and to the ways space within schools is constituted through, and comes to symbolise, social and material relations of control that work to enable and sanction some forms of behaviour and not others. Dixon's study (1997) of identity and sex-play within design and technology lessons also illustrates these processes well. On the one hand, she shows how children's behaviour in the classroom draws on wider social resources, with their behaviour being 'tangible at a macro social level, in that they resonate with global and culturally specific historical forms of masculinity' (ibid.: 89). On the other hand, she also stresses that the micro-spaces of the classroom are important because they are '"overwritten" in specific ways by regulative codes of gender, class and "race"' (ibid.: 92). Implicitly, and occasionally explicitly, this body of work thus draws our attention to the school as a spatial as well as a social project. Not only are different time–spaces within the school constituted in different ways, the school itself is a porous site, constructed and reconstructed through its interconnectivity with wider society (Holloway et al. 2000).

Second, given our interest in the new social studies of childhood (see Chapter 1), we are particularly interested in the attention paid to children's cultures in these analyses of institutional spaces. Their emphasis on multiple cultures and overlapping time–spaces, rather than simply on the importance of top-down management practices, usefully illustrates the importance of children's agency. This is something which researchers in the new social studies of childhood have also been insisting upon over the past decade (James and Prout, 1990; Mayall 1994; Qvortrup et al. 1994; James et al. 1998). Recognition of the multiple spaces within the classroom, for example, points to the importance of children's resourcefulness and agency, even in contexts where they have little formal power. Moreover, the attention paid to teacher practice in association with pupil cultures reminds us that alliances can be built across the adult–child divide, as well as within these categories. In sum, the emphasis in this particular body of work on multiple cultures and overlapping time/spaces usefully stresses children's agency, their power to both resist and ally themselves with adults, as well as the ways in which they are controlled by them. This is particularly pertinent as all cultures are reproduced through everyday practice, and this means they are not forever fixed, solidified in place, but open to change (Holloway et al. 2000).

In the next section of this chapter we go on to examine the importance of school policy, teacher practice and pupil cultures in the way that different children's relations with ICT emerge in our case-study schools. As part and parcel of this analysis, we also take ideas about multi-faceted institutional cultures one step further, and examine the importance of socio-spatial relations and children's agency in shaping children's computing cultures.

Children's computing cultures

Perhaps one of the most noticeable aspects of the ICT lessons we observed in the case-study schools was their relatively relaxed atmosphere. Schofield (1997: 35), in a review of research on computers and classroom social processes, points to a number of studies (see for example Chaiklin and Lewis, 1988; Davidson and Ritchie 1994; O'Connor and Brie 1994; Schofield 1995) that suggest that the introduction of computers into the classroom tends to be associated with 'a shift in teachers' roles away from didactic whole class instruction towards more individualized and student-centred interaction'. Such a shift might have been expected at Westport where greater emphasis is placed on encouraging children to learn the skills required to use ICT, rather than on teaching ICT as an examination subject. However, this atmosphere was equally apparent at Highfields and Station Road where children found ICT lessons more relaxed than other classes despite the fact many would eventually gain an educational qualification in the subject. This is because of the level of autonomy children have in relation to their learning. Pupils at Highfields, for example, described how their work in other lessons is strictly controlled by the teachers, and they are required to concentrate for long periods of time, listening to teachers, taking notes from the board or working from books. In ICT lessons by contrast, the pupils are taught as a group when a new task that will take several lessons to complete is introduced, but are then allowed to work through this at their own pace soliciting help from the teacher as and when required. Fay from Highfields describes what her ICT classes are like:

FAY BEDFORD: I think they're like more relaxing than other lessons, because I mean the atmosphere of it – of the lessons like – I mean it's a warm room to start with – I don't know if that has anything to do with it . . . you're boiling. But it's like, you go in there and it's not like other lessons because people are just more relaxed about it, because you do things at your own pace more. It's not like a teacher standing there doing all the stuff and then you have to get on with a set piece of work. They let you just come in and do it straightaway (Highfields).

This informality is emphasised for those pupils who are good at IT and therefore find the lessons less demanding. Though differences in ability are evident in all classes, they are more emphasised in those which are not streamed by ability. Here, the brighter pupils can handle the work with ease and are left with time to themselves. Identified as one of the benefits of learning with computers, the relaxed classroom atmosphere that such student-centred teaching styles encourage, also have other implications. Most notably, social relations between children are more evident here than in strictly controlled classrooms where adult–child power relations are often more important. The IT lesson is thus a space within the school where teacher practice means pupil culture can come to dominate.

Perhaps the most obvious manifestation of this pupil culture is the highly segregated pattern of seating which develops in most ICT classes, especially in the younger years of secondary schooling. Take one year 9 class at Highfields as an example. In the middle of the Highfields IT classroom are several rows of school tables facing the front, and the computers are arranged on desks facing both side walls and the end wall of the room. In theory, when entering the classroom the children are supposed to sit at the central tables, but in practice many compete to appropriate a computer of their own because unless students are away ill, there are not quite enough machines for everyone to have one each. The seating arrangements these practices produce are highly structured and reflect wider sets of social relations. Most notably, the seating arrangements tend to be gender segregated as boys occupy one side of the classroom and most of the end wall, the girls (of whom there are slightly fewer in this particular class) the other side wall. However, within this gender-segregated pattern other differences also begin to emerge. A group of boys noticeably more keen on computers than the others occupy the computers near the front of the classroom, the other 'white' lads use the remaining computers on this side wall, while the back wall is primarily occupied by a small group of Asian lads. The girls' side of the classroom is split into two discernible groups, one of which contains girls who are more studious than the others (all the girls in this class are white).

Having identified why pupils' cultures are more dominant in the ICT classroom than other lessons, we want to move on now to consider the relationships different children in our case-study schools develop with ICT. For clarity we divide the children into four groups: the 'techno boys', the 'lads', the 'luddettes' and the 'computer competent girls'. We do not want to suggest, however, that these four groups are ever-present and internally cohesive. In what follows we therefore draw out tensions within these groups, their different manifestations within different schools, and ways in which the contours of these groups are transformed as children's relations with technology change over time.

The techno boys

At both Highfields and Station Road there is a group of boys in each class whose interests revolve around computers. The techno boys, as we call them, are generally highly technologically literate. They have mastered a wide range of software applications, have a developing understanding of programming and often the skills to take apart and re-assemble computers. Their interest in ICT is an important influence on their social networks because they choose to 'hang out' with other boys who share their interests. Charles Stevenson, a year 11 pupil at Highfields explains:

CHARLES STEVENSON: Well, one of [my friends], called Jamie . . . was in my form all through school. But then a couple of months ago, about the start of this year, we both realised we really liked computer games. And that sort of made us more friends like. Or closer friends. And then most of my other friends I just made through computer games. Or computers . . . that's sort of all we normally talk about. The latest computer games or how far we got on a certain game or whatever (Highfields).

This enthusiasm for computer games, in Charles's case, also carries over into an enthusiasm for ICT lessons. In the extract below, he describes how he and his friend rush to the ICT class after registration in order to ensure that they can have sole access to, and therefore control over, a PC during the lesson:

CHARLES STEVENSON: There's the odd occasion when there are more people and two of us, we have to share one computer, but it's not that often – we normally sort of – 'cos our form room, it's either in the room just below here or in the actual computer room, so on Friday mornings we can just get in there before anyone else and get to the computer. Like this morning we were in there – me and Daniel were in there before anyone else 'cos we'd just been to have registration (Highfields).

Indeed, this enthusiasm for the educational uses of ICT also extends into some of the pupils' extra-curricular activities. Simon Radford and Gregory Hobson, year 10 students at Station Road, for example, were more than happy to give up their free time to help their teachers build up the school computing resources:

SIMON RADFORD: Yeah, we spent a lot of time after school, before school.
GREGORY HOBSON: We actually came in about half an hour before.
SIMON RADFORD: [interrupts] 8 o'clock in the morning we came in every morning.
GREGORY HOBSON: Yeah, about 40 minutes before school.
INTERVIEWER: So why were you willing to spend that time?
GREGORY HOBSON: Don't know.
SIMON RADFORD: Don't know. It's just – we don't know, its just computers we think. We're just addicted [both laugh]. We are. We're addicted.
GREGORY HOBSON: Better than drugs.
SIMON RADFORD: I know, we're on drugs – computer drugs (Station Road).

In short, ICT usage is central to these boys' lives such that it in part shapes their friendship ties, is integrated into their school work as much as possible and takes up a large amount of their free time.

The presence of this group goes some way towards explaining the gender differences in attitudes to and use of computers, especially the greater numbers of boys using computers out of class time (see Table 3.1). The techno boys' manifest 'lead' in terms of ICT literacy does not, however, mean that they 'lead' the way socially, rather they tend to be a rather marginal social group within their school. On the one hand, some of the other boys, who we refer to here as 'the lads', (see the following section for further details) argue that these techno boys exclude themselves, keeping themselves to themselves and not wanting to make friends with the rest of the lads.

CALVIN HIGGENS: They just sit in one [corner], they stay there, just chat between themselves and . . .
MARCUS JONES: They don't try to make friends with anyone else.
CALVIN HIGGENS: They don't, no.
MARCUS JONES: Except their group kind of thing (Highfields).

On the other hand, we can see that the techno boys' skills are not highly valued by the lads who are more interested in traditionally masculine activities such as football. Far from winning them the respect of their colleagues, the techno boys' skills earn them labels such as 'boffin', 'computer freak' and 'nerd', further compounding their isolation within the classroom.

This is particularly clear in one of our case-study schools, Station Road. Here, widely understood ideas about computer 'nerds' as socially inadequate, rather unmasculine men informed social attitudes within the school leading to the marginalisation of those boys who had an interest in computing. For example, the set of lads quoted below disliked the techno boys in their class partly because these boys preferred computer-related hobbies to sporting activities, a choice which emasculated them in the eyes of the lads, opening them up to insults which imply effeminacy and, consequently, homosexuality. Thus an apparently innocuous question about which boys were best at using computers in their class, produced the following answer:

DARREN BROWN: Giles Chester's a bit of a girl.
SAM COLBY: He's, he's, he's a girl.
INTERVIEWER: Bit of a girl?
MATT DOWSON: Yeah, he's a right weirdo [Edit].
DARREN BROWN: He's like, he acts like a girl in class he's . . .
SAM COLBY: He's a ponce.
MATT DOWSON: Yeah.
INTERVIEWER: A ponce?
SAM COLBY: Yeah, yeah, he is. He's, he is like a lass, he just . . . It's like we, we do our work quick and that, and like boys play football and that. He thinks that he's good at football, can't play football, thinks that he, thinks that he can play cricket, can't play cricket, can't play rugby.
DARREN BROWN: Yeah, he's best at trampolining, like girls' sports (Station Road).

At one level, these comments could simply be read as an extreme response to the techno boys, produced as these lads attempted to show off within the context of the focus group. However, their choice of target, and the logic of their insults is instructive. The link they make from computer nerd, to girl, to ponce is not original. Mac an Ghaill (1996) points out that involvement in sport is often read as a cultural index of what it means to be a 'real boy', and lack of participation in such activities and their associated lad culture is to be a bit of a 'poof'. Thus the lads at Station Road are drawing on wider ideas about gender and sexuality in their derision of the techno boys. What we get from this is a sense of the porosity of the school – it is not a bounded site, rather, it is constructed and reconstructed through its interconnectivity with wider society.

This group of techno boys are also disliked, or privately disparaged, by most of the girls in their class. This dislike does not stem from their intelligence or ability, indeed the girls draw a distinction between these techno boys and those boys who have all-round ability in a variety of classes. Nor does it stem from an interpretation of the techno boys' interest in ICT as in some way feminised, as was the case with the lads. Rather, the girls interpret the techno boys' interests in ICT through wider ideas about marginal heterosexual masculinities. First, the techno boys' interest in ICT is coded as socially unattractive by the girls through its association with a wider range of activities that are broadly defined in popular cultures as 'geekie'. As one group of luddettes – the terms we use to refer to computer-dismissive girls – explains, these boys are only interested in computers, fishing and science fiction:

HANNAH CAMPBELL: You overhear their conversations and its all about fishing and computers [Edit].
LOTTY KENNISON: What computer magazine they're gonna buy this week.
JULIE JAMES: Yeah, how far I got on . . .
HANNAH CAMPBELL: Yeah.
JULIE JAMES: Whatever computer game they play.
HANNAH CAMPBELL: And they all like *Star Trek* as well (Highfields).

Second, the techno boys socially marginal interests are compounded by their bodily presentation – including the wearing of work-style trousers and shirts – which is understood by the girls to be unappealing. They explain:

HANNAH CAMPBELL: Well, they're not very good-looking.
JULIE JAMES: No.
LOTTY KENNISON: Not good-looking and they don't care what they look like and they're immature (Highfields).

Rather than draw on homophobic discourses – which are at their root misogynist because they rest on a rejection of all that is constructed as feminine

(Epstein 1993) – these girls continue to construct the technoboys as hetero-sexual males. Males, however, whose bodies are inscribed upon and constructed through the computers they use (Lupton 1995). Notably the girls draw on imaginings of 'teckies' in popular culture, where computer enthu-siasts are commonly represented as being physically unattractive, wearing glasses, having bad skin and poor fashion sense. These images inform their understandings of the techno boys' bodies as an unattractive product of spending too much time staring at a screen (ibid.). In sum, the girls interpret the techno boys' interests and bodily presentations as socially and physically unattractive through reference to wider stereotypes about 'geeks' and 'nerds' that they regard as the unacceptable, if nevertheless heterosexual, opposite of desirable masculinity.

Both these examples serve to illustrate how wider ideas can shape the school, and thus reproduce the ICT classroom as a space in which certain forms of behaviour are coded as marginal and hence are policed. We do not want to suggest, however, that this is the only way in which an intense inter-est in ICT may be understood by children. At a general level the picture with respect to the gendering and sexing of ICT is subtly different at Westport (an issue we discuss in the following section). On a more specific level, some children, even within schools where boys' interest in ICT is derided, can per-form their technological competence in socially acceptable ways. One boy, Joshua, is a particularly pertinent example of this because his overt perfor-mance of ICT competence at Highfields lead, to his social inclusion rather than marginalisation. Joshua is a loner and the only Afro-Caribbean pupil in the classes we studied at Highfields. He is highly technologically competent and is taking extra IT lessons as part of an attempt by the school to curb his 'behavioural problems', in particular his poor attendance rate. His enthusi-asm for ICT might be expected to contribute to his marginalisation within the class. However, other aspects of his behaviour earn him the respect of the girls in particular. In one sense, his lack of respect for school authority leads to him being seen rather approvingly as a 'bad boy', whereas occasional poor behaviour by the techno boys is constructed as annoying and immature. Moreover, Joshua does not compound an interest in ICT with a bodily per-formance akin to the other techno boys. Rather he performs his bodily identity in ways that are considered fashionable by pupils in general, and attractive by the girls in particular. In this way, Joshua manages to change the meaning of ICT competence, at least for himself if not at a more general level, by combining it with hegemonic performance of attractive heterosex-ual masculinity.

The lads

This generally negative construction of ICT competence at Highfields and Station Road means that the other 'lads', as we call them here, take great care about how they present themselves, lest they be considered 'computer freaks'. The label 'boffin' is something that these lads actively contest when applied to themselves, and use as an insult with which to tease their friends, as this extract from a Highfields focus group discussion illustrates:

SAM BOWDON: I don't know everything, I mean, you couldn't ask me a question on computers and I'd be able to answer it straightaway.
DAVID GOULD: You could.
SAM BOWDON: I don't know everything about computers.
LIAM HENDERSON: You do.
DAVID GOULD: You do.
SAM BOWDON: That's not fair, I don't know how to do everything, there are some things I don't know how to do (Highfields).

Nevertheless these lads are generally able to, and do, use computers in a variety of ways and contexts. The culture of game playing is more widespread and much less 'feminised' than the techno boys' interest in computers as machines and thus provides one way in which the lads gain positive associations with computers. Equally, some of the lads like using the WWW, often searching for stereotypically masculine things, for example, their favourite football teams or bands. These activities are ways in which boys, while downplaying their technical competence, can nevertheless make use of the potential of ICT *and* reinforce their status as lads.

A particularly pertinent example of this is the use a group of year 9 lads from Highfields makes of the Internet during their IT lessons. To encourage them to work, the teacher allows the pupils to play on the Internet after finishing their allotted tasks. Consequently, the lads rush through their work in order to have time to play on the Internet, and sometimes abuse the system by playing on it before finishing their work. Their use of the Internet is both stereotypically masculine, and within normative models of heterosexuality, involving as it does searching for sporting heroes, popular bands and pictures of semi-naked women, particularly actresses, pop stars and super models (see Figure 3.1), as these boys describe:

SAM BOWDON: You type in a name and it gives you a list.
DAVID GOULD: It's got different websites on.
SAM BOWDON: It gives 10 on a page and it'll say one page out of 2743.
DAVID GOULD: So, say, you're searching for Jennifer Anniston [a very attractive actress], it'll say Jennifer Aniston's official homepage.
PAUL ROWLAND: Yes, it might bring up information on her.
DAVID GOULD: And then it'll say exclusive pictures of Jennifer Anniston.
SAM BOWDON: Nude pics XXX or something like that. It'll have that on, and obviously you don't go to that site, you go to the official homepage [in an insincere tone. All laughing].

Figure 3.1 Surfing for pornography on-line reinforces boys' understandings of themselves as heterosexual young men. © Jacky Fleming.

INTERVIEWER: Meaning you ignore the official homepage and go the nude XXX site?

SAM BOWDON: Non, non, no [in a mocking tone].

DAVID GOULD: Yes.

PAUL ROWLAND: Yes.

LIAM HENDERSON: Yes [All laughing] (Highfields).

This particular use of the WWW allows boys to demonstrate an interest in, and aptitude for, computers while also reinforcing their understanding of themselves as heterosexual young men. In searching for websites they bond with each other, sharing pictures and jokes between themselves. The resources they draw upon, both ideologically in terms of ideas about acceptable heterosexual masculinity, and materially, in terms of the websites they visit, extend beyond the classroom. These allow them to reproduce this form of masculinity for themselves within the micro-geographies of the classroom. The boys (correctly) assume that the other lads with whom they are sitting will not 'tell on them' and the male teacher will turn a blind eye, understanding that they have a natural sex drive.

SAM BOWDON: Mr Matthews isn't actually that bad though, he lets you . . .

DAVID GOULD: He lets you go on some sites.

SAM BOWDON: He doesn't encourage it but . . .

LIAM HENDERSON: When he finds us he threatens to [switch the connection to the Internet off] . . .

SAM BOWDON: I think he understands that we are going to look at it.

DAVID GOULD: If it's there, then we are gonna look at it (Highfields).

In this context, the relaxed atmosphere that non-didactic styles of teaching promote (Schofield 1997) allows the lads to reproduce the classroom as a both a gendered and heterosexed space. For example, the girls describe how the boys try to trick them into looking at pictures that they regard as pornographic (these might more accurately be described as 'glamour' pictures because hard-core porn would both be filtered by the school system, and usually require access to a credit card):

JEMMA DELANEY: . . . the boys just like put a porn picture on for like . . .

LOUISE WHEATCROFT: All the lesson . . .

JASMINE TOWERS: And they, like, sit there, laughing at it.

JEMMA DELANEY: Laughing at it or looking at it, and it's really annoying, and they shout out 'Louise, Jemma!' And we, like, turn round and you've just got this picture of a naked woman (Highfields).

The girls' response to this type of behaviour is ambivalent. On the one hand, they regard the lads as 'dirty creeps' (Helen) and 'little perverts' (Louise) who have a poor attitude to women. Interestingly, the girls construct this behaviour in essentialist terms, regarding it as a product of the boys' biology rather than social relations in the classroom as Chloë Robinson and Suzy Frear explain:

CHLOE ROBINSON: . . . they're just dirty. It's just natural for boys to do that.

SUZY FREAR: It's just men isn't it (Highfields).

On the other hand, the sexualised climate in the classroom means some girls feel pressured into appearing attractive to these lads despite reservations about their attitudes to women. Louise explains:

LOUISE WHEATCROFT: You sort of feel sort of special if you are [pretty] 'cos they don't sort of hate you (Highfields).

Contrary to the girls' analysis of the boys' behaviour as natural, we would argue that teacher practice in this particular case allows boys to reproduce the classroom as a space in which the low-level sexual harassment of young women becomes possible. As Dixon (1997: 101) found in her study of a design and technology classroom:

whilst this teacher places himself within a liberal agenda and 'child centred' educational discourse, his abdication from setting the cultural
agenda in the lesson creates the opportunity for students to rehearse and
reconstruct meanings of gender and power in oppressive ways.

Such practices, however, are far from inevitable. The response of Asian boys
within the classroom at Highfields, for example, did not follow the same pattern as the 'white' lads discussed above. These boys used the technology to
search for traditionally masculine interests such as football and cars but not
for sexualised pictures of women. Here, again we see the importance of
children's agency. Like the girls, these Asian boys considered the 'white'
lads' behaviour to be inappropriate in a classroom and at a basic level
argued that it was degrading to women. They therefore negotiate for themselves a significantly different relationship with technology that never results
in their emasculation in the eyes of others, nor to sexualised, hypermasculine
performances. (These differing attitudes to gender were but one of the differences between these two groups of young men: considerable tension also
existed around the issue of 'race', as the Asian boys regarded the 'white' boys
as racist. In turn the 'white' boys argued that they were not racist but that it
was hard to make friends with the Asian boys because they stuck together
and were always looking for a fight.)

The experience at Westport – which as we explained in Chapter 2 has an
official emphasis on computer use rather than computer studies – further
demonstrates that societal understanding of the gendering of technology
can to an extent be reworked within the context of multi-faceted school cultures. Though Westport's classroom culture has much in common with
Highfields and Station Road – pupils, for example, tend to sit in single-sex
groups, and both boys and girls are well aware of the stereotypes about computer nerds – the gendered meanings of computers are beginning to change
for some pupils. Rather than PCs being linked *per se* with certain types of
masculinity, certain Internet-based activities – most notably, browsing web-
pages – are becoming coded as things which boys do, and other activities –
particularly email and chat – are becoming coded as things which girls do
(see also Chapter 6). These year 10 pupils explain:

LOUISE BOSWELL: Boys go on all the boring stuff.
CAROLINE DENNINGTON: Yeah, they go on like the Internet [meaning WWW]
    more don't they and stuff (Westport).

DARREN POTTER: You do get the girls using it a lot, sending emails to each
    other, they love it, yeah.
THOMAS WOODWARD: They go on all the chat pages as well on the Internet.
DARREN POTTER: In fact it's like 90 per cent of the girls know how to use
    these chat pages and the boys don't (Westport).

The gendering of technology persists then at Westport, but on a subtly different terrain. The activities for which the computers are used are important here. Showing the continued importance of wider ideas about gender relations, both boys and girls deploy essentialist explanations for these patterns. For example, boys and girls explain girls' greater liking for email in terms of girls' greater interest in communication: for girls this is a positive feature, a result of the fact that 'girls talk more'; for boys this is room for disparaging humour, seeing chatting as 'women's work'. A final point of interest is the way in which this process of (re)coding has been picked up on by the staff and exploited in a pragmatic way.

JAMES PUNT (IT teacher): Girls will use, have been brought into the use of the Internet by Internet mail, it's had a dramatic impact in the amount of girls who sit in front of PCs (Westport).

Though the introduction of email was not specifically intended to increase girls' use of computers, the staff have capitalised on this result as a way of realising their aim to get a wider variety of pupils to feel 'at home' with computers. In this example, teacher practice encourages a wider range of children to form positive relationships with ICT than would otherwise have been the case.

Computer-competent girls

Turning to look specifically at the girls, we can see that, despite variations in their abilities, most girls at Highfields and Station Road are capable of basic computer operations (including word-processing, setting up databases, transferring files between applications) which to many adults would signify computer competence. As a group, however, girls at Highfields and Station Road display much less overt interest in computers than either the techno boys or the lads, and find the boys' classroom computing culture unappealing (see also studies by Spender 1997; Turkle 1995). As Haddon (1992) has also found, even highly technologically competent girls' classroom conversation is dominated by non-technical concerns, and is more likely to be about general school gossip than computers. Josy Booth, a year 11 student at Highfields explains:

JOSY BOOTH: I mean, Sophie is good on computers but she just – I don't know, she doesn't talk about it or anything. She just uses the computer. She's got loads of stuff at home 'cos her Dad works for IBM [a computer company], so that's handy. So she knows quite a lot about computers but you wouldn't know unless you were a close friend because she doesn't say anything about it or talk about it or anything. It's not really a very interesting conversation, unless you like that kind of thing I suppose (Highfields).

The girls' classroom culture, in which they draw less attention to themselves than the techno boys, and computer talk remain less important in their lives than other more traditionally feminine interests, puts the 'we can/I can't' paradox identified by Collis (1985) in a new light. These girls did not claim that girls as a group were good at using computers, but that they individually lacked the appropriate skills. Rather, they argued that girls as a whole were as good at computing as boys, that some girls were better than other girls, but that girls as a whole just were not that interested in talking about them.

For some highly computer-competent girls this lack of interest in talking about computers is undoubtedly strategic. As Francesca Leighton from Highfields explains, girls may keep their interests quiet as they realise that their technical competence is not highly valued by their peers and they do not want their identities to be re-coded as 'nerds':

FRANCESCA LEIGHTON: I mean 'cos the people who tend to use it in my year, I suppose, at school, there's a lot of quite stereotypical geeky type people who use it and you just get lumped under that so . . . I mean, I'm not going to lie about it [her computer competence and use of the Internet at home] . . . but I don't know, I wouldn't broadcast it, I suppose. Stupid really, but you know people my age can be cruel about stuff like that (Highfields).

What these girls' performances of technical competence display then is their sophistication as social actors. Not only do they possess technical skills that exceed those of many adults, they have developed spatially differentiated performances of these skills, which when used freely at home win the pride of their parents (see Chapter 4), and when used sparingly at school also win them social popularity as well as the grudging respect of their peers for their technical skill.

Even within Highfields and Station Road, which the questionnaire survey shows had fairly 'traditional' gendered patterns of attitudes to, and use of, computers, there are instances in which girls are beginning to rework institutional culture. On the one hand, a number of highly skilled girls are, often inadvertently, beginning to challenge conventional understandings that computers are boys' toys (Spender 1997), and that boys are consequently better at using them than girls. As one lad from Highfields explains, new meanings of technology are therefore beginning to emerge:

DAVID PHELPS: I think computers are changing because Chlöe has obviously proven that she's better than a lot of the boys put together on a computer and that has sort of changed that perspective, but it is still thought in our class to be, you know, a bloke's thing as a console really (Highfields).

The position of Chlöe Robinson is an interesting one. Previous studies have pointed out that girls have less access to home computing than boys, and this means that they are doubly disadvantaged because home computing provides children with the confidence to make better use of school resources (see also Chapter 2, Opie 1998). Our findings show that there are no significant differences between middle-class boys' and girls' access to a home PC,[1] and that some middle-class girls such as Chlöe Robinson also have parents who positively encourage their daughter's ICT skills (see Chapter 4). This development of Chlöe's computer literacy at home pays dividends in terms of her technical abilities in the classroom where she outperforms many of the boys. In this way, experiences in one socio-spatial environment, the home, provide some girls with the resources to challenge the socio-spatial relations in another, the school.

On the other hand, some girls are beginning to positively and publicly value computer use. At Highfields, for example, some of the more school-centred girls use the attraction of Internet use during lesson time both to reject the anti-work ethos of their class, and to perform an overt interest in computers. While they continue to describe the computer club as 'sad', they nevertheless argue that computers in this instance are 'cool' because they can use them during lessons to search for male pop stars such as the Back Street Boys and Jarvis Cocker, and actors such as Leonardo DiCaprio. These are men who in their terms are 'fit' (heterosexually attractive). In this way, they negotiate an overt interest in computers through their heterosexed gender identities, while attributing different meanings to computer use in different time-spaces.

Equally, some girls at Station Road have started to contest their marginalisation within computing culture, and in particular within out-of-class access spaces, by asking for girl-only computer time to be provided. The girls' interest in computers began when they used the Internet to find information for a project that they were doing on bullying. They enjoyed surfing the Net and encouraged their friends to join them, as Tracey Wilson describes:

TRACEY WILSON: I'd had a few days off so I decided to go up to computer room and finish it off [the project on bullying] and that's when Sarah and Ruth started going. I told them about it and then we just started going up from there, looking on the Internet and what we could find and things like that (Station Road).

However, the girls became frustrated because the boys dominated the terminals, and complained to one of the teachers. He suggested that they might like to start a 'girls' computer club' and announced it in an assembly for them. The club is held in an upstairs computing room, while the original computer club meets at the same time in a downstairs room. These girls explain the social and academic benefits of the club to them:

TRACEY WILSON: It's good so you can know computers better.

JULIE PRENTICE: Yeah.

KAREN MASON: You can find out about your favourite pop group or anything.

TRACEY WILSON: And like when you're in IT club, you can say you've got a new skill in IT club, you can go upstairs and practise.

KAREN MASON: Practise at it.

JULIE PRENTICE: And practise your thing and so you can get right better on a computer (Station Road).

Nevertheless, these girls also face an ongoing battle to gain access to computer games that are currently only available in what they term the 'downstairs club'. Thus while the girls have created a space of empowerment for themselves, it is a space on the margins, the hegemony of the boys in the 'computer club' remains largely undisturbed.

The luddettes

A small proportion of the girls we interviewed claimed that they were no good at computing. Julie, Lotty and Hannah are in year 11 at Highfields. Like the adults cited in Chapter 2 they are aware of the potential importance of ICT in a future information economy, but unlike the adults they do not connect this vision of the future to their need to develop technological skills in the present.

JULIE JAMES: For what? [would PCs be useful for]

LOTTY KENNISON: Well, like all the, most jobs now.

HANNAH CAMPBELL: Yeah.

LOTTY: Need computers for . . . with all this technology coming out they'll be useful. That's why my Mum wanted me to go on it [the PC].

[Edit]

HANNAH CAMPBELL: Yeah there's more, more jobs to do with computers, but umm, don't know, I don't want to do computers on a job.

INTERVIEWER: You don't?

HANNAH CAMPBELL: No, not at all.

JULIE JAMES: I wouldn't touch [one] with a barge-pole (Highfields).

Their technophobia, like the techno boys' ICT competence needs to be set within a social context. In one sense these girls are technophobic because they fear the consequences that ICT literacy would have for their lifestyles. These girls see computers as 'geeky', and incompatible with 'having a life'. In turn this association of the PC with 'sad geeks' 'naturalises' its use as boring and socially undesirable activity. As a result the girls imagine a binary division between on-line and off-line activities and spaces in which on-line activities and spaces are regarded as 'dull', 'boring', 'nerdy' and irrelevant, in contrast to off-line activities and spaces, such as going out clubbing. The girls explain:

JULIE JAMES: [referring to using PCs] It's just I've got better things to do with my life.
LOTTY KENNISON: Yeah.
[Laughter]
INTERVIEWER: I wonder what they are [laughing]?
HANNAH CAMPBELL: Yeah, I wonder what they are as well [laughs].
JULIE JAMES: Won't get into that.
INTERVIEWER: What are these better things to do, go on?
JULIE JAMES: Well, going out.
LOTTY KENNISON: Clubbing. Yeah.
HANNAH CAMPBELL: Yeah.
JULIE JAMES: And other things.
LOTTY KENNISON: I mean, I went out last night, I mean, I wouldn't have stayed in to use a computer. If I'd got chance to go out I'd go out (Highfields).

This example demonstrates that the interaction between technology, bodies, identities and peer group relations is 'complex and continuous and all the elements combined are transforming of, and transformed by each other' (Ormrod 1994: 43).

Not surprisingly perhaps, because of the way in which the meanings of PCs have emerged within the girls' peer culture, Hannah, Lotty and Julie are fearful of being seen to take an interest in ICT because of the potential threat it poses to their identities and social relationships. If they show an interest in technology their embodied identities might be re-coded by their peers as undesirable. As they explain below, their participation in the heterosexual culture of the school is at stake.

INTERVIEWER: So how come you can't be, how come you can't be the type of lass that likes going out and the type . . .?
[laughs]
JULIE JAMES: To use a computer.
HANNAH CAMPBELL: You just wouldn't tell anyone that you were using the computer.
INTERVIEWER: Oh right, you wouldn't tell anyone?
HANNAH CAMPBELL: No.
INTERVIEWER: So why not? [edit] . . .
HANNAH CAMPBELL: It's a boffin's thing to do isn't it?
JULIE JAMES: I mean computer boffins, that's what people, well . . .
[Edit]

INTERVIEWER: But you wouldn't want anybody to think you were a computer boffin?

HANNAH CAMPBELL: No.

LOTTY KENNISON: No.

JULIE JAMES: No.

INTERVIEWER: No, why not?

HANNAH CAMPBELL: 'Cos, then, don't get, you don't get invited out or anything like that.

JULIE JAMES: Yeah.

LOTTY KENNISON: You don't pull all these people at little school discos and all that kind of, I don't know . . . (Highfields).

In this way the girls' fears about the threat ICT poses to their identities demonstrate how intimately and complexly the bits and pieces, such as computers, that are part of our everyday worlds are involved in our social relations (Wenger 1998).

Those children who have access to a PC at home have the opportunity to develop their technological competence and keyboards skills away from the surveillance and often ridiculing or hostile gaze of their peers. As a result these children are commonly more confident and comfortable with the technology in the classroom than those who do not have a home PC (see also Chapter 2). Of Hannah, Lotty and Julie, only Hannah has a PC at home and all three describe their parents as afraid of new technologies. Julie claims that her father is so technophobic that he makes his secretary use his computer for him. Perhaps, not surprisingly, given the atmosphere of fear and avoidance which all three girls encounter at home, Hannah, Lotty and Julie are anxious about using computers in IT lessons because of their lack of keyboard skills and understanding of how the PC works. Lotty and Julie feel particularly disadvantaged both in IT classes and other lessons too because they have no opportunity to practise ICT skills at home (see also Chapter 2) or to type up their coursework for other subjects. Lotty explains:

LOTTY KENNISON: 'Cos no one else gives you a chance . . ., 'cos if you don't have a computer at home, you can't do your other coursework, then you've got IT [lessons] and then you've got other subjects that you have to use a computer for as well (Highfields).

Their fears about their lack of skills are compounded by the social context of the classroom where the girls know that they might be laughed at or teased by the boys if they cannot perform at the level and speed of their peers. In this respect they illustrate Brosnan's (1998) argument that the classroom can reinforce anxieties about performance differences. Rather than being stigmatised as the classroom 'dunces', the girls resist using the technology altogether, refusing to do the work or finding ways to subvert the tasks set.

It is a position that commands more social status and respect among their peers than trying and struggling. According to the girls, it is also a tactic which is to some extent endorsed by the male IT teacher.

JULIE JAMES: I don't even use them.
INTERVIEWER: You don't even use them?
JULIE JAMES: No, I can't use them.
INTERVIEWER: So, what do you do, just like turn up [at the IT lessons]?
JULIE JAMES: And, yeah, do stuff. [Edit] He [teacher] says bring some other work in 'cos I'm not gonna learn how to use computer [laughs], 'cos I don't like them.
INTERVIEWER: Yeah, why is that?
JULIE JAMES: 'Cos I can't use them [laughs], they bore me (Highfields).

In this way, the classroom rather than challenging emerging divisions between those who have a PC and those who do not, actually becomes part of the process through which a technological fluency gap is produced.

PCs are supposed to be user-friendly, in other words, to be malleable or controllable. Yet they are often seen as incomprehensible, alien, and a source of anxiety, impotence and frustration. Lupton (1995) suggests that our fear of technology often originates from not being able to understand how it works or how to fix it. Such fears are evident among Hannah, Lotty and Julie who are all deterred from learning computing skills through experimentation because of a fear that they might break the machine.

HANNAH CAMPBELL: . . . because, 'cos you're scared of breaking the computer most of the time [laughs].
LOTTY KENNISON: Yeah . . . know that one [laughs].
JULIE JAMES: That's what I'm like anyway (Highfields).

Likewise, Jasmine and Louise, year 9 girls at Highfields, describe how their inability to control the technology makes them anxious.

JASMINE TOWERS: I get stressed out with computers.
LOUISE WHEATCROFT: Yeah, I can't work them.
JASMINE TOWERS: Yeah, and they don't print when you want them to.
LOUISE WHEATCROFT: They don't do anything you want them to, they're just stupid (Highfields).

Fears about 'control' run deeper, however, than an anxiety about not being able to work or damaging the technology. Rather, as Louise Wheatcroft's comment 'they don't do anything you want them to' implies, PCs are often credited with the intentionality to deliberately obstruct or frustrate their users. Ross (1991) observes that notices are often pinned on office walls by computers, photocopiers and other machines attributing them with the ability to sense the moods of users and to respond to their degree of urgency by breaking down. He writes:

> the notice assumes a degree of evolved self-consciousness on the machine's part. Furthermore, it implies a relation of hostility, as if the machine's self-consciousness and loyalty to its own kind have inevitably lead to resentment, conflict and sabotage.
>
> (Ross 1991: 1–2, in Lupton 1995: 104)

Hannah and Julie employ similar sentiments in this account of Hannah's work experience.

HANNAH CAMPBELL: When I was on me work experience this girl wiped off everything about this important case that was coming up in about two weeks. If I'd , I'd, I'd, I don't know I just wouldn't like that. All she did was just press like a button with her little finger. I mean they could . . .

JULIE JAMES: And it just wiped everything (Highfields).

Hannah's explanation that *all* the girl did was 'press like a button with her little [and therefore most insignificant] finger' implies the user's innocence and lack of responsibility for the loss of the document. Julie's comment that *it* just wiped everything clearly attributes blame for the loss on the maliciousness of the computer. The girls' technophobia is not therefore just about the fact they feel they do not have the knowledge or confidence to 'control' the computer but also that the technology itself might have the potential power to undermine them (see also the discussion of anthropomorphism in Chapter 5). Lupton (1995) suggests that it is the blurring of the boundaries between human and machine inherent in ICT that inspires feelings of anxiety and fear. She writes that:

> There is something potentially monstrous about computer technology in its challenging of traditional boundaries. Fears about monsters relate to their liminal status the elision of one category of life and another, particularly if the human is involved, as in the Frankenstein monster . . . While there is an increasing move towards the consumption of technologies, there is also anxiety around the technologies' capacity to consume *us*.
>
> (ibid.: 106)

To summarise this section, children's technophobia is not a fear of computers *per se* but a fear of how ICT may transform their individual social identities and relationships within the everyday context of the school and their peer group cultures. Use of technology is a social act, such that the PC plays an important role in changing or stabilising social relations in the classroom. As a consequence, some children are fearful, first, about the social consequences of their performance relative to the technological competencies of their peers. Second, they are anxious about their ability to control the PC. Third, they are concerned about the ways in which their identities might be read by their peers if they show an interest in technology. In the concluding section we reflect on what these understandings of children's identities, peer group cultures and relationships mean for the Government policies about ICT and social exclusion that were discussed in the previous chapter.

Tackling social exclusion: the importance of classroom practices and children's cultures

Contrary to much popular and policy discourse which assumes that the computer will have a number of inevitable impacts upon society, we have argued here that institutional cultures are exceedingly important in children's experiences of ICT in schools. These institutional cultures are not homogeneous but multi-layered as Hickling-Hudson (1992) suggests, reflecting not just official school policy but also informal teacher practices and diverse pupil cultures. For example, the official approach of equal access for all at Highfields has led to gender-differentiated experiences of computer use because the male teacher's non-didactic approach allows pupils' gendered cultures to dominate classroom practices (cf. Dixon 1997). Similarly, the official emphasis on use (rather than teaching) of technology at Westport, that has resulted in the provision of email accounts for students, has led inadvertently to smaller gender differences in out-of-class use. The girls' already gendered interests mean that they are attracted into computing through the potential to communicate with others, whereas their counterparts in other schools are not. Moreover, these cultures not only vary between schools, but also within them (Shilling 1991; Dixon 1997), such that the same technology can mean different things in different time–spaces. For example, one group of girls could argue that computers were 'cool' as you were able to surf the Net during lessons, but equally that computer clubs were 'sad', because these were associated predominately with socially marginalised boys. What all this suggests is that policy-makers at both the national and school level need to take into account teachers' classroom practices and pupil cultures when formulating policies, if they want to promote social inclusion.

Indeed, these institutional cultures do have important effects being both a space through which gendered differences in boys' and girls' attitudes to, and use of, computers are (re)produced, and an arena through which gender and sexual identities are constructed and contested. Looking first at gender differences in attitudes to, and use of, computers, we can see that boys' greater liking for and use of computers are reproduced in all three schools (though there a number of important caveats to this statement for Westport). Confirming the results of a number of other studies (Hickling-Hudson 1992; Shashaani 1993; Comber *et al.* 1997; Nelson and Cooper 1997; Reinen and Plomp 1997; Brosnan 1998), we found that boys like computers more, are more likely to consider computer skills as being very important to their future, and are more likely than girls to use computers in a range of setting for a variety of activities. In contrast, many girls are alienated by computing culture (Turkle 1995; Spender 1997), and only tend to claim their place within it when the communications aspect of ICT are emphasised.

However, while our results do confirm the gender differences highlighted in other studies, they also suggest that simple boy–girl distinctions in attitudes to, and use of, computers are inappropriate for two reasons. First, our findings point to the importance of the range of computer functions on offer – for example, whether or not they are on-line, whether or not pupils have access to email accounts – in shaping gender differences in pupils' attitudes to computers. Computers have a variety of potentials, some of which appear to be more attractive to girls, others to boys, and thus the specifics of what is available in particular situations must be taken into consideration because this in part shapes the emergence of gender differences in attitudes and use. Moreover, the study of classroom practices highlights the importance of competing masculinities and femininities, suggesting that important differences exist within the male and female categories as well as between them.

Looking at this second point in more detail we can see that the different cultures of computing are negotiated through both hegemonic and marginalised understandings of masculinity and femininity. In all three schools computer competence is not socially valued despite the considerable numbers of children who think that computer skills will be important to their future. Instead computer competence is often associated with marginalised forms of masculinity. The techno boys' interest in computers is constructed in 'feminine' terms by the lads, and thus leads to the policing of such masculinities through homophobia. Equally, in the girls' heterosexual codes of desire the techno boys are considered both socially and physically unattractive. Despite this, the lads are able to deploy a number of strategies that allow them to demonstrate an interest in, and aptitude for, computers while also reinforcing their status as lads. Most notably, they play games, and surf the Net for things of traditionally masculine interest. Most girls at Highfields and Station Road manage their technological literacy in a different way. In the classroom they generally draw less attention to themselves, and, for many, computers remain less important in their lives than other more traditionally feminine interests. Despite high levels of competence among some girls, they tend to be protective of girl-only spaces in which they can use computers without having to compete with boys. However, new associations between femininity and technology also appear to be emerging, most notably in Westport, where availability of email is contributing to the development of a girls' computer culture.

The bonding of friendship groups through shared activities, mutual help and boundary making – what we might term communities of practice – reinforces children's sense of who they are, and who they are not. The lads, in using the Web for traditionally masculine things, reinforce their identity as 'lads', while making their difference from the techno boys clear to both themselves and others. Equally, they reinforce their identities as 'lads' by marking their interest in, but difference from, women through the use of sexualised jokes and harassment. The girls both respond to this on one level, wanting to appear attractive to these lads despite their dislike for them, and resist it by making disparaging remarks about their behaviour, thus simultaneously reinforcing their sense of themselves as more mature. While we can discuss these differences between boys and girls in terms of the reproduction of gender identities, it is equally clear that the silence on sexuality in schools' research noted by Epstein (1993, 1997) and Mac an Ghaill (1996) is inappropriate. The gender identities of the different boys and girls are not only shaped through ideas about gender, they are also reproduced through the heterosexual economy of the classroom. This heterosexual economy is evident both in the power that the lads can muster to harass the young women in their class, and in the pressure young women feel to remain attractive to lads whose harassment they sometimes manage to contest. Equally, it is clear in the attitudes of both the girls and the lads to the techno boys. The girls' reaction to these boys is shaped by their understandings of desirable heterosexual masculinity; while some of the lads make jokes that suggest that the techno boys are gay because they do not, in their eyes, behave as 'proper' boys. Given the importance of this heterosexual economy in structuring patterns of classroom interaction, the silence on sexuality in schools is untenable. Both gender and sexual identities are being performed and contested within this institutional space.

In thinking about the reproduction of such institutional space, we also want to build upon Philo and Parr's (2000) suggestion that we might think about institutions as precarious geographical achievements. Following the work of feminist geographers (see Laurie *et al.* 1999 for a summary), we would argue that the school as an institutional space is (re)constructed through a series of different geographies. At one level, all parts of the multi-layered institutional culture are informed by wider sets of ideas embedded in British society (and beyond), with, for example, teachers drawing on the jargon of wider educational discourses about the entitlement curriculum, and pupils drawing on wider understandings about appropriate masculinity and femininity. In this sense, the school is a porous space, constructed through its links with the wider place, the wider sets of interlocking social relations within which it is embedded. Equally, this chapter has shown that the school is an important site through which gender and sexual identities are reproduced. The multi-layered institutional cultures of the schools sanction, through both social and material relations of control, certain forms of behaviour, for example, that which conforms to pupils' and teachers' stereotypes of gender-appropriate behaviour. In doing so these cultures make other choices less likely (cf. Shilling 1991; Dixon 1997). Moreover, our cultural discourses about gender and sexuality can shape the meaning of places, for example, the normalisation of heterosexuality means that schools can be characterised as asexual spaces (which are nevertheless implicitly assumed to be populated by heterosexuals). This can in turn influence behaviour, with the result, for example, that the importance of sexuality in structuring classroom interaction is ignored by most teachers and researchers alike. In this way, we can indeed characterise institutions as geographical achievements: they are embedded within wider places; they are important sites for the negotiation of gender and sexual identities; and as spaces they are in part shaped through our notions of gender and sexuality. This achievement is precarious, however, because these institutions are not forever solidified in their current form. Rather, they are open to change, both inadvertently (for example, in the case of the introduction of email in Westport), and through the concerted actions of individuals (for example, when the girls at Station Road demanded their own computing club).

These understandings have a number of consequences for the questions of social inclusion and exclusion in relation to children's use of ICT that we explored in the previous chapter. In Chapter 2 we showed how the emphasis within the UK Government's IT for all policy is on the need to provide access to hardware and software for all children (an approach also mirrored in the USA). The evidence of this chapter, however, suggests that this is a naïve approach because it assumes that all those who have access to the technology will take up the opportunities that they have to engage with it, and that they will develop the competence to use it. Rather, the children's accounts presented within this chapter demonstrate that ICT emerges differently for different individuals and groups of users. While many users of all ages take to, and become adept at, using Internet-connected PCs, others are fearful of them and resist their incorporation into their lives. This means that those children who currently have access to ICT, but resist or reject the opportunity to become technologically literate, may still be socially excluded in a future Information Society because without these skills they may be unable to participate in 'normal activities'.

The understanding of social exclusion that we have developed in this chapter and the previous one – as both about the large-scale distribution of resources and as something reshaped through everyday practices – presents radical policy implications. Namely, it is not enough for governments merely to provide access to computer provision within schools, rather, there is also a need to explicitly address how ICT is introduced within the school context. If UK and US governments are serious about trying to promote an inclusive society in the Information Age, they need to ally their efforts to provide access to hardware and software for all with a recognition of the need to tackle technophobia, particularly among the young. Currently, adults' techno-fears about the projected future mean that they are presenting ICT to children as something that they must become competent at because it will be important to them in a future society. In doing so adults are suggesting that PCs will impact on children's lives in potentially negative ways. Yet, children are not future oriented, nor concerned about the broader transformation of society. Rather, they are more worried about the present, and the local context of the peer group social relations within which they have to negotiate and manage their own identities.

Children's technophobias are rarely a fear of machines *per se* but rather are fears centred around their performance in the classroom and how the technology might transform their social identities and relationships in the context of their highly gendered and heterosexed peer group cultures. In order to encourage children to take up the opportunities that they have to use ICT rather than to resist it, adults need to promote the use of technology in ways that relate to the social context of children's everyday lives and communities of practice. For example, by emphasising the educational uses of ICT for word-processing, spread sheets and programming, adults contribute to the technology emerging as a tool which is considered to be boring and the preserve of 'boffins' and 'geeks'. In contrast, by encouraging children to use email and the Internet – on-line activities which children understand as connected to their off-line lives and activities – adults can contribute to helping ICT emerge as a 'cool' tool in more children's eyes. This in turn will encourage them not to see technology as a threat to their social identities but rather as something exciting and relevant to their off-line world. So the fact that technology, identities and peer group relations are transforming of, and transformed by, each other will be regarded by children as offering them a range of positive possibilities rather than presenting a threat to their identities.

In the following two chapters we switch our focus from the school to the home. In Chapter 4 we address contemporary moral panics about children's safety on-line by examining constructions of their technical and emotional competence within 'the family'. In Chapter 5 we focus on how different households domesticate home PCs, the multiple time–spaces implicated in these processes, and the consequences of these practices for 'family' togetherness and children's use of outdoor public space.

Chapter 4

On-line dangers
Questions of competence and risk

In Chapters 2 and 3 we have focused on the Government's promotion of ICT as an essential, though potentially divisive, ingredient for Britain's future competitiveness in a global information economy. In doing so, we have concentrated not only on the Government's agenda of ICT for all, but also on the ways this is translated, transformed and experienced by different actors, and within different spaces, within individual schools. By combining these different levels of analysis we have highlighted the importance of an overall agenda that promotes inclusion, and of the need to pay attention to the specificity of social relations in different learning contexts. In this chapter we build upon, but also extend our analysis to date, in two ways. First, we broaden our consideration of the discourses surrounding children's use of ICT to look at questions of children's technological competence. Second, we introduce another spatial context to the debate by focusing on the home (a theme which continues in Chapter 5). This not only gives us a more rounded understanding of children's everyday lives, it also allows us to consider the views and practices of their parents. To date, children's use of ICT at home has attracted relatively little attention (though see Livingstone *et al.* 1997), especially in comparison with the volume of work undertaken by educational researchers on children and computers in the school context (see Chapters 2 and 3).

In this chapter we show how current public and policy understandings of children's use of ICT contain paradoxical ideas about childhood and technology. On the one hand, 'boosters' celebrate children's command of technology; on the other hand, 'debunkers' raise fears that this technology is putting children's physical and emotional well-being at risk. In examining these discourses we consider both how ideas about childhood in these debates resonate with understandings of the child that have a much longer history in Western thought, and the ways that technology is constructed as impacting either positively or negatively on society (see also Chapter 1). We go on to argue that these discourses are problematic both because they essentialise the child category, denying children's diversity and their status as social actors, and because they rest on technologically determinist understandings of ICT. Drawing instead on research in the new social studies of childhood and the sociology of science and technology, that inform much of our theoretical perspective in this book (see Chapter 1), we suggest an alternative agenda. This highlights the need to trace the different understandings of childhood and technology that emerge for parents and their offspring as they negotiate and make sense of not only children's technical, but also their emotional competence, in the domestic setting.

The discursive construction of children and technology

Contemporary public and policy debates about children's use of ICT are mobilising 'traditional', often paradoxal sets of ideas about both childhood and technology in new ways (Buckingham 1998; Bingham *et al.* 1999; Holloway and Valentine 2001a). On the one hand, boosters are celebrating children's command of a technology that is assumed to be our future. This celebration relies on essentialist assumptions about children's 'natural' ability to learn technical skills as these quotations demonstrate:

> Sit your average adult today in front of a computer screen and tell him or her to start navigating, and the person will look at you like you're nuts. But sit a kid – a really young kid, 2 or 3 – in front of a computer screen filled with colourful graphics, and she or he will immediately grab the mouse and cruise.
>
> (Kornblum 1998: 1)

> Because N-Gen [net generation] children are born with technology, they assimilate it . . . they soak it up along with everything else. For many kids, using new technology is as natural as breathing.
>
> (Tapscott 1998: 40)

As a consequence of children's so-called 'natural' learning abilities, 'traditional' sets of power relations that construct children as less developed, less able and less competent than adults (Waksler 1991) are, according to the media hype, reversed:

> The usual order is upside down. When my wife can't figure out something on the computer, she'll ask 6-year-old Alison if she knows – and she often does. Teachers get taught the Internet by students. Managers defer to just-graduated new hires about technology.
>
> (Maney 1997: 1–2)

This reversal is assumed to be truly transformative because, in this booster discourse, the society of the future is a digital one:

> Children in the digital age are neither unseen nor unheard; in fact, they
> are seen and heard more than ever. They occupy a new kind of cultural
> space. They're the citizens of a new order, founders of the Digital
> Nation.
>
> (Katz 1998: 1)

On the other hand, debunkers counter such boosterist views by arguing that
children's very competence at using ICT is placing them in potential danger.
Notably, some commentators (e.g. Sardar 1995; Squire 1996) argue that the
relatively unregulated nature of cyberspace means that sexually explicit discussions, soft and hard core pornography, racial and ethnic hatred, Neo-Nazi
groups and paedophiles can all be found in the space dubbed by some on the
moral right an 'electronic Sodom'. A cover story in the 3 July issue of the US
magazine *Time* (Elmer-DeWitt 1995) headlined 'Cyberporn!' claimed that
83.5 per cent of the pictures on newsgroups were sexually explicit[1] (Cate
1996). The Australian magazine *New Women's Weekly* took a similar
approach in an article titled 'Virtual Nightmare' (Evans and Butkus 1997).
While on 25 August 1996 the British broadsheet newspaper *The Observer*
ran a series of articles on 'child abuse' which collapsed a range of issues
including child pornography on the Internet, child-sex tourism and child-sex
abuse into a single panic about 'child protection' (Oswell 1998). Although,
some of these concerns appear to be more about protecting children's 'innocence' by attempting to stop them from gaining access to information about
sexual practices and alternative models of sexuality (Lumby 1997) than they
are about on-line 'stranger-dangers'. In other words, they are fears about
knowledge (and implicitly the leaky and unstable boundary between childhood and adulthood) as well as violence. Lumby points out that:

> Concerns about children and the Internet point to broad cultural anxi-
> eties about the way the labile world of the Internet and the possibilities
> of virtual life are changing traditional social hierarchies, including the
> boundaries between adults, adolescents and children . . . Access to
> power is dependent on access to information in contemporary society.
> Children learn this early – to move up a class in school is to move
> another step up the ladder of status and power. It's for this reason that
> kids often harass adults to give them access to books, games or television
> programs considered 'too old' for them. But the flood of new media for-
> mats . . . has made the job of filtering information increasingly
> difficult . . . The Internet represents the apotheosis of this undermining
> of the graduated and hierarchical world of print media. The proliferation
> of information is rendering the social body and its competing identities
> increasingly unstable.
>
> (Lumby 1997: 45)

For these reasons Wilkinson (1995: 21) argues that:

> We are all having to face up to the fact that our children's familiarity with technology is bringing a new set of risks, especially if we want them to take full advantage of computers as tools of empowerment and education.

The subtly different understandings of childhood and technology that these debunkers draw upon are evident in debates about the regulation of the Internet. Oswell (1998: 138) examines how two figures, the 'child in danger' and the 'dangerous child' (see Chapter 1), that have a much longer genealogy in Western thought (see Jenks 1996; Valentine 1996a), are being mobilised in these debates. The first figure is that of the angelic child. This draws on historical imaginings of children as innocent beings who are gradually corrupted as they become inculcated into the adult world (see Chapter 1). The vulnerable figure of the innocent child plays a central role in the moral panic about children and the Internet that has developed in the Australian, UK, and US media. Here, the innocent child is represented as being at risk from dangerous strangers and paedophile groups using chat rooms and email (McMurdo 1997; Evans and Butkus 1997). As Rubins (1992: 271) has observed, 'no tactic for stirring up erotic hysteria has been as reliable as the appeal to protect children'. This is a fear that is being fuelled by some academic commentators too. Durkin and Bryant (1995) for example, claim that cyberspace allows paedophiles to feed their fantasies and helps them to identify and get together with other like-minded people, and in so doing also contributes to their opportunities to actualise their fantasies. While Lamb's (1998) study of individuals who visit on-line chat rooms putatively for youth found that less than 10 per cent of those browsing the sites appeared to be young people and two-thirds were adults passing as children to engage in cybersex fantasies. In these discursive constructions of children and the Internet it is not only individual children who might be at risk but the state of childhood itself.

The second figure is that of a little devil (see Chapter 1). In contrast to the angelic child who is regarded as passive and weak, the 'dangerous child' draws upon imaginings of children as delinquent, innately sinful and in need of control and discipline (Valentine 1996a). The troublesome child is evident in popular anxieties about the way that children can use their technological skills to intentionally seek out pornography on-line and to commit crimes such as fraud or hacking into secure databases. The US Government has noted for example, that '. . . the Internet threatens to give every child with access to a connected computer a free pass into the equivalent of every adult bookstore and video store in the country (Levendosky 1997, cited in Evans and Butkus 1997).' These fears are shared by Spender (1995: 214) who argues that:

whereas parents can keep a check on Penthouse or Playboy (or the even worse publications that appear in print), and can insist that certain programmes on television be switched off, there is no ready way they can implement an 'appropriate-use' policy on the superhighway.

In using both these figures, debunkers concur with boosterist views about children's greater technical competence. However, they mix these with older ideas about children's lack of emotional maturity (whether that be in the guise of innocence or lack of moral control) to argue that these skills merely place them at risk in cyberspace. Here they represent virtual space, not as the space of our future, but as a dangerous space which risks all our futures (Holloway and Valentine 2001a).

These contrasting interpretations of children's relationship to ICT – that children can command a technology that is our future, and that children's emotional well-being is placed at risk by their ability to use such technology – are problematic. First, both interpretations rest on essentialist understandings of childhood identities which ground children's abilities (or lack of them) in their biology (see Chapter 1). For example, both interpretations see children as 'naturally' technically skilled (or at the very least better able than adults to learn new skills), while the debunkers also construct children as lacking the emotional competence of adults. As we argued in the introduction to this volume, such biological essentialism is not new to debates about children's relation to ICT. It is inherent in the construction of childhood that has dominated since the Enlightenment, a construction upon which both boosters and debunkers draw. Research which shows that this construction is both historically and spatially specific (Ariès, 1962; Jenks, 1996; Holloway and Valentine 2000a) – because children's supposedly 'natural' qualities vary over time and between places – demonstrates that 'child', far from being a biological category, is a socially constructed identity. Indeed, to follow Connell's (1987: 78) arguments about gender, age is 'radically unnatural', being inscripted on the body through a lengthy historical process (Holloway and Valentine 2000a).

As with many other (biologically or strategically) essentialist understandings of identity (Rutherford 1990; W.G.S.G. 1997), this marking of children's difference from adults results in an implied homogeneity of experiences between children, who, for example, are all presumed to have the same capabilities with, and relationship to, technology. This homogeneity is not borne out in practice, as we saw in Chapter 3, not least because the category child is also fractured by other social differences such as gender, 'race' and class. Moreover, the assumption that children are human becomings, whose behaviour stems from natural tendencies until shaped by adults through the forces of socialisation, denies them the status of social actors. Rather, as highlighted in Chapter 1, we follow researchers in social studies of childhood in understanding children to be 'active in the construction and determination of their own social lives, the lives of those around them and of societies in which they live' (Prout and James 1990: 8).

A second problem is that these interpretations of children's relation to ICT are technologically determinist, assuming technology to be a stable entity that will impact upon and change society in predefinably positive, or negative, ways. Again, as outlined in Chapter 1 we are influenced by work within the sociology of science and technology (Callon 1987; Latour 1993; Star 1995). Writers within this field have shown that computers are not invariant objects with a predictable set of effects, but rather are 'things' that materialise for people in diverse social situations and which may, therefore, vary as much as the contexts in which they are used (Law 1994; Bingham *et al.* 2001). In the following sections we therefore examine how children and technology come together in different households to explore the different ways in which children's ICT competence is constructed. In this way, our empirical work both stems from a critique of essentialising, technologically determinist 'stories' about children's relation to ICT, and involves an analysis of the ways in which these discourses are both mobilised and reworked by children and adults through their everyday practices (Holloway and Valentine 2001a).

Role reversal?: 'adults are toast', children are the net generation

In many households, where parents are willing, and able, to buy a PC, children's technological competence exceeds that of adult family members. In discussing this, parents commonly draw upon and re-articulate the wider discourses outlined above about the supposed naturalness of children's technical competence. Children, adults assume, are curious and fearless beings who automatically develop skills through experimental play as these three parents describe:

MR LAW: If something new comes out, obviously kids are first to know about it (Station Road).

MRS LEIGHTON: It comes automatically to them, they're not frightened of it (Highfields).

MR BAINES: Kids aren't [frightened of it] by their very nature, they'll just dig in and experiment (Highfields).

Adults, however, are not assumed to share these skills. This is evident in Mr Wilcox's explanation of his son's superior computer skills. His son, he explains, is good with computers because he has grown up with them; however, there is no sense in which the time Mr Wilcox has spent surrounded by computers as an adult should lead to the same 'automatic' skill development:

MR WILCOX: Chris has actually been brought up with them from, from young, so that's why he's alright with it now, you know. But we've just, I mean, I still shied away from them even, even though they've been in the house (Station Road).

For most of these parents, their children's technological proficiency is a source of great pride. They appreciate their child's skill both as an abstract achievement, and because as we described in Chapter 2, they assume that it will be important in their children's future. We have a sense, then, of how homes are spaces where 'communities of practice' that are very positive about children's technical skills develop. On an everyday basis, however, it can leave a competence divide within households – a computer chasm to use Maney's (1997) terminology – as some parents are unable or unwilling to share their children's interest:

MRS STEVENSON: But I think in, in those of us who are sort of over 40, it's just unknown territory to us, um, depending on, I mean, obviously some adults, older people, I mean, go work in offices where they, they see stuff or use it. But I think for the, the vast majority of us, it's absolutely unknown territory (Highfields).

MRS READ: Baz goes into too much detail, what programmes he's using, completely loses you and . . .
MR READ: And just looses you. And so you just switch off and just let him rabbit on like . . . and then say, 'Oh right, Baz.' (Station Road).

CHARLES STEVENSON: Mum doesn't really like the computer and so I don't normally talk to her about that. Other things though. Mum doesn't normally like me talking about computers or anything in front of her (Highfields).

More often, however, parents draw on their children's technological competence to their own advantage, for example, by asking children to undertake particular tasks for them or to provide support for their own learning. As Sibley (1995) reminds us, however, the family is a locus of power relations and such 'role reversal' situations where children help teach their parents, rather than learn from them, can involve reinterpretations of 'traditional' power relations within the household.

DARREN BROWN: Children . . . do know a lot more about the Internet and different things like that than adults do at the moment. Even though it's the adults that design most of the things that go on the Internet.
[Later he returns to the same theme]
DARREN BROWN: I was just showing him [his Dad] just some of the basics –

I was showing him like the encyclopedia and how you basically use it, like search for anything you wanted and I was showing him some of the screen savers I've got – he was quite impressed with them.
[Edit]
INTERVIEWER: How do you feel about kind of knowing something – you obviously know quite a lot more about computers than your Dad, say, how does that make you feel?
[Edit]
DARREN BROWN: I suppose, it makes you feel a little bit, erm, older in a way – more experienced – more like an adult really (Westport).

Some children clearly enjoy their position of power as knowledge holder, and use this to tease their parents. This is particularly the case where parents are unable to admit they need the child's help. Sisters Rachel and Helen Oats describe their father's struggles:

RACHEL OATS: Well, he doesn't [ask for help], often he has a big panic attack, and he has a big stress and he says 'Urr, can't do it. Stupid computer', and then you say, 'It's only as stupid as you are', and then he says, 'Oh shut up' and things like this and then he doesn't, he won't ask for help straight away like if he can't do it, he'll, you know . . .
HELEN OATS: He'll kind of sit there going . . .
RACHEL OATS: . . . he'll progress until he just can't go any further and then he'll say, 'I need some help', and you go, 'Pardon?' and he says, 'Help.' 'What was that?' [laughs] and make him feel really guilty and really bad and he'll just go . . .
HELEN OATS: And then he's there going, 'Help me!'
RACHEL OATS: 'I need some help.' 'Oh help.'
HELEN OATS: And you kinda go, 'Well, if you press that', . . . and he's like 'I knew that. I was just testing you.' It's like, 'Yeah, right' [in a disbelieving tone of voice] (Highfields).

Papert (1997) seeks to caution children against such an approach, and it is clear that other children are more sympathetic in these circumstances and underplay their own competence in order to help their parents more discreetly, as Francesca Leighton explains:

FRANCESCA LEIGHTON: You kind of have to do it surreptitiously, like pretend, you just go 'Oh well, what would happen if you did that?' when you know exactly what would happen if you did that! (Highfields).

In some cases, parents seek more structured help from their children, asking them to introduce them to new applications rather than simply troubleshooting problems that occur in everyday use. In this way, children are helping their parents respond to the changing demands of the labour market, thus improving the overall socio-economic position of the household. Such help was more often given to mothers than fathers, though in some households men were also benefiting from their children's technological skills. For example, Anthony Harvey who attends Station Road school has been teaching his father how to use the word-processing, desktop publishing and spreadsheet packages that his father needs to know how to use for work:

MR HARVEY: I used to work for the Council, but we have been contracted out so I now work for a company called CTD. And computers are pretty important to us. But the training we have, actually had from the Council, has been terrible. So Anthony has spent that much time on computers that he can teach me things I need to know. I mean, some of the applications he doesn't know how to apply them to the job. But basic computer work he can teach me. And I am supposed to do so many lessons with him every week (Station Road).

These occasions can be both beneficial and frustrating for both parties. Children are often irritated at their parents' slowness to pick things up, but this is combined with a sense of superiority and pleasure in the power that they hold over them, as Anthony Harvey describes:

ANTHONY HARVEY: I tend to show off about it really . . . that I know more than them 'cause – well – well, sometimes – I don't know, I just – you know, it just tends to be like if they need any help it tends to be me they come to (Station Road).

Parents, while sometimes critical of their children's poor teaching skills, feeling that the trial and error learning process has not equipped them with the overview and patience necessary to teach, are nevertheless generally grateful for the help they receive. This is both in terms of the improvement they experience in their own skill levels and the tasks that children undertake on their behalf, such as typing up letters and searching the Web for information. For Mrs Newton, the help that her children provide is a sign of their growing competence and maturity:

MRS NEWTON: I'm very into the fact that as soon as they can start 'giving back', they do [laughs]. Yes, they can't do anything themselves [when they are born], you teach them well and they will then teach you (Highfields).

Similarly, Mr Akram in asking his son for technical assistance saw a change in their relationship. He describes how he cannot give orders to his son like a 'sergeant major' in the same way that he sees other fathers issue commands to their children, because his son might refuse to give him the technical support upon which he depends. Instead, he regards negotiating this help as an opportunity to maintain a good, if subtly different, relationship with his son. One that is predicated on mutual respect rather than on an adultist assumption that as the father he is automatically more knowledgeable and in control:

> MR AKRAM: You're maintaining a good relationship between yourselves – it may not be a father and son relationship, but it may be a friend to friend relationship, in order for, to get that work done. [Edit] But I don't mind being taught by somebody younger than me because I mean, I respect him all the more for it (Highfields).

Nevertheless, though many children do have greater technical competence than their parents this is not always the case, belying the myth that 'adults are toast' (Maney 1997: 1) and that children are 'the Net generation' (Tapscott 1998: 1). In some families, parents' and children's competencies are in different fields, allowing for the possibility of knowledge sharing that has echoes of Papert's (1997) recommendations for a positive family learning culture:

> MR GOULD: I mean, David was teaching me how to cut and paste stuff off the Internet. I show him how to turn a table into a graph, different kinds of graphs (Highfields).

Equally, some children have helped to develop their parents' skills to the degree that their parents have now become able to offer help in return:

> LUCY THOMAS: I help Dad with, like, his quotes. He'll say, like, you know, 'How do I get [this in the centre] – 'cos he is still a bit like funny with how do you get this in the centre or this, you know, 'I want this down a bit' and that's what I help him with mainly. [She continues later] But he's got better now so I don't have to show him so much, and sometimes it like, it's quite bad when he . . . has to show me stuff, and that feels like, you know, I've been doing this longer than you! So he's picked up a lot of stuff and he's quite good now (Westport).

In other cases, parents' competencies far exceed those of their children, and this is particularly the case where parents have jobs involving significant use of ICT. Given the monetary rewards associated with high-level ICT skills in Britain, these households are all middle class. The parents are also keen for their children to develop technical competence so that they too can use computers as a future work tool even if they do not want to go into dedicated ICT work. To this end they provide them with ICT support at the home (see Chapter 2 for a commentary on the importance of these domestic cultures of support). For example, Mr Robinson describes himself as working at the 'bleeding edge' of ICT innovation, and encourages his children to develop their skills. He has provided them with computers from a pre-school age, bought them educational games and continues to provide them with technical support where required. His practices are important not only in the home, but in the ways that they shape his daughter's relation to technology at school. As we saw in Chapter 3, Chloë Robinson's evident technical ability is beginning to challenge the idea held by many of her peers that computers are simply boys' toys. In doing so, Mr Robinson is encouraging his children to develop economically valuable skills, and is thus reproducing them as future members of the middle class (Holloway and Valentine, 2001a; see also Chapter 2).

Trust and trouble-makers: questions of children's emotional competence

Children's technical skills are not, however, the only skills at issue in these domestic communities of practice. Equally important to many parents are questions about children's emotional competence or vulnerability, and their ability to deal with the 'risks' of corruption or abuse that, as we outlined earlier (see Chapter 1), are sometimes associated with children's use of ICT.

Those parents who are highly computer competent rarely take the panics about children's use of ICT seriously. Mr Robinson, discussed above, was perhaps the most vociferous in countering the idea that the use of technology brings 'new' dangers for children. His argument is based on a banal rather than an exoticised understanding of technology. Rather than imagining on-line space to be a new realm that threatens to provide a gateway for dangerous strangers and pornography to pollute the home, he constructs on-line and off-line spaces in the same terms. For example, he recognises that his children are just as able to access printed pornography in the local newsagents as they are by downloading it from the Internet. He is also dismissive of fears that spending time on-line isolates children from the 'real' world and turns them into 'zombies'. Fears about on-line dangers in his mind are media hype:

MR ROBINSON: There's people that've worked all their lives with computers and they're not sort of, you know, zombie, you know. They're perfectly capable of holding a conversation with you, and I think that kind of view [of the threats computers pose to children] tends to be, come from a sort of, you know what, I call it the gutter [press] element, doesn't it? I mean it comes, it comes from the typical *Sun* [a tabloid newspaper with a reputation for sensational stories] reader who is looking for another one-liner to latch onto. So it's rubbish (Highfields).

Other parents are less quick to reject popular fears about children's use of the Internet out of hand, accepting that there are dangers on-line. However, while they recognise that children as a whole may be at risk, they argue that their own offspring will not come to any harm because they have the emotional competence to deal with what they might encounter on-line. In terms of pornography this understanding of children's competence is played out in two ways (Holloway and Valentine 2001a). On the one hand, some parents regard their children as mature and emotionally competent enough not to want to access, or take any opportunities that they might have to access inappropriate material. Mrs Stevenson, for example, who lacks confidence when it comes to her own computer use, trusts that her son will not access pornographic images because he knows that his parents would disapprove. In this instance, her trust in her son seems to be well founded, because in a separate interview he described how he 'nuked' (crashed) the computer of someone who was offering porn in a chatroom that he visits. Mrs Stevenson's approach is also shared by Mrs Jackson. As the quote from her daughter Teresa (which follows Mrs Jackson's words) testifies, this trust is respected because of the high regard in which Teresa holds her parents and because she acknowledges their status as adults.

MRS JACKSON: Well, we have this thing where we try and say to her, it's a two-way thing. We need to give you enough responsibility and you must show us that we can trust you so if you want us to, you know, let you do more, then you have to keep within those boundaries that we've set for you (Westport).

TERESA JACKSON: I have, have a lot of laws set down and I daren't break them. I have a lot of respect for my parents and they said I'm allowed, that I have a certain time to be back – I'm always back by that time. [Edit] I love Mike [her step-father] and I have a lot of respect for him. I love my Mum and I have a lot of respect for her and I know they are a lot wiser than me, they've been on this planet a lot longer than I have and I just have a lot of respect for them and I think it's, it's wrong all these kids that back chat their parents, that break the rules that are set down and you, you know. One, I know I'm gonna be in a lot of trouble if I do break, and two, it's just respect (Westport).

On the other hand, some parents recognise that their children will encounter unsuitable material on-line but believe that their offspring have the emotional competence to cope with the images that they might find and are sensible enough not to get drawn into anything serious. Indeed, some even suggest that a little experimentation is 'natural' for teenage boys. Mr Thyme explains:

MR THYME: I mean, to be quite honest, we don't watch them, we trust them, I mean – and we can go into the history folder [a file on the PC which records all the sites accessed] and see where they've been anyway. So well, I mean they're clever enough to know how to delete that if they wanted to anyway so you probably can't win. But I mean it's all about trust, isn't it [Edit]. I mean, I think the worst thing that Andy and his mates have downloaded is some Pamela Anderson pictures, so, I mean, that's 13-year-old boys for you, isn't it? I mean, we've all been there.

[Edit]

INTERVIEWER: It's trust and a broader picture as well.

MR THYME: That's right and, to be honest, I think we're quite lucky in the fact that our children are quite sensible you know. I mean, Lorna is old enough now to know about things like that but I mean she's sensible enough not to worry about them, not to want to get involved with it, I think – I hope. That's all you can do, isn't it, with children, let's be honest . . . you can guide your children as much as you want but you can only hope that they'll turn out like you want them to (Westport).

Such perceptions of trust are facilitated for some parents by their understanding of on-line space as less 'real' than off-line space. As Mr and Mrs Stevenson explain below, this is because their son Charles is spatially distanced from strangers that he might talk to ('they are not in your house') and because disembodied social relationships are somehow less authentic than face-to-face encounters ('they are not real people'). They also appear to conceptualise violence as a physical act, something that's done body-to-body ('there's no physical interaction over a machine'), rather than an emotional act that might be done mind-to-mind.

MRS STEVENSON: I haven't come across it yet [my child talking to strangers via email or chat functions], of course, but I haven't got a problem with it. 'Cos, like I say, at the end of the day it's somebody on the end of a phone line, they're not in your house, they're not invading your privacy. There's no physical interaction over a machine so, at the end of the day, I haven't got a problem with it.

MR STEVENSON: I don't think I'd have any worries about that because, when all is said and done, they're not, they're not real people. It's all very well chatting, I mean he does it at school. [Edit, continues later] And then again, Charles is old enough – I think he could probably tell if questions were leading the wrong way and also it's not as if he would actually meet anyone like that.

MRS STEVENSON: Yeah. You've got far more danger, I think, answering an advert in the local paper, you know, and the lonely hearts column or whatever (Highfields).

Indeed, for some the Internet PC actually emerges as a tool that can both protect the 'innocent child' and 'the dangerous child' from potential sources of harm in outdoor public space. By keeping children indoors to use the screen, the computer protects vulnerable children from embodied assault, and keeps children whose immaturity and lack of trustworthiness mean that they get into trouble on the streets, out of temptation (we return to the relationship between on-line and off-line space and indoor and outdoor space in Chapter 5). Ms Lake explains the role that the home PC plays in keeping her sons out of trouble:

MS LAKE: I think to meself, yeah, in one sense, they're there [at home using the PC], they're not on the streets, they're indoors. They're not causing problems on the streets, they're not. I haven't got the police coming round the door thinking 'your son's done this, your son's done that'. At least they're indoors and they're keeping out of trouble. If they're indoors they're on the computer, yeah, fine. I don't worry so much. . . (Westport).

As Ms Lake's comment suggests, not all parents share the ability to trust their offspring enjoyed by Mrs Stevenson and Mr Thyme who were quoted earlier. However, while Ms Lake is less fearful about her children's on-line activities than their off-line activities, for other parents their lack of trust of their offspring spills over from the off-line world to the on-line world. Tim Simpkin explains the reason why his father will not let him use the PC unsupervised:

TIM SIMPKIN: I think he's a little distrustful at the moment. I were in some trouble with the law in Year 8.
INTERVIEWER: Oh right. What kind of trouble?
TIM SIMPKIN: I got arrested for shoplifting, and that put his trust right up his head, you know. Won't let me go out at all for about a year. And he's still a bit wary I think from that (Station Road).

The anxieties of some parents about what their children might do, or encounter on-line, are exacerbated by their own lack of ICT skills which mean that they neither know, in the words of Mr Price, 'where they go' or 'what is out there'. As such, the fears this group articulate most often echo those raised in the media. Having little technical knowledge, the Internet emerges for these parents as a potentially dangerous technology that is out of their control.

MRS JACKSON: I mean, like with the TV, you can go and turn it off or I can take the TV out of the room or whatever so there's a certain amount of control. I think with that, that would worry me slightly because I think with that [the Internet which they don't have] your control is maybe gone a little. It would be harder to control maybe (Westport).

MR LAW: You've the files on like cases in America, aren't there, where they've gone to meet somebody and it's ended up being a bloke or something like that. It'd happen turn out to be a kid [if my children went to meet someone] but like you don't know (Station Road).

MR AKRAM: I've also heard that young kids now are very, very streetwise, they can go through one programme onto the adult version, shall we say, and I'm a little bit reluctant, although Sohail has mentioned that he would like to join the Internet and I have made initial enquiry that it doesn't cost all that much. But it's just the amount of information he'll be exposed to which I feel a little bit will be detrimental at this stage (Highfields).

In Mrs Jackson's, Mr Law's and Mr Akram's cases, their fears are sufficient to stop them signing up with an Internet provider. It is only by refusing to go on-line that they feel they can protect their children from a new set of risks that would otherwise invade the home: a space that wider social discourses suggest ought to be a haven of safety for their children, protecting them from the dangers of the outside world (Holloway and Valentine 2000a; Valentine and Holloway 2001a). Papert (1997: 7) argues that this group need a 'Dr Spock for the computer generation', a manual which would explain how to raise their children in the 'digital age' (see Figure 4.1). This need is something

Figure 4.1 Parents need guidelines to help them raise children in the digital age. Reproduced by kind permission of *The Sheffield Telegraph*.

the UK Government, which as we discussed in Chapter 2 is keen to encourage the development of ICT skills, plans to meet through the production of a new guide for parents (Smithers 1999).

It is evident from the range of attitudes and practices discussed in this section that parents do not share the unanimity of view on children's emotional ability to manage the potential or imagined dangers on-line that were in evidence when they discussed the benefits of technical skills. For some parents the Internet-connected PC emerges as a potential gateway to harm. For others, children are credited with the emotional competence to deal with any potential dangers. For another group still, on-line and off-line environments are not imagined in binary terms leading parents to reject the terms of this debate altogether. The diversity of the ways that ICT emerges for parents within our study highlights some parents' complicity with, and others' rejection of, binary understandings of children as little angels (Apollonian) or little devils (Dionysian). It also demonstrates that the Internet-connected PC does not have any inevitable impact on children within families. Rather, the meanings of ICT are negotiated as children, parents and technology come together in markedly different household formations or communities of practice (see also Chapter 5). Notably, as our diverse examples demonstrate, while parents' understandings of the children's technological competence can shape social relations in the family (especially the adult–child relationship/boundary), the children's social competence also shapes the way, and extent, to which their technological competence is allowed to develop. In other words, social and technological competencies co-develop. We pursue these points further in the following section where we explore parents' attempts to control and restrict their children's on-line activities.

Negotiating on-line temporal and spatial boundaries

Temporal restrictions are one means through which some parents limit their children's play in off-line public space (Christensen et al. 2000). Both parents who regard ICT as a potential source of danger and those who understand it to be a refuge from the dangers and temptations of outdoor public space employ similar methods to control their children's virtual activities. These take the form of limits on the length of time children are allowed to be on-line or using a screen, insisting on being informed of where children are going in cyberspace, and establishing a time by which machines must be switched off. These time–space boundaries are also supplemented by domestic geographies of surveillance that again bear striking similarities with some of the tactics that parents use to control their children's independent use of outdoor space. For example, in some homes computers are deliberately located in a particular room to enable the parents to maintain a Foucauldian gaze over the children's use of the Internet (a point that we return to in

Chapter 5). Some parents even go so far as directly supervise the Internet sites where their children visit. These range of supervisory tactics are described in the following quotations:

DARREN BROWN: Dad's not the strictest person in the world but he does try and make, set rules that I have to follow.

INTERVIEWER: How does that work, can you give me an example?

DARREN BROWN: Well, usually I'm not allowed on the computer more than a couple of hours a night, I usually do what he says (Westport).

CHARLES STEVENSON: During the weekdays I'm not allowed to watch TV and play computer games or anything after ten o'clock. But then at the weekends they don't mind so much. But I think that, that, the rules any screens after 10 o'clock. 'Cos if I'm still doing work they'll say 'you've got to stop now' (Highfields).

MARTIN JONES: Yeah, sometimes Dad is – he's not you know – if I say I'm gonna go on a page, then he trusts me and lets me go on the page. Like, say I wanna go on a chat page, he says all right, and I show him what I'm going on first and then he just goes – but most of the time he's there sitting, you know, and then I get off and Dad has a go and I just watch him as well (Westport).

While parents' temporal and spatial tactics to control children's activities in cyberspace bear some similarities with the practices that they adopt in public space, they are also constituted somewhat differently because of the way that ICT emerges in the context of their specific household and parent–child relationships. Notably, technology itself offers possibilities for policing children's activities. As Ackrich (1997: 205, 206) points out: technical objects 'simultaneously embody and measure a set of relationships between heterogeneous elements', in other words, 'technical objects can constrain actants in the way they relate both to the object and one another'. For example, filter systems, such as the one advertised in Figure 4.2 can restrict access to particular websites, computerised records of the websites that have been visited can map children's on-line geographies and the telephone bill can uncover irregularities in, or excessive use of, the Internet. In this way, the technology itself can establish norms and expose those who transgress them (Valentine and Holloway 2001a). Parental rules about children's use of the Internet are not just social but are also technical as these quotations demonstrate:

MR GROVES: Oh yeah, I had a look at the porn sites myself and, er, but there is a history [a computer record of the sites accessed]. I can if I want to put a block on it but I wouldn't do that unless I saw evidence that you know, if Pete looked at something once just out of curiosity then I'd let

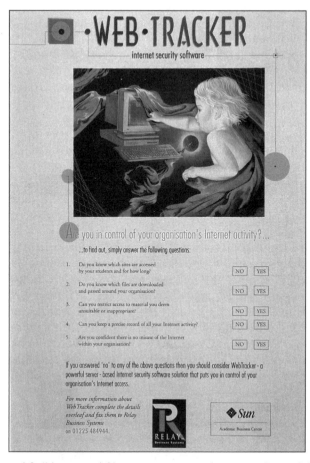

Figure 4.2 'Net nanny' filter systems provide one curb on childen's on-line excesses.

it go like that but if the history file [on the PC] showed that he was doing it all the time I'd put a block on it. I tend not to try and access the history file too much, once in a blue moon just to double check, but you know there's gotta be some sort of trust I think, but then again you've gotta balance the responsibilities of parent. It's a bit, you know, yeah, I do check the history file occasionally to make sure he's not doing anything stupid and from what I see it's the normal sort of BMX bikes and mountain bikes you know the usual . . . (Westport).

MRS GRAYSON: But they know that when the [telephone] bill comes through.
INTERVIEWER: Then you, they'll be found out [local calls in the UK are not free].

MRS GRAYSON: Yeah, they will be found out and we're not likely to say to them 'oh well, you pay for this, this and this', but we will say, 'well, that's it, you've had your chance'.

MR GRAYSON: I'll disconnect it [the PC from the Internet] 'cos I don't make much use of it.

MRS GRAYSON: You've abused it and we don't need it, it's not a service that we need so you're not gonna be able to have it (Highfields).

In the process ICT can also allocate parenting roles and responsibilities within the household. As Pringle (1989) points out, men and women (and we might add parents and children) are not automatically and passively inscribed into existing power relations. Rather, to take the example of the PC, gender relations and adult–child relations must be negotiated, accepted, created and recreated as part of the process of the organisation and incorporation of the technology within the home. For example, in several homes where the father uses computers/Internet at work and considers himself to be technologically competent and the mother defines herself as technologically incompetent or technophobic, the children are not allowed to use the Internet-connected PC when their father is not at home. In this way, differential levels of technological competence can define the parenting roles of mother and father and their individual relationships with their children. In other words, Internet-connected PCs and people are brought into being in a process of reciprocal definition (Ackrich 1997) in which the technology is defined by parents' social rules about its use, while the parents' policing strategies and own roles are defined by the technology. Mr and Mrs Simpkin explain their household rules and roles:

MRS SIMPKIN: Tim . . . don't go on it if his Dad's not here.

MR SIMPKIN: He's not allowed on it unless I'm actually in the house.

INTERVIEWER: Right.

MR SIMPKIN: No. If I'm at work he's not allowed to use it unless he's had prior permission.

INTERVIEWER: Right.

MR SIMPKIN: But it's got to be important for school work, he's not allowed to use it for chatting on Internet or 'owt [anything] like that, he knows that – he wouldn't do 'owt [anything] like that.

[Edit]

INTERVIEWER: So why is that, why do you like to be in the house when he's using it?

MRS SIMPKIN: 'Cos he's liable to mess about [as Tim explained earlier in this chapter, his parents do not trust him because he has been in trouble for shop-lifting].

INTERVIEWER: Right.

[Edit]

MRS SIMPKIN: But if Tim goes on it whilst his Dad's out but I'm in, I don't know what he's doing [because she does not know how to use a PC or surf the Net].

INTERVIEWER: Yeah.

MRS SIMPKIN: So he could be messing about for all I know (Station Road).

Despite Mr and Mrs Simpkin's efforts Tim still manages to dodge his parents' attempts to control his on-line activities. He has several different strategies for doing so. The most subtle is to exploit differences in his mother's and his father's approach to parenting. Echoing other research that has shown that mothers tend to apply a more flexible interpretation of household rules than fathers, who are usually the disciplinarians (Valentine 1997a, 1999c), Tim enlists his mother's support to (re)negotiate his cyber-boundaries with his father. When these sort of tactics fail he adopts a more straightforward approach, waiting until his parents are out of the house to go on the PC, using his technological competence to cover his cyber-tracks:

TIM SIMPKIN: Me Mum's alright. Me Mum's easy. She's alright. I can usually get around her. Sweet talking and charm and all. Me Dad's a little bit more hard, like you know, puts his foot down. So usually I try and get me Mum to talk him round.

[Later the interviewer asks]

INTERVIEWER: Yeah. Do you ever sneak on it behind his back?

[Edit]

TIM SIMPKIN: Well, on like school holidays and me Dad's on afternoons [his father works shifts] and Mum's working, sometimes I'll sneak on [the Internet-connected PC] and put a game on. I make sure to cover me tracks.

INTERVIEWER: How do you do that then?

TIM SIMPKIN: Well, if I've viewed any text things they show up on document on the Start menu bar, so you delete that. And one time it was pretty close. They both went out – a night job, and all of a sudden I heard this car and I went, oh my God! I had this CD on this game and I turned it off straight-away with the CD in and I thought, oh well. And I sat down [hums] – the TV's not on! Turned the TV on . . . Whoosh! [as the CD comes out of the PC]. And they just came in and I went, 'Hi!' (Station Road).

As Tim's story demonstrates, although children's position is weak relative to that of adults, children do not passively abide by parental rules (Solberg 1990). Rather they often resist, oppose and find gaps in adult restrictions. Geographical studies (Katz 1991; Valentine 1997b; Breitbart 1998) have drawn attention to young people's ability to subvert and resist the production of public space and rules surrounding its use. This work particularly highlights young people's ability to win extensions to the spatial restrictions imposed on them by their parents and their success at resisting adult-oriented urban space through neighbourhood environmental activism. Similar struggles over parental rules take place within the home in relation to the use of ICT. Francesca Leighton and Andrew Noble describe some of the methods that they employ to get round restrictions about when, and for how long they can use computers:

INTERVIEWER: And do you have any ways of getting round your parents' restrictions?

FRANCESCA LEIGHTON: Well just staying on and not telling them usually. I mean they don't have an itemised bill or anything . . . They just get the bill and because it's a fax modem, you know, my Dad uses the phone on it for work so they can't tell [whether call times relate to his use or Francesca's], they haven't a clue (Highfields).

ANDREW NOBLE: She [his mother] only tells me off if she hears me. I have to be very quiet, 'cos she's like, she's a very very light sleeper and I have to like type the keyboard really lightly like that [gesturing, to indicate he tries not to make a noise]. And I just have to make sure I don't wake her up . . . (Highfields).

Children not only duck and dive in order to use avoid time restrictions on the use of ICT, they also go to sites that are forbidden. Andrew Noble and Andy Gardener describe webpages where they have been:

ANDREW NOBLE: I had one thing. It's called the Anarchist's Cook Book, it's basically just, just a text plan, haven't got it anymore. I just got to see what was in it. All sorts how to make things, don't know if you know what it is called, thermite [??], things like just that, you can burn through steel and stuff.

INTERVIEWER: Oh God, sounds lethal.

ANDREW NOBLE: Yeah, does things like that. You have to try and like make really good smoke bombs, that sort of thing. Nothing that bad. Well, there is if you look for it but you can look for how to make dynamite equipment, explosives and stuff if you wanted (Highfields).

INTERVIEWER: Have you ever been on pages where you are not meant to be on?

ANDY GARDENER: [laughs] Yeah.

INTERVIEWER: What's that, what sort of things?

ANDY GARDENER: [laughs]

INTERVIEWER: Don't worry, you're not going to . . .

ANDY GARDENER: I've been on porno ones [in very embarrassed laugh].

INTERVIEWER: What at your friend's house?

ANDY GARDENER: Yeah.
INTERVIEWER: Is it easy to find?
ANDY GARDENER: Well, it is quite hard, 'cos it keeps saying 'are you 18?' . . .
INTERVIEWER: And how do you feel when you're on it?
ANDY GARDENER: Well, it's a laugh really (Westport).

This behaviour is very gendered. Many of the boys brag about seeking out unsuitable websites (especially pornography). As we described in Chapter 3, using the technology in this way is for some boys an important way of negotiating their masculinity within the heterosexual economy of peer group social relations (Holloway *et al.* 2000). No girls admitted to using the Internet to access inappropriate material. Rather, they describe their brothers' and their male peers' on-line activities either as 'natural' (as indeed Mr Thyme did above) or as evidence of their immaturity. Instead, girls are most likely to break parental rules by talking to strangers, reflecting their preference for using computer technologies for communication (see Chapter 3).

Girls – though few of the boys – recognise the need to be alert to potential stranger-dangers in cyberspace. Yet, while acknowledging the possibility that they might encounter what they frequently characterise as 'dirty old men' online, the girls also argue that they are not at risk because they are competent and mature enough to take sensible precautions when talking to strangers (a view shared by some of the parents cited above). The girls have a strong sense of invulnerability which research in psychology suggests is a product of having a sense of control or self-efficacy (Perloff 1983). Here, the girls often draw on each other for support. Indeed, several children appear to conceal potentially 'dangerous' experiences from their parents in order to maintain their parents' innocence and protect them from worry. These tactics of nondisclosure might also be underlain by an awareness that parents might impose tighter restrictions on their on-line activities if they realised the extent of their daughters' on-line/off-line encounters. These girls describe their ability to manage their own safety. While Hannah Campbell and her friends explain the sort of precautions it is sensible to adopt in cyberspace, Caroline Mason and her friends outline their role in protecting another friend, Jenny, who wanted to meet an on-line acquaintance face-to-face, and Francesca Leighton describes her self-efficacy at handling unwanted on-line attention.

HANNAH CAMPBELL: I mean, you don't know who you could be talking to, you could be talking to a rapist or anything like that and you wouldn't know and if you met him then you would be putting yourself at risk. It's all right to talk to him on the thingy [the Internet] and on the phone.
LOTTY KENNISON: Just don't tell him anything personal.
JULIE JAMES: Yeah.
LOTTY KENNISON: Don't tell him the address or anything like that (Highfields).

CATHERINE MASON: Jenny . . . she, she met someone on the chat line and she met them in Portsmouth not long ago.

INTERVIEWER: Is that right?

CATHERINE MASON: And she started going out with him.

REBECCA STILES: He's really funny.

LUCY HOPWELL: We all went [the first time she met him] in case he was a mass murderer or something. We'd thought we'd all better go and scare him.

CATHERINE MASON: So we all went and met him.

INTERVIEWER: And he was alright, he was who he said he was?

LUCY HOPWELL: Oh yeah, he was a normal person, not strange.

INTERVIEWER: He lived in, he was at school at Portsmouth?

CATHERINE MASON: No, he lives in Norwich but he was like staying with his mates in Portsmouth (Westport).

FRANCESCA LEIGHTON: Yeah it's worse [than going into an off-line bar or pub], it's worse, 'cos people just go for it. I mean, that's what they've gone on there for, some people you know, the kind of people who go on porno pages and stuff, sometimes they think, oh well, I'll go in the chat room and see if I can pick someone up and they, they'll like come onto you and stuff and say a load of rubbish. But I mean, normally if you tell them to go away they do and then that's it (Highfields).

As we outlined above, some parents represent on-line and off-line space as two distinct worlds. Here, the off-line world – particularly the home – is imagined to be a space of childhood innocence where children are assumed not to have access to pornography or other forms of sexual knowledge. Indeed, sexuality is constructed as an adult and potentially dangerous activity and therefore as the anthesis of childhood itself (Jackson and Scott 1999). Rather, materials such as pornography are imagined to be contained within virtual space. This is a world that some commentators and parents (though not all as we explained above) believe threatens to contaminate the so-called 'real world' by invading and polluting the home with sexually explicit images and 'dangerous information'. However, it is an imagining of both 'childhood' and on-line and off-line space which children themselves regard as naïve and misplaced. As the quotes below illustrate, several children challenged parental assumptions about their innocence, pointing out that they are sexually well informed. Rather than assuming an artificial distinction between the corruption of on-line space and the sanctuary of the home, these children argue that there is nothing available on-line that they have not found in pornographic magazines, seen on television or videos or heard discussed within their own peer groups. Just as some parents describe their children as naïve and in need of protection from the adult world, many children use a similar language of naïviety to describe adults. They are dismissive of their parents' lack of recognition of their own sexual knowledge and the extent to which sexually explicit material is part of their off-line as well as on-line worlds.

JONATHON CARLOW: I mean at our age you've probably seen everything yeah . . .
INTERVIEWER: Uhm, so it's not so . . .
DAN ABRAMS: In science and there's films like *Basic Instinct* just watch em, just learn.
INTERVIEWER: So it's no challenge to go out and find it?
ALL: No.
DAN ABRAMS: I mean, your parents can't and the school can't really keep you under their wing all the time. You just go round your mates and they've got Sky TV and you just watch porn . . .
[Edit]
JONATHON CARLOW: You see a lot of it on TV now anyway (Westport).

JUSTINE LONG: I think when you're with your friends, say [addressing her brother], I think and like, they're, if they go to a page that's not actually that good [referring to pages with unsuitable material] . . . they [her brother and his friends] could get that from other sources anyway, it isn't exactly like that's the only place you can get it (Westport).

In other words, as the examples in this section demonstrate, children are often actually more knowledgeable and competent at managing their own lives (in particular potentially dangerous situations) than they are assumed to be by some adults. The so-called hallmarks of adulthood: maturity, rationality, social competence, knowledge and so on are just as readily performed by a child as a grown-up. Likewise, adults can sometimes demonstrate naïvety, gullibility and other less reasoned responses that are usually ascribed to children. Emotional and social competence is not therefore a stable attribute of a particular age but rather is a fluid, context-dependent performance that can be staged by children and adults alike (Valentine 1997b).

In the conclusion to this chapter we draw together the discussion of adults' and children's negotiations of competence, risks and boundaries to evaluate the boosters' and debunkers' discourses that we outlined in the introduction.

Challenging boosterist and debunkers' discourses

Current popular and policy debates tend to portray children's relation with ICT in either highly positive or very negative terms. Both these mirror-imaged interpretations are problematic, resting as they do on essentialist ideas about children, and overt technological determinism (see Chapter 1). Drawing instead on work within the new social studies of childhood (Prout and James 1990; Brannen and O'Brien 1995; James *et al.* 1998), and research in the sociology of science and technology (Law 1994; Wenger 1998), we have sought in this chapter to examine what happens when children, parents and computers come together in diverse communities of practice. Specifically focusing on the home environment, we have traced the spatiality of children's performances of ICT competence, and the way other children and adults influence and respond to these performances. In so doing, our aim has been both to highlight the different ways that children perform competence in this socio-spatial environment, and to explore the ways in which this space of everyday life is constructed through interconnecting geographies (Holloway and Valentine 2000a).

Our empirical work shows that different communities of practice (Wenger 1998) develop in different off-line spaces. In the home, parents and children are generally very positive about children's technical abilities. Though socio-economic differences mean not all children can gain access to ICT in the home, in households where it is available parents encourage their children's technical abilities, and children feel free to perform these skills openly in an environment where they are socially valorised. These practices represent a stark contrast to many children's experiences of using computers in school. As we saw in Chapter 3, many children draw on gendered discourses about technology in the school environment that construct technical competence in negative terms. As such, all children have to take care about the ways in which they perform their technical abilities or else risk marginalisation by their peers. The picture regarding parents' assessment of children's emotional competence is more mixed: while some parents reject the idea that technology brings new dangers, and others emphasise their children's emotional competence, a smaller minority of parents fear for their children's safety in cyberspace (Holloway and Valentine 2001a; Valentine and Holloway 2001a).

While at first glance moral panics about the threats posed to children's safety and innocence in outdoor public space appear to map neatly onto cyberspace, on closer inspection, parental fears about off-line space are not completely replicated in on-line space. Rather, ICT emerge in different ways in different households depending on differential levels of technological and emotional competencies between household members and differential understandings of technology and conceptions of off-line and on-line space. In this way, parents, children and Internet-connected PCs mutually enrol, constitute and order each other. When individuals and objects such as Internet-connected PCs are brought together in practice, they themselves can undergo transformation. For example, parents' roles and responsibilities, or the extent to which a child is regarded as mature or socially competent, may be transformed by the incorporation of the PC into the home. Likewise, the properties of the Internet-connected PC may also be changed in interaction (e.g. from dangerous tool, to source of entertainment, to referee or source of conflict in familial relationships).

The varying relationships that children and adults develop with technology have a very interesting connection to contemporary public and policy debates about children's use of the Internet. As we argued earlier, these contemporary discourses are both essentialist and technologically determinist, providing an unsatisfactory understanding of children's relations with ICT. Nevertheless, we cannot simply dismiss these 'stories' about children and technology out of hand as they continue to have considerable power in practice, and are sometimes reworked through the everyday activities of adults and children. Looking first at childhood, we can see that essentialist ideas about children's natural technical abilities underlie many parents' understandings of their children's abilities in the home (it is interesting to note that children do not mobilise similar understandings at school, and instead construct themselves as a diverse social group with varied relations to technology). In contrast, some, though not all, parents do rework 'traditional' understandings of children's emotional incompetence, stressing their ability to manage everyday dangers.

Similarly, when looking at the meanings of technology which emerge in these diverse communities of practice, we can see both links with powerful technologically determinist discourses, as well as times and places when these are reworked. For example, understandings of the positive, transformative impacts ICT will have on future society underlie children's and parent's enthusiasm for ICT skill development in the home. However, the same technological determinism that debunkers employ to suggest cyberspace is an inherently risky place is rejected by some parents who construct technology in banal ways, emphasising the similarities between on-line and off-line spaces. What this analysis suggests is, first of all, a need to deconstruct the stories surrounding children's use of technology in public and policy discussion (Buckingham 1998; Bingham *et al.* 2001), and, second, empirical work that can trace the enduring and changing power of these discourses as they are mobilised and occasionally reworked by children and adults in different communities of practice (Holloway and Valentine 2001a).

Finally, this chapter also shows the need for geographical analyses that explore how these communities of practice develop in different off-line spaces. At one level, the contrast between our descriptions of children's negotiations of technical competence at school in Chapter 3 and at home in this chapter reminds us that off-line spaces matter. While studies of on-line socio-spatial relations are essential (e.g. Turkle 1995; Stone 1992, see also Chapter 6), so too are analyses which explore off-line communities of practice because, to make a simple but often overlooked point, on-line worlds are accessed from off-line spaces. At another level, such a geographical analysis allows us to show that these spatialised ideas and performances are not simply rooted in particular spaces, but are constituted through the socio-spatial relations which shape the off-line spaces of home and school.

For example, the home and the school are in part shaped through wider social processes. This can be seen in the influence of ideas disseminated by national government and commercial interests – about the educational benefits and future economic importance of ICT (see Chapter 2) – have on the value parents placed on ICT skills in the home, and in the effect socio-economic differences have on levels of home-PC ownership. Equally, the ideas about computer nerds which children use to tease each other in the school reflect the wider development of microcomputer use in this country, which was initially the preserve of hobbyists (Murdock *et al.* 1992). Moreover, these off-line environments are also shaped by others, as individual actors move between different spaces. Some children, for example, use the greater ICT skills that they have developed at school to renegotiate power relations within the home.

At the same time, these off-line environments are also shaped (and reshaped) as children and adults work through ideas about the behaviour appropriate for different social actors in different spaces. The home and school experiences of highly technically competent girls, for example, reflect the different ideas about gender-appropriate behaviour in these spaces. While many girls are encouraged to develop technical skills at home by their parents, the regulative codes of gender are different among their peers at school, where such behaviour is seen as 'uncool'. The different performance of technical competence these girls manage at home and school illustrate their competence as social actors and their sophistication in managing their own life worlds. They not only develop the ability to read and work within the social structures of different environments, but in some cases also deploy their agency, in understated ways, to change these rules (Alanen 1990; Mayall, 1994). Equally important are the ways in which ideas about childhood spaces shape the meaning and use of different off-line environments. The attempts by some parents, for example, to protect their children by refusing to go on-line at home is shaped by the discursive construction of home as a sanctuary.

In summary, what this chapter shows is that children's and adults' understandings and performances of technical and emotional ICT competence are both spatialised in themselves, and are shaped by (and reshape) the socio-spatial relations involved in the production of the different sites of everyday life. This demonstrates the importance of studying off-line, as well as on-line, communities of practice if we want to understand children's use of ICT. Moreover, it makes clear that to fully grasp the dynamics of these off-line communities of practice we need both to consider the changing importance of discourses about childhood and ICT within them, and to include an analysis of the socio-spatial processes shaping the off-line spaces in which children and technology come together. In the next chapter we therefore focus on the role of the PC in the family home in more detail by looking at how this object is domesticated within different households.

Life around the screen

The place of ICT in the 'family' home

As we argued in Chapter 1:

> [H]umans stand apart from other animal species not only because of their upright posture, the size of their brains, their use of language and the opposition between thumb and forefinger, but also because of the way they create, use and live with a wide variety of material objects.
>
> (Dant 1999: 1).

These objects with which we share our lives have agency. They can make and transform meanings as well as articulating human subjectivity (Callon 1991; Latour 1993). In Chapter 3 we looked at some of the ways that children and computers come together in the context of the school to show how technology, classroom practices, pupils' identities and peer group cultures are transforming of, and transformed by, each other. Here we adopt a similar approach to explore what happens when children, parents and computers come together in the context of the home. While the previous chapter focused on how parents and children negotiate and make sense of children's technical and emotional competence in a domestic setting, in this chapter we broaden our interest to think about the way that the PC is incorporated into 'the family' as a whole. Our concern in Chapter 4 with moral panics about children's safety on-line is mirrored here in our examination of contemporary popular fears about children's potential addiction to home PCs and the consequences that this addiction might have for family time and unity, and for children's use of outdoor public space.

The chapter is structured into four sections. We begin by outlining previous research that has identified a fourfold classification of the way that people absorb objects into their households. We then go on to use the evidence of our own research to argue that this typology artificially separates out processes that are in practice mutually constituted. Specifically, we explore the complex ways that PCs are both absorbed into, and transform the time–spaces of the home. In the third section we connect the home to the wider space of the local neighbourhood. Here we evaluate popular concerns about the perceived impact of the home PC – an indoor technology – on children's use of 'public' outdoor space. In the concluding section of this chapter we reflect on the notion of everyday practice and its role in shaping the way that ICT emerges for different households.

And the PC makes five: the domestication of ICT

The home PC market emerged in the late 1970s. At the time, assemble-yourself micros were aimed at hobbyists who had the technical competence to cope with their user unfriendliness (Murdock *et al.* 1992). Murdock argues that they were 'self-referring' in that the pleasure of using them lay in the challenge of making them work and solving technical problems rather than what you could do with them in terms of their applications or uses. In the 1980s and 1990s, discourses about the dawning of an Information Age that accompanied Government policies to put a computer in every classroom (see Chapter 2) motivated computer companies to try to conquer the domestic consumer market. Advertising campaigns targeted at adults played upon the fact that parenthood has become an increasingly responsible task, with parents expected to give their children every opportunity to make the best start in life (Beck and Beck-Gernsheim 1995), by emphasising the educational value of home PCs (see Chapter 2). At same time, they also highlighted the creative possibilities of the Net as a new more fun way of learning than traditional educational methods. The sub-text being, you may not have enjoyed your own school days but you will enjoy this (Nixon 1998). In contrast, advertisements aimed at children promoted computers essentially as toys. Indeed many retail stores such as Toys R Us now include family multi-media computer centres. A new genre of magazines and books for inexperienced converts to the digital age, including titles such as *Parents and Computers*, and *Family PC*, also began to appear on bookshelves (Nixon 1998). What these marketing tactics shared in common was a representation of computers as part of the family, in which the PC was positioned within the home among 'naturalised' domestic items such as furniture, books and toys (ibid.).

When objects, such as computers, are purchased and introduced into the home they cross a boundary from the 'public' world where they are designed, made and distributed into the home where they are absorbed into the life of the household (Silverstone *et al.* 1992). Through the everyday practices of the household, objects become part of a personal world of meanings in which the public meanings associated with them may be re-negotiated and transformed (Kopytoff 1986). At the same time, as we alluded to in Chapter 4, objects themselves also have the potential to change household social relations. These complex mutually constitutive relationships between people and things are never static but rather change over time. Notably, for example, there is often a transition from the novelty period when an object is first brought into the home to when it becomes taken for granted. Silverstone *et al.* (1992) suggest that the domestication of technologies involves four distinct processes: *appropriation, objectification, incorporation* and *conversion.*

An object is appropriated when it is taken possession of or owned by an individual or household. Through this process an item becomes invested with the traces of its owner, taking on autobiographical meanings and in Kopytoff's (1986: 65) terms becoming effectively 'decommodified'. Objects can be used to define and distinguish both individuals, and households from each other (Silverstone *et al.* 1992). In other words, Nippert-Eng (1996) suggests that when an object is appropriated it can become an extension of the self in wider space.

The process of objectification refers to the ways that an item is used and displayed in the home. Here the focus is on the way that domestic space is constructed and arranged to facilitate this, and the way that objects can be used to mark out space as belonging to particular individuals or to create more comfortable social environments (Nippert-Eng 1996).

While objectification is about spatialities, the process of incorporation emphasises domestic temporalities. This is the process through which objects are incorporated into the domestic routines and schedules of everyday life. Different patterns of use may result in time saving, time shifting or the maintenance of household rhythms.

Finally, conversion captures the process through which objects both facilitate and become the subject of conversation. By talking about things we can turn our knowledge about them into social and cultural capital (a point we have already identified in Chapter 3 in relation to children's use of computers at school, and will return to again in Chapter 6). In other words, objects play a role in embedding individuals and households into the wider environment.

This classification of the ways that objects become domesticated into four distinct processes has been adopted as a valuable framework for many studies of consumption. Yet our research on the way that computers are absorbed into households with children suggests that this classification artificially separates out processes that are complexly interwoven. For example, as we show in the following section, the spatial organisation of the PC within the home (objectification) is intimately bound up with issues of how and by whom the computer is taken possession of (appropriation). This in turn is intertwined with questions of conversion. Perhaps more significantly, however, the distinction between objectification and incorporation artificially separates out spatiality from temporality. It is a common failing. May and Thrift (2001) observe that geographical research has often set up this unhelpful dualism, see-sawing at different times between prioritising either space or time. For Massey (1994) this dualism constrains geographers' understanding of space and place, but May and Thrift (2001) point out that social theory on time is equally guilty of overlooking the way that the temporal patterns of social life are inseparable from the spatial. They argue that we need to think about the way we both make/live multiple time–spaces and imagine them.

In the next section we therefore explore the complex ways that PCs are both absorbed into and transform the time–spaces of the home. In doing so we continue our focus on children's agency. For while Silverstone *et al.* (1992) do point out that individuals within households may engage in processes of appropriation, incorporation, objectification and conversion in differential ways, the power of children's voices within the home is at best implicit and certainly never spelt out in their thesis. Following on from our consideration of technophobia (see Chapter 3), and differential levels of technical competencies (see Chapter 4), we also draw attention in this chapter to the way that some individuals resist the domestication of the computer. Although Silverstone *et al.* (1992) observe that individuals within a household may have different levels of identification with domestic technologies they are perhaps guilty of focusing primarily on positive relationships between people and things, notably the way people tame technologies, and make them their own. In doing so they fail to acknowledge the ways that technophobes can regard the home PC as an object of fear and dread, one which they try to limit the influence of, or expel from the home.

Living with objects: domestic time–spaces

Enhancing their children's educational (and future employment prospects) opportunities is, as argued in Chapter 2, one of main factors which motivates parents to purchase a home PC. For the same reasons parents often invest in children's bedrooms in order to provide an appropriate space for them to 'work'. Dixon and Allatt (2001) point out, it is not just what young people study but where they study that is important to independent learning outcomes. As such, and given the fact that figures for the amount of time spent using domestic computers suggest that they are used more intensively (i.e. more often and for longer) by children than adults (Riccobono 1986), it is perhaps not surprising that these technologies are often located in children's bedrooms.

The ability of families to do so, however, is in part shaped by wider socio-economic processes. Preliminary findings from a pan-European study of children's media use (Livingstone 1998) indicate that more boys than girls, and children from higher compared to lower socio-economic status households, have access to a PC in their own bedrooms (Livingstone *et al.* 1997; Johnsson-Smaragdi *et al.* 1998; van der Voort *et al.* 1998). This pattern is also evident in our research (Holloway and Valentine 2001c). Many of the middle-class households own multiple computers, allowing children to have access to their own machines independently of the equipment that is reserved for parents' own work or for general use. This proliferation of domestic technologies is often a result of households upgrading their machines in response to technical advances allowing older machines to be passed down to each child in turn, with the oldest having priority. In such cases while the children usually do not own a PC either in the sense that they purchased it or in the sense that it is permanently 'theirs' to keep, they do own it in the sense that they 'possess it'. This relationship is constituted and articulated through the location of the computer in the bounded space of the child's bedroom. In turn because children are often allowed to have some control over the 'private space' of their own room, they are then able to restrict the time (when and for how long) other members of the household are able to access 'their' machine which further reproduces their status as its 'owner'. In other words, appropriation and objectification are mutually constituted processes:

MR ROBINSON: Chlöe's got a computer in her room . . . Ashley, our lad, has got a computer in his room. Sort of, they get passed down, so mine is the newest – I've got, I've got like a 22, 233 megahertz Pentium jobby . . . Chlöe's is a slightly older one which is 166 megahertz Pentium and Ashley's is a bit older again, it's a 90 megahertz Pentium but they've all got the set 32 mega memory and mine's got 64, I think . . . And, again, hard disks – you can, you can see the geography of, you know, of computing sort of going backwards [laughing]. Mine's got a 4-gig hard disk and Chlöe's got a 1-gig hard disk and Ashley's is probably a 1-gig now as well . . . It was half, half a gig before (Highfields).

BOB HIGGENS: If Mal's [his brother] been on for a length of time and then it kind of, I get a bit itchy sort of thing, like, I don't mind him being on it but I think, I don't sort of like him being on it for any length of time and I guess that causes a bit of friction, it has done befor (Highfields).

Boys who are techno-enthusiasts (see Chapter 3) are more likely to have a computer in their bedroom. These children have often contributed to the initial purchase financially or in kind (for example, by doing chores) or have spent money that they earn outside the home (for example, by delivering newspapers) on regularly upgrading the machine. In this way they 'own' the machine in a more conventional way than children such as the Robinsons. Alex Newton, for example, was active in persuading his mother to buy a second computer that is located in his bedroom for his sole use, contributing to the cost of its purchase.

Livingstone et al. (1997) argue that the increasing availability of media in children's bedrooms, primarily television, but also videos, PCs, and games machines are part of the development of a bedroom culture. For some commentators, this raises fears that children may be withdrawing (spatially and temporally) from the household, thus abdicating from family life. These concerns about the location and use of ICT within the home also link to general anxieties about the decline of 'the family'. The home is supposed to be a site of togetherness (both physically and metaphorically) where its members can spend dedicated time with each other to the exclusion of non-family members (Christensen *et al.* 2001). Particular time–space routines such as the shared family meal have traditionally played an important role in constituting these moments of togetherness and consequently in producing 'the family' (Charles and Kerr 1988; Valentine 1999a).

However, at the end of the twentieth and beginning of the twenty-first centuries a loss of 'family time' is, according to some commentators, threatening family life (Mellman *et al.* 1990). This 'time famine' (Zeldin 1994: 352) is a product of factors such as: the growth of dual income households, the extension of working hours, the introduction of more flexible working patterns, and teleworking. All of these are claimed to be eroding the ability of family members to create and maintain a spatial and temporal divide between work time and home time (Shaw 2001). Mr Davies, for example, describes how a home PC has made the boundary between his home life and work life more porous:

MR DAVIES: The computer that's here actually belongs to my company, I purchased it with the company. On the justification that I, you know, I bought it primarily so that I could be in contact. We do a lot of work in different time zones. You don't always want to be getting up, you know, at the moment we're working in Australia and in America. You don't really want to be getting up to go to the office at the crack of dawn and staying late at night and doing the normal working day, so it makes sense [to have one] somewhere at home (Westport).

Middle-class children's lives are also becoming more institutionalised in that their out-of-school time is increasingly being taken up by adult-organised formal activities such as after-school clubs, sports training, music lessons, and so on (Valentine and McKendrick 1997; Smith and Barker 2000). This is a trend which further reflects the extent to which in an individualised world contemporary parents are being held responsible for their children reaching their full potential educationally, emotionally and even aestheically (Beck and Beck-Gernsheim 1995). As a result of such processes Gillis (1996: 4) argues that the temporalities (though we would term these time–spaces) of individuals have become both less standardised and less synchronous with those of other family members. She writes:

Families have been the losers in the competition for scarce days, hours and minutes. Even though the time spent by Americans on housework began to fall in 1970 after a steady rise over the previous century, parents complain they do not have enough time for their children, much less for one another. Mornings and afternoons have long since been lost to school and work, and now the evening is endangered, as both parents in two-earner families arrive home late, with only minutes to spare before the children's bedtime.

(Gillis 1996: 5)

This is an argument that is supported by a survey that shows that a quarter of all fathers in Britain with young children work over fifty hours per week (Smith and Ferri 1996, in Shaw 2001). Such is the importance placed on parents and children spending time together at home that some people argue that families who do not, for example, share meals together are not 'proper' families (Charles and Kerr 1988).

For a minority of children in our study, having sole access to a computer in their bedroom does indeed mean that they spend less time with their family. Anthony's description of his computer use, for example, would seem to confirm fears that computer use can isolate children from their family within their own homes. He explains that he spends most of his time using the PC in his bedroom rather than another computer that is located in a living room because the presence of other household members and the television interferes with his concentration. Free from familial distractions in his own room, Anthony is able to spend considerably longer on his computer. Although Anthony does use the PC for school-work, it primarily emerges for him as a leisure tool. He regards his homework merely as something he must 'get out of the way' before he can continue the more pleasurable pursuit of exploring the computer's seemingly endless possibilities. Anthony's enthusiasm for spending leisure time on the computer is shared by other techno-addicts such as sisters Vron and Teresa Jackson and brothers Paul and Doug Brady.

TERESA JACKSON: . . .'cos you look at the clock when you start and it's like half past one and then by the time you've finished it's half past seven and you're like, 'Oh my back. Oh, I feel sick' [Edit]. They [her parents] control the time [Edit] because they know I make myself ill because I keep going and going and going until I just flop down on the floor (Westport).

VRON JACKSON: . . . I mean, I live in my room practically now with my stereo and TV. I've got most of my main things upstairs but I mean I'm very arty. I get lots of – I do tons of poetry and I'm constantly getting like things in my head and everything and I'll have to write them down but I'd be just straight on the computer – I'd be designing this, doing that, doing stories, doing course work all the time. I just wouldn't be off it (Westport).

INTERVIEWER: So when do you use yours, what sort of time do you tend to use yours . . .?
PAUL BRADY: Internet at the weekends when phone calls are cheaper, but otherwise, erm, it's after school mainly for, like, school work – homework. It's basically from about 4.30pm till probably 10. But we don't use it constantly 'cos it hurts my eyes . . .
[Edit]

DOUG BRADY: Yeah, like, I go almost every night to have a couple of games on my football [computer] game.
INTERVIEWER: Right.
DOUG BRADY: Because you can have a league [on the computer] and you get like 48, 50 games in a league, if you play one a night it'll last you about 50 (Highfields).

As these quotations hint, ICT are shaping the use and understanding of time within the home. The Jackson sisters' descriptions of forgetting about clock time when they are on the computer support the findings of studies of tele-working that suggest that computer users find it hard to establish temporal routines and construct limits to their working day. Indeed, Lee and Liebenau (2000) argue that the Internet-connected PC is robbing us of important temporal anchors in the routines and rhythms of our daily life. This is because it allows individuals to find information and engage in work, leisure and social activities that have traditionally been defined and restricted by school and office hours, playing times, and shop/library opening and closing times, any time of the day or night. They claim that 'both the seven-day week and the currently patterned day are weakened by the Internet' (Lee and Liebenau 2000: 49). As such, when individual household members give precedence to spending time on the computer over spending time with other family members, it can cause domestic tensions (Failla and Bagnara 1992, Steward 2000).

LOUISE LANGTON: My Mum's always complaining about it, but I'm not bothered, 'cos my Dad's sometimes on it [the PC] for like all day or something and she'll get mardy because he doesn't talk to her (Station Road).

MRS PHELPS: Sometimes I think that if David's up there all evening [in his room using the computer], which he can be, er, if I go out, I mean there might be a meeting or we may just have dinner together or something, well, that's it, we just have a ten minute chat, he's in bed, next morning we're up and off to school – so it can be like that [they never spend time together]. Erm, it can do that, I think (Highfields).

Women traditionally have made time for family and spent time on it. In contrast, men's time is more often their own and rather than spend time on producing and sustaining the family they tend instead to spend time with it (Leccardi 1996). Women also tend to make up the greatest percentage of non-ICT users across all age groups (Riccobono 1986). Not surprisingly, therefore it is mothers who are most often (though not exclusively) hostile towards the computer regarding it as an interruption to family life. In this regard, their fears echo the attitudes of a previous generation towards the television. Spiegel (1992; 47) describes how in the 1950s the television was regarded as a 'monster that threatened to wreak havoc on the family' by seducing children to watch it at the expense of engaging in family activities. Veneered wooden casing and doors over the screen were employed to conceal the television as an item of furniture.

Similar expressions of fear or hatred of 'it' [the PC] were evident among some women (see also the discussion of technophobic children at school in Chapter 3). People often deny that they have an emotional relationship with objects and yet the way they think or talk about them often betrays the fact that we all do indeed anthropomorphise them (Lupton 1998) as these quotes illustrate:

INTERVIEWER: Your Dad was saying that your [PC] is broken down at the moment and that's quite frustrating for you as well as him, how important do you think the computer is in your life now?

DARREN BROWN: It is important 'cos you definitely miss it when it's not working and ready – it's something that I do miss (Westport).

TODD GARRETT: Say if it crashes, you get, you can get really annoyed . . .

KAREN GARRETT: In the middle of a piece of work.

TODD GARRETT: Yeah, or it hasn't saved something for you. Then you can get annoyed. When I'm playing the football game as well, if I lose I sort of get annoyed with it. But it's not its fault (Highfields).

Callon (1991: 137) observes that objects 'order humans around by playing with their bodies, their feelings or their moral reflexes'. This ability of things to influence our emotions (bringing comfort, confidence, sensual pleasure, evoking memories, etc.) is after all, the basis of most consumer advertising and the reason we keep or carry around objects long after they have ceased to be functional (Campbell 1995; Nippert-Eng 1996). The emotions computers often evoke, however, are not of pleasure but of fear, anxiety, frustration, anger and impotence (Lupton 1998). As we observed in Chapter 2 in relation to teachers and Chapter 4 in relation to parents, adults often have less technical competence than children. Some are anxious about their ability to control PCs and the consequences that this lack of skill will have for their identity and status as an adult, and their authority over their pupils or children. They also often attribute the computer with the agency to transform household relations in a negative way. These feelings are often expressed in terms of technophobia: a fear and dread of the computers themselves (Valentine and Holloway 2001b). These fears of 'it', and the way 'it' might disrupt family time–spaces are commonly articulated in a desire to banish the computer from the central time–spaces of family life. Such emotions are evident in these quotations:

TERESA JACKSON: Mum . . . they frighten her, she said, she's frightened of computers (Westport).

MR BROWN: We thought about having it [the PC] down here [in a living room] – there's like an alcove in the lounge which is quite a nice little place for it – but then the amount of time we'd use it – that's like a social area and I thought it's going to impinge . . . and I thought well, no thanks (Westport).

MRS GARRETT: I felt very strongly and I still do, that it won't ever come in a living room. I like it out of the way. [Later she returns to the same theme: her dislike of ICT] And it's unsociable, which means you can carry on with your work all the time if you want to, or do something on it, just because it's readily available. And I don't like that. I don't like it. I think you need to use it and shut it down and then have another time for using it . . . It kills the art of conversation completely, I think (Highfields).

Tapscott (1998) suggests that talk of children's addiction to computers, and the threat they pose to family life is evidence of an anti-technology bias. He points out that people do not talk about book addiction but rather use more positive terms such as voracious readers to describe children who spend time on this hobby. Gillis (1996) also cautions against setting too much store by reports of contemporary threats to family time. She argues that moral panics about 'time famine' have a long history that pre-date the computer, and that in any event families may well have exaggerated their togetherness, reporting more shared moments than were actually the case.

For other children, however, a computer in their bedroom means something quite different and does not promote a withdrawal from family life within the home. Chlöe Robinson, for example, has a much more instrumental relationship with her computer. She likes having a PC because it can improve the presentation of her homework and will retreat to her bedroom to use it to study but she rarely uses it for fun, preferring to spend her spare time at dancing lessons and going to the local youth club. For children such as Chlöe, then, the computer is not a leisure machine but instead emerges as an educational tool.

It is also important to remember that the time children spend alone in their bedrooms playing, rather than working, on computers is not necessarily negative. Children spend most of the weekday in a very time-disciplined environment at school where all their activities from arrival, registration and lessons, through to eating and playing, are governed by the daily rhythm of timetables and bells which signal the choreographed mass movements of pupils within the school (Adam 1995; Valentine 1999d). Young people are commonly under a lot of pressure to perform well at school and in their leisure pursuits. Like adults they, too, often feel that they do not have much spare time (Dixon and Allatt 2001). Solberg's (1990) study of Norwegian children found, for example, that they valued the time they spent at home after school before their parents arrived back from work as time to themselves. Using a computer in the privacy of their own bedroom is another way that some children make a time–space for themselves to escape or block out the negative aspects of family life such as: marital conflicts, squabbles with siblings, nagging parents and domestic chores.

Academic and popular commentaries often represent on-line life as a poor substitute for the sociality of the so-called 'real world'. Yet, children's off-line lives are not necessarily positive social environments. Rather, individuals – particularly those who are different in some way – are often bullied and excluded by their peers (James 1993; Valentine 1999d). Indeed, as we explore in the following chapter, on-line PCs can enable children to develop global social relationships. Mrs Richardson explains how computers have provided an antidote to her son's off-line social isolation.

MRS RICHARDSON: He's always been terrible, always been a loner on his own. He's one of them kids, who are always sat in corner of playground on his own, all the other kids will be running around but Ben would just, always sat on his own . . . [later she returned to the same thing] . . . it's done what I hoped it would do, he's not, he's not so lonely when he's on a computer, you get what I mean . . . I've always known that Ben is one of them people, as he gets to an adult I think he'll be completely different, he's an adult-oriented child. He prefers adult company, and I think as he gets to an adult he'll find it a lot easier. And computers have just given him something to do, take his mind off things and he just, that keeps him occupied don't it. So he doesn't feel that he's getting left out as much now (Station Road).

The micro-geography of computer location reveals different sets of ideas and practices at work in those homes where the computer is located in a family room, such as the sitting room, dining room, kitchen or study[1]. For some poorer households, this decision to place the computer in a family room reflects a lack of space for a desk in children's or parents' bedrooms. Equally important, however, is the need to place computers in a room that is accessible to all. The appropriation and bounding of bedrooms by both adults and children (Sibley 1995) make them an unsuitable space for computers that are regarded as owned in terms of access/usage (even if they were not purchased) by the whole family as these quotations illustrate:

TERESA JACKSON: Well, we couldn't put it in a bedroom because me and Vron [her sister] don't, it's like a war zone upstairs so we wouldn't dare put it in anyone's room, not in Mum and Mike's [their step-father] room. [Edit]

INTERVIEWER: Do you think, I mean, if it was in your or Vron's room? [Edit]

TERESA JACKSON: If Vron crosses over into my room, which is like a bomb site, I'd freak 'cos we can't stand each other in each other's rooms (Westport).

INTERVIEWER: Where would you put it [discussing the family's plans to buy a PC]?

STEVE LAKE: I'll put it in the kitchen.

INTERVIEWER: In the kitchen?

STEVE LAKE: Yeah, because my Mum might use it as well to do her projects and things.

[Edit]

INTERVIEWER: So you think it's important that it was somewhere that other people could use it?

STEVE LAKE: Yeah.

INTERVIEWER: Not just you, you wouldn't want to have it in your room?

STEVE LAKE: No, because it would be unfair on my parents, so they won't be able to see it and that (Westport).

MR THOMAS: It's a problem where to put it actually because it does take up a big corner and it is a problem where to put it. We wouldn't have it in any-body's bedroom because so many people – it's got to be in a place that's accessible because so many people use it. I mean, if it was in our bedroom we don't want all Abe's and Lucy's friends messing around in our bed-room. The children are a little bit possessive of their bedrooms, aren't they? Lucy doesn't like Abe in her bedroom and Abe doesn't like Lucy in his bedroom so it's got to be somewhere everyone can go (Westport).

Indeed, the location of the PC in a shared family space rather than in the individualized time–space of a bedroom also encourages the computer to act as a gathering point for members of the family (see Figures 5.1 and 5.2). Gillis (1996) suggests that shared activities such as family meals and Sunday drives first became important in instantiating the family during the nineteenth century. It was in this period of industrialisation that family mem-bers began to live separate lives in that men were divided from women, and children from adults, by the emergence of the time–spaces such as work and school that were distinct from the household's living space. It was also during this period that the home first became a sacred space for close kin. She writes:

> One could say that family was put into cultural production, represent-ing itself to itself in a series of daily weekly and annual performances that substituted for the working relationship that had previously con-stituted the everyday experience of family life.
>
> (Gillis 1996: 13)

Figure 5.1 The computer is implicated in the development of children's bedroom culture.

Figure 5.2 The location of the PC in a shared space can provide a gathering point for members of the family.

Through such activities households not only began to come together as a family but also imagine themselves as a family. In contemporary times the television set (see Spiegel 1992), and now also the computer have become part of the glue that binds some families together. Mitchell writes:

> When attached to a display device (like a television set or personal computer monitor), such an appliance presents itself as a hearth that radiates information instead of heat. Just as the fireplace with its chimney and mantel was the focus of the traditional living room, and later became

the pivot point for Frank Lloyd Wright's box-busting house plans, so the display – the source of data, news and entertainment – now bids to become the most powerful organiser of domestic spaces and activities. In most rooms, it's what most eye-balls are most likely to lock onto most of the time.

(1995: 99)

Indeed, the PC is such a part of the Simpkin's family life that they not only use it together in the evenings but they even take it on holiday with them.

TIM SIMPKIN: We're planning to take computer down there to the coast in the boot. It just about fits in the caravan. [Edit] She'll [his mother] watch us [he and his father] . . . she'll watch us but she won't go on it [the PC] . . . Sometimes when I'm playing with the dog outside or something like that she'll be in here watching me Dad go on Internet. She doesn't know what's going off like, but she'll watch. And you know, me Dad will try and bring things up for her.

INTERVIEWER: Yeah. Do you want to take it on holiday with you?

TIM SIMPKIN: Yeah. Because like if it's raining and I can't go out then there's nowt to do, only watch TV, and if there's nowt on there then that's the only thing to turn to. Me Dad will be on it all the times when I'm outside. I know him. 'Cos I'll be outside with mates that go down as well, you know, 'cos I've got a couple of mates that go down. That's why I like going down there (Station Road).

MRS ZISEK: It [using the PC together] pleases them and their Dad and it's something that they can, all three, because they're all that way inclined, you know, it's an interest that they can have separate from me, which is important, that goes with their Dad [from whom she is separated]. So yeah, fine.

[Edit]

MRS ZISEK: It actually brought the boys [her two sons], 'cos these two boys, you know, have had a little bit of, because they're so different in personality and it actually brought them common ground where they, one would know one bit and one would know another bit, because one's more practical and one's more academic. So it actually brought them together quite a lot, so I was quite pleased about it. [Edit, later she continued on the same theme] . . . for the boys as a brother and brother relationship I think that it [the PC] made them communicate more with each other and learn to respect the different ways that people learn things, instead of you know beforehand if one would get the grasp of something practical and the other would say 'Oh God!', you know 'Don't be so stupid, it's done like this' and do it for them. Whereas this, for some reason, this seems to have been a connection where they can appreciate that different people learn at different levels in different ways, 'cos there's more than one way to do it, you know (Westport).

As the quote from Tim Simpkin above about his mother's relationship to his use of ICT with his father implies, families do not have to use the computer together for it to bring them together. In a study of children's experiences of time Christensen *et al.* (2001) found that young people aged ten to twelve defined quality time as being in the house together with other family members. This they argue contrasts with adults' understanding of quality time as a perceived set of shared activities designed to promote togetherness, such as playing games or going to the park together. In children's terms *being* together in the same room with the computer is just as constitutive of the family as *doing* computer-related activities together. Sebastian describes the importance of family life around the screen:

SEBASTIAN BAKER: It's [the PC] in the kitchen as well so that if anyone's cooking you can talk to them . . . [Edit] [comparing it with TV which disrupts family exchanges] because you know you can stop the computer half-way through but if you want to watch the television, you can pause a computer but you can't pause the telly (Westport).

Indeed, in some homes, parents actively place the computer in the centre of a family activity space in order to promote its use and these sorts of family relations. Mr and Mrs Oats, for example, moved the computer from an upstairs box room into the dining room (which is next to the kitchen and linked to the sitting room by glass doors) to encourage their daughters to use the computer more frequently and for longer periods of time. Their daughters' interest in the home computer is limited because their parents construct the computer as an educational tool, for example, through the purchase of learning games and resources. Though the girls are very keen to convert the computer into a leisure machine by connecting it to the Internet and thus the wider world, their parents are unwilling to bend to their wishes. Nevertheless, the placing of the computer in the dining room rather than the box room has increased the girls' computer use by transforming the machine into a more social tool. Rather than feeling 'stupid' sat by themselves in a 'diddy room' with an 'electric thing' (Helen Oats), they regard computer use in a family room as less individualised and more social and, consequently, as more socially acceptable. Moreover, the computer has agency too. Its very physical presence in the midst of the family encourages the girls to use it, once again demonstrating the mutual constitution of processes of appropriation, objectification and incorporation.

RACHEL OATS: It was next door to my bedroom and I, we didn't really go on it very much at all 'cos it was sort of away and we could just shut the

door and say, 'I don't wan go on it', or 'I've got something else to do' but
when it's downstairs then . . .

HELEN OATS: Staring you in the face.

RACHEL OATS: You just, it sort of calls you and says, 'Come on'.

HELEN OATS: 'You know you want to.'

HELEN OATS: But it's easier for, like, when it's, like, work and stuff 'cos, say,
'cos Mum's usually in the kitchen or downstairs and you can just shout
through 'How do you do this?' or whatever. Not like computer stuff but
like spellings and things like that (Highfields).

The difference between Mr and Mrs Oats' attitude to the appropriate use of
the home PC and that of their daughters reflects common differences
between adults and children in terms of their understanding of time. Time
after all is not just linear or cyclical, nor objective and universal, rather
there can be multiple social, biological and physical meanings of time. For
parents whose lives are governed by the dominant time economy, clock time
is often regarded as a resource to be budgeted, allocated, sold and controlled (Adam 1995). They view time on the computer as time that should be
spent productively in educational pursuits rather than being 'wasted' on
computer games and on-line chat. In other words, times are hierarchically
ordered with leisure time subordinated to work time (Leccardi 1996). Here
parents' fears about technology and waste (see also Chapter 2) resonate
with other moral panics about male youth sub-cultures (e.g. Cohen 1967) in
public space (Marshall 1997). Mrs Thyme's attitude to the Internet is reproduced in Darren Brown's anxieties about the need to justify the time that he
spends on the computer by supplementing its use with other activities.

MR THYME: I mean, I just got intrigued and in the end I must say much to
Sheila's [his wife] disapproval I got it [the Internet].

MRS THYME: Yeah, I don't agree with the Internet really.

INTERVIEWER: Why is that?

MRS THYME: Well, because they [the children] spend hours on there, in these
chat rooms and I think that's a waste of time (Westport).

INTERVIEWER: Your Dad says sometimes you have the TV on and using the
computer at the same time – is that right?

DARREN BROWN: Well, I like to, er, listen 'cos the thing that I feel when I'm
using my PC is that time seems to go very quickly and I feel like I'm
wasting some time for some reason – and just by turning on the TV I, it
somehow allows me to listen to what's happening elsewhere as well as
doing something on the PC (Westport).

Children, it is assumed, should learn to postpone pleasure now for success
and rewards in the future (Adam 1990). Yet a sense of the future as a reality

is slow to develop in children (a point we also noted in Chapter 2, and return to in Chapter 6). Rather than using the computer as an educational tool, many children prefer to use it for messing around (Giacquinta *et al.* 1993; Sefton-Green and Buckingham 1998). Most notably it is a good way of killing or filling in time as these quotations illustrate:

LORNA THYME: Like, if you're, like, waiting for a programme [on TV] to come on and you're just waiting for something, you just sit down and you get these little games, these simple games that you just like, yeah, you just sit down for those (Westport).

COLIN BOWNESS: . . . nothing to do, then you just go and play on the computer, go on the computer (Westport).

Murdock argues that:

[I]n contradistinction to the diffusion of innovations model which presents the home computer as a simple technological commodity with a stable identity defined by its applications . . . [it is] a site of struggle between contending discourses, notably those emanating from government and the education system on the one hand and from the entertainment industry on the other. This struggle is regularly played out in conflicts between parents and children as to the proper use of the machine.

(1989: 233)

As we argued in Chapter 4, some parents often do not yet consider their children to be competent enough to be responsible for their own time and so limit or supervise their on-line activities. Here placing the computer in a family room also serves to reduce the risks of improper use either by their children, or in the actions of others on-line towards their children. Contrary to Livingstone *et al.*'s (1997) suggestion, these parents' fears of outside dangers are not leading to the development of a bedroom culture among children encouraged to spend their leisure time indoors rather than on the street. Rather, some parents also see the bedroom, linked to the wider world by an Internet connection, as a potentially risky space, and thus try to encourage use in family rooms. In comparison to other parents discussed above (who allow children to have Internet-connected PCs in their bedrooms), these parents have less confidence in their children's ability to manage everyday risks, and intervene more often to influence and protect them (see also Chapter 4).

INTERVIEWER: I mean, you say you use the Internet sometimes at home?
SEBASTIAN BAKER: Yeah, well, Mum and Dad usually, like, supervise me on it to make sure I'm not wasting too much time or anything. I mean, I've

got, I go on a few websites of like drum companies and music places, so it's mostly music but I've gone on to find a few, you known fact things for projects and stuff at school.

[Edit]

INTERVIEWER: Do you feel constrained about what you can do?

SEBASTIAN BAKER: Well, if they weren't there [parents] I mean, because I go, I used to go on [the Internet] and Dad used to always be over me so that if anything happened or I wanted to do anything, he'd do it, so I felt a bit, you know, constrained as you say, but it's really so that I don't do anything wrong and so I don't waste too much time (Westport).

MR LYNDON: And it's like, like, we have it down here [PC in dining room] so that if they're down here we can see what they're doing, if it's up in their bedroom you don't know what they're doing.

INTERVIEWER: No, no. So it's . . . [trails off].

MR LYNDON: They, they could be doing anything, couldn't they? Anything on it.

INTERVIEWER: Yeah. So you'd rather have a bit of control over what they're doing?

MR LYNDON: Yeah. No, I, you know, 'Oh well, what you doing on there?'. You can see what they're doing (Westport).

Though the primary distinction we have made in this discussion is between homes with computers in the children's bedrooms and those where they are kept in family rooms, some households encapsulate both patterns. Charles Stevenson, for example, has access to a PC in his bedroom and one in the sitting room. As Sibley (1995: 134) argues, though some middle-class children such as Charles have a degree of autonomy in their bedrooms:

> Elsewhere in the home, children may still constitute a polluting presence, requiring regulation or exclusion. Parents commonly determine what are adult spaces and adult times, creating a mixed regime with elements of separation and little concern about the control of the child's space, combined with regulation and strong boundary maintenance [in family rooms].

Charles' description of when, and for what, he uses the two machines is illuminating, revealing intersecting hierarchies of use. Specifically, Charles' educational use comes first, followed by his father's computer use, and parents' leisure use of the family room, with Charles' leisure use of the computers relegated to time–spaces not otherwise required by adults:

CHARLES STEVENSON: If Mum and Dad are in the sitting room reading or doing tapestry or whatever, then I won't, I probably won't use it [the family PC] as if I want to play a game or whatever, they don't want the volume on. I'll probably stay in my bedroom, play games [on the PC] in there. But then if Mum and Dad are outside, or in bed, or something I'll come in here [the dining room] and play it. Or at the weekend when Mum and Dad go out, I usually use that. But if I'm just doing work, I'll just use it whenever, as long as my Dad, well, if it's school work, my Dad will move and clear off. But if it's just to play games he'll say go away and play on your own [PC] 'cos he wants to use it (Highfields).

Such examples, where computers are available in a variety of rooms within the household, neatly illustrate the power relations in operation within the family home. Although the home is often imagined as a space where people have control over their own space and time (in contrast to work and school), in practice time and space are scarce resources and so the different time–space requirements of individuals have to be juggled and reconciled (Glucksman 1998). As Charles Stevenson's quote illustrates, these allocations are not necessarily equal. Family rooms are far from equally available to all family members: rather, adults' use is favoured over that of children, unless children's learning is at stake. In this example, only when Charles' educational development was a consideration could he control the use of 'family' space within the home on his own terms.

Charles Stevenson does not have any brothers or sisters and so only has his parents to contend with when negotiating when and where he can use a computer. In larger families, however, children also have to enter into negotiations about their everyday use of particular time–spaces with siblings. What is at stake is often not only who has the right to use the computer, when and for how long, but also their right to have the space to use it in privacy without interruption from other household members. These are domestic disputes that parents, usually mothers, are often called upon to arbitrate by establishing priority uses (which are once again usually educational) or rationing individual's access to time–spaces in the form of household rotas. Although family times tend to be anticipated and fondly remembered, they are often in practice stressful and conflictual, with generational and gender tensions particularly apparent. Gillis (1996: 14) observes that 'modern family time is perversely dialectical, dividing even as it unites, creating the very discontinuities it is meant to resolve'. These children illustrate the sort of disputes that fracture family unity:

LISA WEBB: If she's [her sister] doing her homework, I need to get mine done. We always fight over it [the computer] and say it's not fair, someone else is always on it all the time, that we never get a go (Station Road).

KAREN GARRETT: And he [her brother Todd] used to take that time up [the time he was allocated in the family rota] with like computer, with his games, and then he'd say 'Oh, but I've got homework to do'. And then he was surprised when Mum would say 'Tough, get off and go hand write it or something.' And then he'd come out with this argument 'Yeah, but you said homework was more important than games, I've got to do it now.' [Edit, later she continues . . .] Sometimes we [she and her younger brother Jason] can't even get on that computer 'cos he does it deliberately. He'll go out up the scout hut and leave the football [a computer game] on so that nobody else can get on the computer. 'Cos you can't close it without finishing all the stuff off. And nobody knows how to do that except him. And he does it on purpose so that nobody else can play on it (Highfields).

INTERVIEWER: So whereabouts is the PC in the house?
MIKE KING: In the kitchen.
[Edit]
RICKY KING: My brother [Phil] hates it [being in the kitchen]. Not him [referring to Mike], he's [his other brother Phil] at work at the minute, Phil. 'Cos he used to do college work and he hates people looking over his shoulder at his work and so he screams at everyone to go (Station Road).

Though sometimes quite fraught, these contestations over the use of time–spaces within the home are important ways through which children's understandings of the family and their contribution to it are realised. The family is not a pre-existing structure but rather is a 'doing', something that is produced through everyday practices (Morgan 1999). In other words, negotiations such as those described above are not an effect of the computer in the family home, but are constitutive of it.

To summarise, we have argued that aspects of appropriation, objectification and incorporation are all evident in the way families – as communities of practice – domesticate computers. However, contrary to Silverstone *et al.* (1992) we do not regard these as distinct and clearly identifiable processes. Rather, the evidence of this research is that ownership, and domestic spatialities and temporalities are actually mutually constitutive. For example, ownership of the PC is not necessarily defined in terms of who contributed financially to its purchase, rather it is something that is claimed through spatial possession and time occupancy. Likewise, where the PC is located (for example, in a bedroom or shared family room) can shape whether it is used by individuals or collectively and for how long and how frequently, and therefore who is deemed to own it. Finally, the amount of time household members spend using the computer for different purposes can determine whether it emerges as a family tool or individual tool, an educational tool, work tool or play tool and therefore its most appropriate location. Through these examples it is also evident that while household negotiations over time–spaces can transform the meanings of the PC, the PC itself can also help to produce time–space differently. For example, it can be used to create shared family time–space, to bound personal or private time-space or to reproduce time–space hierarchies.

Indoor and outdoor worlds

Taking a lead from feminist and other work (Hanson and Pratt 1988; Moss, 1997) that argues the need to expand our notions of home outwards, our second reading of children's use of ICT in the home comes from an examination of the position of the home in the neighbourhood. Early academic and popular commentaries on ICT suggested that because households can connect directly with the wider world through the Internet, their members will no longer need to engage with their local communities, becoming 'home-centred' (Graham and Marvin 1996: 206). This process in turn is also claimed to potentially undermine the nature of off-line 'public' space. Gumpert and Drucker (1998: 429) observe that: 'In our mediated home, we extend our ability to communicate beyond place, and simultaneously, we become disconnected from our surroundings.' Likewise, McCellan (1994: 10) predicts that:

> rather than providing a replacement for the crumbling public realm, virtual communities are actually contributing to its decline. They're another thing keeping people indoors and off the streets. Just as TV produces couch potatoes, so on-line culture creates mouse potatoes, people who hide from real life and spend their whole life goofing off in cyberspace.

Indeed, some commentators have gone so far as to suggest that on-line simulations might erode face-to-face relations with personal appearances becoming precious and rare. These anxieties replicate panics about previous 'new' technologies such as the telephone, which was once seen as an exotic depersonalising form of contact and is now regarded as important for sustaining face-to-face relations and get-togethers (Fischer 1994).

These anxieties are often articulated in relation to children in terms of a concern about the potential impact of computers on their use of 'public' outdoor space (Valentine *et al.* 2000). Like television before it, the PC – a sedentary indoor activity – is accused of displacing the time children used to spend getting exercise playing outdoors. As a consequence technology is being blamed for undermining children's physical well-being and friendships within the local community, as well as robbing them of the capacity to enjoy the sort of imaginative outdoor play which adults recall from their own childhood. Yet, the time budget diaries (see Figure 5.3) children completed show that they spend only just over half (54 per cent) their non-school time at home. Computer use takes up a small fraction of this time (around 5 per

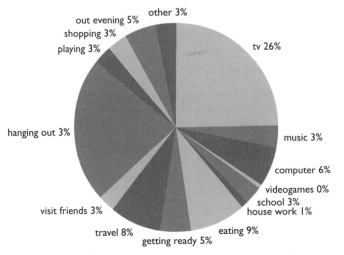

Figure 5.3 How the PC 'fits' into children's everyday lives: a Westport after-school time-budget diary.

cent overall compared to 25 per cent of time watching TV). Most of the children we interviewed argued that they would prefer to be outdoors: hanging on street corners, shopping, at the movies, or playing sport than indoors using the computer. Indeed, use of the PC is very seasonal, being largely determined by the weather and number of daylight hours. On dark winter evenings children prefer to stay indoors and enjoy the freedom the Internet gives them to communicate with friends and escape other members of the family without getting cold and wet. When it is warm and light most of the children – with the exception of the most enthusiastic PC users – are usually outdoors in public spaces with their friends (Valentine *et al.* 2000).

PAUL BRADY: Well, I've always been up for every single sport there is, so I prefer to be playing football or basketball 'cos we've got a basketball ring at home, playing at home, go down to the park to play football, tennis or stay here and play basketball rather than play on the computer 'cos the computer I can lose! (Station Road).

COLIN BOWNESS: I don't usually use the computer much during the summer, I'm outside all the time, but in the winter when it's like, you know, miserable weather, you come in and put the computer on or watch a video something like that.
INTERVIEWER: It's something you can do when it's . . .
COLIN BOWNESS: Yeah, something extra to do, but in the summer I'm always

working or down the beach. I'd rather spend my time down the beach than in front of the TV or computer (Westport).

INTERVIEWER: And how does things that you do on the Net or the computer compare with the things you do in real life, in terms of what fun you get out of it?

ALEX NEWTON: Say if I was on the Internet talking to somebody [an on-line friend] and then somebody [an off-line friend] phoned up and said 'D'you wanna go to the cinema?' I'd go to the cinema. So it's not like it prioritises or anything (Highfields).

When children do use computers it is often to find out information about their off-line hobbies and so enhance, rather than to act as a substitute for, their off-line activities (this is a point that we return to in Chapter 6). Thus although Karen Garrett thinks that her brother Todd leads a very narrow life, this is because his on line interest replicates rather than replaces the focus of his off-line world.

KAREN GARRETT: It's boring [to her brother Todd]. Your life has shrivelled to this amount [indicating a small gap between her fingers].

TODD GARRETT: I hate . . .

KAREN: Two little levels. Football games [on the computer] and football outside.

TODD GARRETT: Yeah but I hate you, I hate you talking to your friends on the phone saying what, what you're going to wear and what you're going to buy and everything (Highfields).

Ironically, one of the very few instances where we found households withdrawing from previous activities in the locale was through 'proper' (Murdock *et al.* 1992; Johnsson-Smaragdi *et al.* 1998), that is to say educational, uses of the machine. Whereas trips to the local library, particularly among children from Westport, had previously been part of the household routine, the purchase of a home computer with an encyclopaedia CD and access to the Internet rendered these visits unnecessary. The presence of a PC in the home mediates family activities, reducing the intensity of their use of neighbourhood resources. Yet, parents argue that this does not change family dynamics: they still assist their children with their homework, it is only the information sources that have changed.

MR DOYLE: I don't think it's noticeably changed the dynamics of the family. I think it's a case of possibly . . . looking at the computer rather than wading through text books or going down the library, but it's a different technique, but I don't think it's altered [the family dynamics] (Westport).

The activity that is most likely to be cut back to allow children to spend time on the computer is an indoor, not an outdoor activity: watching television. A survey by Jupiter Communications and KidsCom Company found that 40 per cent of their respondents claimed that the amount of time they spent watching television had declined because of their Internet use (Tapscott 1998). Likewise, the American Internet User Survey conducted by Cyber Dialogue revealed that one-third of Internet-user households reported that they watched less television (URL 1). While some of the children in our study did claim that the computer was reducing (though not replacing) their television viewing, generally it did not appear to be displacing other indoor activities. Again this finding mirrors the results of other studies that suggest that people who use new technology are more, not less, likely to use print media and other technologies (Robinson *et al.* 1997). This is because books, magazines and the telephone are often used in tandem with a computer, while radios, stereo systems or even televisions are commonly used as background accompaniments to working or playing on ICT.

MR BROWN: He tends to have the TV on at the same time so he's fiddling around in there with a match on – so he's into two or three things – but, er, I don't know, I think it's not too bad (Westport).

INTERVIEWER: So, do you think using the Internet is like replacing magazines [the question is in response to Paul stating that he looks up basketball scores and match reports on-line rather than waiting for them to appear in magazines]?

PAUL BRADY: Use them both because I like the pictures from magazines to put on my wall 'cos it takes a long time to print the pictures out from computers because they're quite big [trails off].

INTERVIEWER: So there's not much point in it?

PAUL BRADY: Yeah, it's slow loading up some of the good pages – like they have lots of graphics on. I mean, I prefer the Internet to magazines because you can get, you don't instead of having to buy like five magazines, you can just visit five websites (Station Road).

Indeed some children argued that their use of the PC does not displace any of their regular activities because they are able to carve new 'special' times in which to use ICT out of previously marginal times when they were 'doing nothing' or out of gaps between other activities. Teresa Jackson and Pete Groves describe the ways that computers can be fitted into existing personal schedules:

TERESA JACKSON: . . . find a special time to fit into my schedule where I'd be on the computer because I can't miss the TV for anything. [Later she returns to this theme] . . . find that hour, that I've got space between when I start watching TV, which you can't get me out off, I'll probably find that,I might not be on it for the whole hour but probably schedule off half an hour and then I'd probably just go and listen to music or go to sleep 'cos if I'm not watching TV or doing homework or at school, I'm sleeping, reading or watching telly (Westport).

PETE GROVES: We usually like to go out and play football and stuff like that, and then like, about 6 o'clock which is like teatime, watch TV and then play on the computer for a bit and go out again at about 8 or something (Westport).

Overall, then, most children use ICT in a balanced way. The technology is fitted into their lives rather than displacing other activities; as such it does not make them narrowly home centred, nor erode their use of outdoor space. Rather, its use is taken for granted as an unremarkable part of everyday life – a finding replicated by other research. Katz and Aspden (2000) for example, found no statistical differences between those who use Internet and those who do not in terms of their membership of a range of community organisations. Francesca Leighton and Mr Groves describe these concepts of 'fitting in' and 'balance':

FRANCESCA LEIGHTON: I mean, it's [the computer] not, like it's not like doing that has stopped me from doing anything else so, I mean, people see using computers as this intrusive force and it's gonna wipe everything out but it's just something I do like snowboarding and something that I do or play the drums or something (Highfields).

MR GROVES: It's a bit like what the TV used to be to us as kids, you could say, I mean, they used to say it about our generation 'you're watching too much TV'. Well, I think everybody goes through spells where you watch it, and then one day you'll get up and turn it off and think, well, I'm going for a game of football, you know. But both my children are physically active, I mean, so it's a balance, you know, I'm quite happy with the balance (Westport).

The local also continues to remain important in children's lives because their domestic use of ICT is often a highly social activity (cf. Suss *et al.* 1998). This is not only in terms of the way that it is used together with other family members as we outlined in the previous section but also the way it is used with friends drawn from school and the local neighbourhood (see also Chapter 6). Even most of the techno-enthusiasts who have PCs in their bedrooms, and might therefore be expected to fit the stereotype of rather solitary computer users mediate their activities through local friendship networks. Anthony Harvey, who, as we outlined above, spends many hours in his room working on his PC, taking less part in his family life than previously, has a friend to visit most weekday evenings during which time they use the PC together:

ANTHONY HARVEY: [My friend comes round] nearly every day. Well, [he] usu-
    ally pops in after school. We usually walk home and he comes in for a bit
    and then goes down t'papers [to do an evening paper round].
[Anthony continues later]: [We] mainly talk about computers, like we do all
    time at school, things like that. As I said, mainly it is to put software on
    or if we've been talking about something to try something out or some-
    thing (Station Road).

Computers, rather than isolating children within the home, can then play an important role as the common link around which friendship groups can form. Indeed, some previously isolated children have found their interest in computers provides a way of making connections with others, reducing their social isolation. Alex Newton, for example, was previously a rather isolated child, not getting on well with his peers whose interests he did not share. However, he has now developed a circle of friends also interested in computers who visit each other to play games and work with computers. Children such as Alex not only construct computers as leisure tools; PCs are also important in shaping these children's childhoods, in Alex's case by changing him from a socially marginal child into a more sociable child with a network of friends with common interests (see also Mrs Richardson, p. 109). For the most part these friendships are performed in off-line environments; however, where children also have access to the Internet, they can be reinforced on-line with children emailing each other, visiting the same chat-rooms and playing computer games against each other while sitting in their respective homes (see also Chapter 6). Communities such as these, where children's technology use is embedded within local social networks, are rarely, if ever, the focus of cyberspatial studies of 'community' (see Kitchen 1998b, for a review). However, as Kitchin (1998a: 402) argues in a different context, 'life on-line is not divorced from non-virtual life but highly situated within it', and such unremarkable communities of practice are as (if not more) important as those more seemingly revolutionary virtual communities that operate only in on-line spaces (Holloway and Valentine 2001c).

Computers play a less pivotal role in the lives of most children than they do for the relatively small group of techno-enthusiast users. Nevertheless, even less 'techy' children's computer use is often negotiated through local social networks (a point we will return to in Chapter 6). Some children, more often those from less affluent backgrounds, who have access to a home PC explained that they allow school friends who do share this privilege to use it to write up special assignments. In this way they make use of the computer as a social machine, not simply as a social activity. Similarly, a wide variety of children use their computer for leisure as well as work when their friends came round to visit.

JASON BOWNESS: It's good fun [chat rooms on-line] when all your mates are around and you're on it but when you're on your own, it's just a bit boring. But when you're talking to your friends as well, it's funny (Westport).

SARA PURDUE: It depends – if we're doing a subject, um, project at school, then we'll choose the *Encarta* for references and stuff, but we're in a band and we tend to do our songs on the word processor and do ballads and songs and stuff like that, graphics and stuff (Westport).

Fears about anti-social 'digital junkies' (see Fenton 1998; Wynn and Katz 1998) who are connected to others on-line but are disconnected from off-line local places are thus far from the practices we observed. Children's use of computers is at one and the same time a highly social and a highly local activity, because much computer use is negotiated through local social networks. This does not, however, imply homogeneity in children's experiences. The mutual constitution of the technical and the social means that computers emerge as different tools in different communities of practice, for some children being seen as educational tools, for others as leisure machines (and for others as a mixture of the two). Moreover, the place of the PC in children's social networks is diverse, with computers sometimes bringing children together, and on other occasions being an incidental part of existing relationships (Holloway and Valentine 2001c).

In countering the idea that domestic use of ICT simply dislocates homes from the local environment, and isolates users from off-line friendship networks, we do not, however, want to suggest that the access to the wider world provided by the Internet is of no relevance to those children able to use this technology at home. In the following chapter we therefore go on to examine children's on-line identities and social relationships.

Everyday practices

In this chapter we have explored the complex relationships between ICT use and domestic life around the screen. Contrary to previous studies we have argued that the processes of appropriation, objectification and incorporation, through which it is argued technologies become domesticated, are not distinct. Rather, we have shown that they are mutually constituted. In particular, by exploring PC use in terms of domestic time–spaces we have challenged the way that time and space are often dichotomised.

In this chapter we have also further reinforced our critique of techno-determinism (see previous chapters, particularly Chapter 1). By showing the variety of ways that ICT is made sense of in everyday life we have implicitly illustrated that computer use does not follow the pre-defined logic or pre-scriptions of designers, manufacturers and retailers. Nor do computers impact on domestic life in particular ways, for example by eroding family relations or undermining children's use of outdoor space. Rather, this chapter emphasises the importance of everyday practices, defined in terms of 'repetition and invention' (Horning et al. 1999: 297) in shaping the ways that computers emerge or come into being for different households. This process is relational in that while computers may reconfigure the time–spaces of the family (for example, by creating bounded personal time–space or collective time–spaces and shaping whether the home is understood as a haven from external threats or a space that needs protecting from pentration by outside dangers), household members' definition of time–spaces can also transform and redefine the meaning of the technology (for example, from work tool to social tool etc.).

In this chapter we also refute popular discourses about the alleged impact of ICT on children's home lives and use of outdoor space. We have shown that on-line activities are not displacing off-line activities, the home is not becoming dislocated from the locale and computer users are not becoming more home-centred in a narrow sense. Rather, children's on-line activities complement and enhance their off-line interests; their use of ICT is mediated by the local social networks within which their lives are embedded; and their computer activities fit into rather than displace their regular time–space activities. Instead of becoming increasingly monochronic (pursuing one activity at a time), young people's use of computers is often polychronic in that it is something done with others or while watching television, listening to the radio or talking to other household members.

In the following chapter we move on from our focus on the off-line space of the home to consider children's on-line activities in more detail.

Chapter 6

Cybergeographies
Children's on-line worlds

While the previous chapter focused on children's off-line lives – what happens around the screen – in this chapter we turn our attention to children's on-line activities: what happens on the screen. We begin by looking at how children can extend the scope of their knowledge by using the WWW to access information from around the globe and explore what this means for the local cultures in which their lives are embedded. In the following section we move on to explore the ways that children use ICT to communicate with both off-line and on-line friends/acquaintances, and to consider how they represent their own embodied identities in the process. In the third section we think about how these connections might be shaping children's sense of place in the world, and question popular representations of cyberspace as a placeless social space. The conclusion to this chapter reflects on the cybergeographies that are evident in children's on-line activities, and emphasises the extent to which children's on-line and off-line worlds are mutually constituted.

The Information Age: accessing the wider world

Janelle (1973) uses the concept of extensibility to measure the way that people can use transportation and communication technologies to overcome the tyranny of distance. The WWW is one such technology, enabling pupils to extend the scope of their sensory access and knowledge acquisition beyond the boundaries of the place where they live. This form of extension is regarded by both parents and teachers from Westport as a particularly important way of helping rural children to reach their educational potential. The town's rural location, and its lack of quality research library resources, mean that children from Westport are more isolated from wider sources of off-line information than their urban peers (Valentine and Holloway 2001c). Mr Thyme describes how the Internet facilitates his children's school work (a point also touched on in Chapter 2). Although, in Lorna Thyme's case this advantage appears to be vicarious, being achieved through the on-line activities of her father.

MR THYME: I mean, the reason we bought it [Internet-connected PC] is for the information. I mean, Lorna's doing a history project at school on Stratton and I spent hours in there [on the Internet] one night getting, I mean, you wouldn't believe that there was even information on a little place like this on there, you know what I mean. And I actually [edit] emailed a chap who was doing a book on King Alfred because I couldn't find the quote that was mentioned in the will about Stratton and I actually emailed this chap who was doing it and he emailed me back with the quote that was in the book that mentioned Stratton which has helped her [his daughter] with her project (Westport).

Indeed, several parents argue that the Internet is important not only because it allows children to extend their knowledge acquisition but also because of the opportunities it offers young people to extend their personal horizons as social actors. Again this is regarded as particularly important in Westport because it is a rural town. The rural environment is often imagined to be an ideal setting to raise a family. It is regarded as safer space than the city to bring up children and a space where children can have more freedom and independence than their urban peers (Little and Austin 1996; Valentine 1997c). The countryside is also attractive to parents because it is assumed to be devoid of the commercial pressures of the fashion industry and peer group pressures to engage in activities such as drugs, underage sex, bullying and violent crime that are evident in urban environments. As such the rural is imagined to provide a more innocent, less worldly, and purer experience of childhood than that offered by the city (Jones 1997; Valentine 1997c). However, some Westport parents recognise that as children grow into young adults these benefits can rapidly become disadvantageous. In particular, the close-knit nature of rural 'communities' can encourage children to be inward rather than outward looking, which can mean that they lack awareness of possible education, employment or travel opportunities elsewhere and as such set their personal horizons too low. The Internet overcomes these limitations by enabling rural children to benefit from the advantages of living in a small community while also allowing them to extend themselves in space and time.

MRS GARDENER: If it's [the Internet] going to widen a child's view of what is happening out there, across the sea, you know up the country, whatever, it's got to be a good thing. It's no good living in this little compact environment you know . . . [edit] there's got to be a place for it when it gives children with limited, erm, funds to travel and see different ways people live, etc. It's got to be, there's definitely a place for it (Westport).

MR GROVES: I think it's [the Internet] very positive because I think the trouble like, especially here in Westport, people here in Westport don't even

know what's going on down the road, thirty miles down the road [edit] . . . they [children using the Internet] get exposure [on-line] to a different way of life, there is more to, there are more ways of living a life than just the way that we were brought up you know (Westport).

As the quotation from Mr Thyme above hinted at, many of the children themselves prefer to use the Internet to extend the scope of their everyday knowledge and social activities rather than in the pursuit of the sort of educational enlightenment favoured by their parents. Popular on-line activities among children from all three schools include: surfing the Internet for information about celebrities from the worlds of film, sport and music, using shopping sites in order to find out about fashions and designer labels, and looking up information about off-line hobbies and leisure activities. For example, Sarah Gould enjoys playing netball and uses the Internet to look up the All England Netball Association (AENA) news, results of international matches, and world rankings. Her local team has also taken advantage of on-line tactics pages, and has copied the AENA emblem from its webpage to use as a letterhead in correspondence with other rival teams. Information gathered on-line in such ways can be used as social capital to enhance children's off-line social status (a point we return to in the third section of this chapter) as Sebastian Baker explains below. In this sense, children's horizons are set in terms of their present position within their contemporary peer group social relations – a perspective which contrasts starkly with their more forward-looking teachers and parents.

SEBASTIAN BAKER: Well, we, people talk a lot about PC games and stuff like that and we've swapped a few of them within each other and I, I've given a few websites to people who like play the guitar or something if I can get them or any decent ones that I give to my friends (Westport).

The information resources, in terms of the pictures of pop stars, movie stars, and international footballers etc., that the children draw on in this way, while given significance by the framework of their local peer group relations (see Chapters 3 and 5), are not purely rooted in the place where they live. Rather, they are part of a globalised youth culture (Massey and Jess 1995; Massey 1998). Patrick Redwood followed up his off-line interest in Oasis on-line, in order to follow their global activities and international releases but in doing so he also found out about upcoming tour dates and consequently was able to get tickets to see them at a local venue:

PATRICK REDWOOD: I go on the Oasis webpage to find out tour dates and album releases and things like that. 'Cos they don't tell you they released *Stand by Me* as a single but only in Japan – it was for an aid thing, a charity sort of thing. And you get pictures, I get pictures from concerts

and like tour dates. 'Cos that was what I used, 'cos I went to see Oasis
when they came to [local venue], so I got the tour dates off the Internet
(Highfields).

In other words, the children's on-line activities clearly demonstrate that their
worlds of meaning are simultaneously global and local. They are global in
terms of their interconnections with the youth cultures in the wider world
upon which they draw, but these global cultures are also interpreted through
the lens of local social relations and as such are re-made in the process
(Holloway and Valentine 2000b; Holloway and Valentine 2001c).

   This is also evident in the following section where we consider the ways
that children communicate with others on-line and make sense of these
global relationships in the local context of their everyday off-line lives.

Making connections: identity, sociality and friendship on-line

It is ironic that despite the fact that one of the main uses of ICT is for communication, these technologies are often imagined to be anti-social. The
computer is often derided as the refuge of geeks and loners. Yet, as shown in
Chapter 5, on-line activities can be both social and 'public', binding domestic users together in off-line space through their shared use of ICT. This
sociality is also evident in on-line. As Curtis (1992) observes:

> If someone is spending a large portion of their time being social with
> people who live thousands of miles away, you can't say they've turned
> inward. They aren't shunning society. They're actively seeking it. They're
> probably doing it more actively than anyone around them.

Indeed, one of the most heralded aspects of ICT is the opportunity that they
offer to extend ourselves in space and time by connecting with others across
the globe. While other means of communication such as the telephone and
postal service offer similar possibilities, ICT have the advantage of being
cheaper to use than the telephone and being a quicker and more informal
means of contacting others than writing a letter. Further, in contrast to
media such as the television and radio, which are one-to-many forms of communication, the Internet is a many-to-many form of communication that
links over 40 million people in a global network (Elmer-DeWitt 1995). As
such, it blurs the boundaries between interpersonal and mass communication
(Parks and Floyd 1996). Holderness (1998) argues that because there is
little difference in terms of the costs and convenience of communicating on-
line with people locally and those globally, everyone who is on-line at the
same time is effectively in the same place.

   Children in our study, for example, use email to keep in touch with distant relatives. In particular, ICT provides an important means of binding dislocated families together.

LOUISE NEWSON: I email my Dad a lot 'cos he's in Kettering at the moment but he's just moved house, he normally lives in Warwickshire so I haven't got his new phone number yet.

INTERVIEWER: But you do know his . . .

LOUISE NEWSON: His email address.

INTERVIEWER: So that's at work?

LOUISE NEWSON: Yeah. But he really likes getting emails at work, he thinks it's really funny (Westport).

As highlighted in the previous chapter, the networked PC also emerges for some young people as an important means of connecting with friends who live locally. In many cases it has become a substitute for the telephone, being used to arrange get-togethers. For these children their on-line relationships are effectively a virtual manifestation of their off-line social relationships in much the way that Beamish (1996) envisioned that ICT might be employed. At Westport children even use email to contact their friends in other classes (both at break and in the middle of lessons) or those sitting on the opposite side of the same room. Indeed, as a disembodied and asynchronistic means of communication, girls find email a useful way of talking to boys in the school whom they would be too embarrassed to approach face-to-face. Steve Lake and his friends also used the anonymity of an email to send a message to a school bully telling him to stop picking on other children, a request to which he responded.

INTERVIEWER: Why, why do you say it's easier to talk to people, kind of, send them a message rather than going up to them?

RACHEL BONNINGTON: You're not there when they read it.

LOUISE NEWSON: You can tell them more how you like feel.

INTERVIEWER: Right, is that people you know quite well or would like to know?

LOUISE NEWSON: Yeah.

CAROLINE DURRANT: Both really.

LOUISE NEWSON: If you want to get to know someone, just send them an email and see if they write back (Westport).

TERESA JACKSON: My best friend Jason sends me a lot of messages 'cos I'm on the French side and he's on the Spanish side [sections of the school] and we, I've been with him all my life [in primary school] and we got split up when we went to Westport [the secondary school] and we don't like it so we try to communicate as much as we can (Westport).

COLIN BOWNESS: You can get access to information on the other side of the world, or other people in Westport. If you know their email addresses then you can just email people all round, all round Westport and everything, and you know, it's good that way (Westport).

While ICT emerge for some children as tools to facilitate or extend existing local off-line social networks, others use communication media such as email and chatrooms to develop new forms of interaction on-line and new kinds of social relationships (Thompson 1995). The Internet is one of the technologies that allows people's social activities to extend or spill over into distant spaces. A friend of brothers Paul and Doug Brady supports the Italian football team Sampadoria. The boys often use the Web to follow the club and check on its progress. Paul explains how ICT has enabled his friend to develop new international relationships with other football fans. Likewise, Alan, a keen sea surfer, has befriended an American surfer with whom he exchanges surfing techniques and product tips and, through talking about her off-line hobby, drumming, Francesca has also made new friends on-line whom she has subsequently met face to face.

PAUL BRADY: One of the players Sampadoria bought came from the, one of the Spanish teams. And there was someone he [the friend who supports Sampadoria] found who – he was in the sports room [a chat room for sports fans] and he found someone who supported that Spanish team. So they were having an argument about how good this player was, and the Spanish one [the on-line contact] didn't like him because he'd gone [left the Spanish club] and my friend liked him because he'd come [had joined Sampadoria] and he was really good. Things like that, so if, if you both, if you like a common theme then you can have a good conversation (Station Road).

ICT not only enable young people to make those who are physically distant present, these technologies also offer opportunities to bring those who are socially distant closer too. Colin Bowness's brother Jason, and Teresa Jackson, are just two of those who use email to try to contact their celebrity heroes and heroines.

COLIN BOWNESS: Like Jason [his brother] talking to Phil Mitchell, he's a pro body boarder, he's been talking to him for about four months now, you know, on and off like every week.
INTERVIEWER: They actually reply, do they?
COLIN BOWNESS: Yeah, they reply, like he's got replies off the best body boarder in the world, and . . . a few other people, you know that he admires and he talks about – and they give him tips on body boarding.
INTERVIEWER: So it makes him feel quite close to his heroes in a way?

COLIN BOWNESS: Yeah, you know, a bit closer and it's also on the other side of the world as well, so it makes it look like they're just like, like in the next room really, 'cos it's that quick (Westport).

TERESA JACKSON: I've got my Oasis CD, it gives you the Internet address which you can email them on and sometimes I send messages and I ask information on, Aqua and Will Smith are my favourite ones. (Westport)

These examples of football fans, body boarders and music lovers further support the point we made in the previous section about the glocalised nature of children's cultures (see also Holloway and Valentine 2000b; 2001c).

Computer-mediated communications are often celebrated as disembodied forms of communication that enable participants to escape from the limitations of their bodies and to connect with others mind-to-mind (Stone 1992; Heim 1993). Bodies can get in the way of social relationships because of the meanings that are read off from them, or the judgements which are made about particular physical characteristics such as age, attractiveness and gender (Van Gelder 1996). Steve Lake who is insecure about his appearance describes the advantages of on-line versus face-to-face communication:

STEVE LAKE: Yeah, because one girl, if a girl comes up to you and they think you're ugly, they just carry on walking, so if you speak to them on the Internet, they don't know what you look like so they just carry on talking to you which makes it easier (Westport).

As these quotes suggest, the anonymity afforded by ICT allows on-line users to construct 'alternative' identities, positioning themselves differently in on-line space than off-line space. These identities – which are often played with and then abandoned (Plant 1993; Turkle 1995) – open up liquid and multiple associations between people and create spaces of concealment and masquerade (Benedikt 1991; Plant 1993). Perhaps the most famous example of this identity play is that of a middle-aged male psychiatrist who in the course of being mistaken as a woman on-line discovered that he was privy to more intimate, richer conversations with others as a woman than as a man. He therefore set about creating the on-line persona of 'Julie' a totally disabled, single woman and over a period of time 'she' developed a wide circle of virtual friends. When 'Julie' was eventually exposed as an able-bodied man 'her' on-line friends, who had confided intimate details of their lives to 'her', said that they felt 'raped' by the deceit (Stone 1992).

Despite salutary stories such as that of 'Julie', playing with identity is often promoted as a fun thing to do. Numerous writers have described the 'thrill of escap[ing] from the confines of the body' (Springer 1991: 306) while Plant (1993: 14) claims that cyberspace is 'a grid of reference for free experimentation, an atmosphere in which there are no barriers, restrictions on how far it is possible to go'. Children from all three of our schools described various playful and often spontaneous casual on-line exchanges in which they have misrepresented their off-line identities in order to make themselves appear more interesting or attractive to other users. The most popular ways to do this are to claim to be older, and to live somewhere more interesting than their own home town. Jason Bowness describes how he likes to 'be someone different', masquerading as older than he is, while Paul Brady plays with his geographical location:

JASON BOWNESS: Well, about 15, 16 sometimes.
INTERVIEWER: So, like, two or three years older than you are.
[Edit]
JASON BOWNESS: I don't know why it is, it's just easier really – just you don't have to worry about what you look like or anything like that, and you don't have to worry about your speech or say you make mistakes.
INTERVIEWER: You just create.
JASON BOWNESS: Yeah, you just – you can pretend you're somebody else, can't you, an' say you're from Japan or something like that – you can be somebody different (Westport).

PAUL BRADY: If you see there's someone who's, er, say 18 and they live in a really exotic place then, er, you'll think oh, well, I can hardly say I'm from here, so you'll say, you'll say somewhere. If . . . you say about London then you've got more of a talking point. London's the capital city, er, so we, you've got things like saying oh, all the big shops, go to Harrods [a famous department store] and, er, everything like that so – I don't know you can, you can normally tend, er, pick a city if you know a bit about it then – er, the only problem is if they say that they also live there [laughs] (Station Road).

Thu Nguyen and Alexander (1996) suggest that disembodied forms of communication are particularly appealing to young people because in the adultist world of off-line space they are commonly treated as less knowledgeable, less serious and as less competent than adults. As the quotes above from Donny Wade and Steve Lake imply, teenagers in particular are often self-conscious about what other people think of them, and about how their bodily identities are read. Indeed the body is a crucial marker of sameness and difference in young people's peer group relationships (James 1993; Valentine 1999d). According to some of our interviewees, ICT gives them more control over their identities than spontaneous face-to-face encounters because they have time to think about what they want to say and how they want to represent themselves. There are also fewer consequences of making a fool of yourself in virtual spaces where no one can see you blush. Clive Stone, Helen Oats and her sister Rachel explain that they find it easier to take risks with their self-presentation on-line because of the anonymity and privacy afforded by ICT ('no one knows who you *really* are', 'you are not *really* seeing them', 'they can't *really* judge you . . . 'cos they don't really know you'). It is also easier to disconnect from uncomfortable disembodied on-line encounters than it is from those which take place face-to-face, in off-line space.

CLIVE STONE: . . . because you don't, sort of, have to introduce yourself [to people in on-line spaces], you, you're not really shy 'cos people can't see you and you just talk to them anon, anonymously, so, yeah, I think it makes it a bit easier.

INTERVIEWER: Yeah, yeah, you haven't got those same barriers.

CLIVE STONE: Um. You just go on and start talking. Anyone who listens might reply but if they don't, it's not that embarrassing, 'cos no one can see you. No one can be there to laugh at you if you say something really stupid. So you can just disconnect and sulk away without anyone seeing you. It makes it a bit easier and less embarrassing (Highfields).

HELEN OATS Often when you meet new people you're really, sort of, you're nervous and you, you don't really know what to say. But you can, when, when you're on the Net you don't have to say, oh, you, you can be somebody who you're not really and you can be all outgoing and everything because you're not really seeing them. Like sometimes when you look at people in the face and you've never met them before then you're quiet and you're sort of. [laughs]

RACHEL OATS: Yeah.

HELEN OATS: No one knows really what to say but if it's somebody, if it's just a computer then it's not gonna talk really.

RACHEL OATS: Yeah.

HELEN OATS: You're never gonna see the face unless you decide to meet them or something and then you probably feel you know 'em 'cos you've been talking to them for days and days.

RACHEL OATS: Yeah. But, like, whatever you say, they don't, they can't really judge you on it 'cos they don't really know you, so it's really good (Highfields).

While young people's on-line sociality is often fleeting and casual, some of those we interviewed have established national and international virtual friendships (see Figure 6.1, p. 151), some of which have been consummated by face-to-face meetings. These relationships represent the possible beginnings of a re-scaling of young people's social networks. Advocates of ICT argue that these technologies enable users to meet others with whom they share the same interests. As a consequence, on-line friendships are argued to be potentially stronger than off-line friendships which are often formed through the coincidence of proximity rather than mutuality (Bruckman

1992; Rheingold 1993, Turkle 1997). The Internet is particularly useful to those who are socially or physically isolated, such as lesbians and gay men or disabled people, because it offers them the opportunity to locate others who share their identity (Correll 1995; Valentine and Skelton 2001). Indeed, Turkle (1997) suggests that some people use the medium of ICT to work through identity issues. Lorna Thyme describes the way ICT enables users to seek out 'sameness' which she illustrates through reference to her musical taste (a point we will return to in the next section):

LORNA THYME: Well, you can find out more, like, you can talk to people that are into the same things. Like, with your [off-line] friends they're into some similar stuff but they've got their own kind of, you know, music that they like and everything. But on the Internet you can pick up like people that actually like almost the exactly the same kind of stuff you like so you're talking to like somebody who is, you know, knows what you're talking about on different things.

INTERVIEWER: So is that quite – do you think that's an advantage?

LORNA THYME: Yeah, like, 'cos, like, I like a lot of American artists and like you know . . . in America they've heard of them and they're like, oh yeah, you know, she's good, she is good and everything and they know, you know, what he's released or she's released and it's like they're telling me stuff.

INTERVIEWER: Sure, so are many of your mates [off-line] into the same sort of music?

LORNA THYME: No they're into like pop things like the Back Street Boys (Westport).

On-line relationships are credited with sharing all the characteristics usually associated with close face-to-face ties, they are: frequent, companionable, voluntary, reciprocal and support social and emotional needs. Their place-lessness is even considered an advantage because while geographical mobility can threaten or destroy face-to-face friendships, on-line relationships can always be maintained (Wellman and Gulia 1996). All of these qualities are evident in Francesca Leighton's description of her on-line relationships (which include regular and close contacts as well as fleeting exchanges). She claims that her virtual friendships are based on genuine shared interests rather than the accident of geography or the coincidence of age and gender. In contrast to the close-knit and incestuous nature of Francesca's local face-to-face friendships, she characterises her on-line relationships as more particular (and some are also very transient), and thus more discrete than her off-line relationships. This is because the information she shares with people on-line is socially and spatially distanced from her off-line everyday life. In other words, Francesca's on-line world effectively constitutes a 'private' space, a space of separation or escape from the intensity and gossipy nature of her locally based everyday social relationships. She explains:

FRANCESCA LEIGHTON: I mean, people [on-line] tend to go straight for the jugular you know, they talk about all this deep stuff [e.g. music, philosophical theory] on there which you don't chat about everyday over a cup of tea or whatever. Yeah, so I mean a lot of my [off-line] friends, they're not interested in exactly the same stuff as I am, so I can go there [Internet] and just find someone who is and have a chat about it and stuff [Edit] . . . people listen to you more. I'm not saying it's [ICT] a replacement [for face-to-face friends] or anything but it's quite good to be able to go on and do that. [Edit . . . later she continued on this theme] . . . I don't know, like, my [off-line] friends are all my own age, whereas the people I write to [on email and in chatrooms] tend to be older and, I don't know, it's definitely a different thing, the kind of things you talk about and stuff, I mean, it's kind of good to have someone that's not that close [in the sense of physical proximity] and you can tell them something, you know it doesn't mean anything to them it's just what you've written, whereas you know if you discuss kind of personal stuff with other people [i.e. local face-to-face friends], it gets out of hand and it gets round (Highfields).

Taken at face value, the quotes from children in this section (for example, from Steve Lake, Francesca Leighton, Clive Stone and Helen and Rachel Oats) all seem to suggest that there is a clear divide between children's off- and on-line spaces in which the virtual is conceptualised as a space of separation, an escape from the social and bodily constraints of the 'real' world (a construction we also identified being drawn upon by some parents in Chapter 4). However, while young people may position themselves differently in on-line spaces from how they represent themselves in off-line spaces, the alternative (often banal) on-line identities that they construct are still usually situated and contingent upon their off-line identities and everyday peer group social relations. As such, their virtual activities do incorporate the 'real'. First, for some children the sites which they choose to go to, the nicknames they give themselves and the things they choose to talk about on-line are a product of their off-line lives. Myers (1987), for example, describes how the 'Professor' was chosen as a nickname by a user because it was his favourite comic book character. Likewise, Francesca Leighton describes below how her on-line personas reflect her off-line interests and bodily identity, while Paul Brady explains how he initiates on-line friendships by talking about his everyday off-line activities:

INTERVIEWER: So, do you create an identity for yourself? How do you sort of represent yourself when you go on-line?

FRANCESCA LEIGHTON: I just have a couple of handles that I use from books that I've read that I like, people's names and stuff. I think it's kind of fun, but I don't have an alter ego or anything, you know, I just go on there and talk about stuff that I'm, I, me actually I'm interested in. I know you get people on there who pretend they're models or whatever but I don't really see it like that (Highfields).

PAUL BRADY: It's, like, oh, we had a really great weekend and I played basketball and what the score was and, like, tennis I'll be two sets to one – how do you like tennis? What's the weather like there? You just sort of develop a theme (Station Road).

Second, as the quotes from Steve Lake and Donny Wade above imply, on-line identities are constructed within the off-line context of the heterosexual economy of the classroom (Holloway *et al.* 2000). As we demonstrated in Chapter 3, heterosexuality is important in a whole repertoire of pupil–pupil and pupil–teacher off-line interactions including: name calling, flirting, sexual harassment, homophobic abuse, playground conversation, graffiti, dress codes, and so on. Through these relationships both young men and women are under pressure to construct their material bodies into particular models of heterosexually desirable masculinity and femininity. These pressures are equally evident on-line. Turkle (1995), for example, argues that from age ten upwards on-line sexuality, including everything from flirting to virtual sex, is an important part of children's use of Internet-connected PCs. On-line, symbols (known as emoticons) and text are employed to describe touch and bodily gestures and to enable participants to develop a sense of each other's bodies. In this way on-line words can pierce off-line bodies causing feelings of desire, hurt, anger, and so on (Argyle and Shields 1996).

Bodily characteristics such as gender and age in particular are used to get a 'fix' on other participants, while as we explained above, alternative on-line identities are commonly constructed in what is imagined to be a heterosexually desirable way. Usually these are stereotypical or highly stylised identities based on famous models or sporting heroes. Despite being willing to play with their identities in these ways most of the children we interviewed claimed not to alter their gender on-line. Turkle (1995) suggests that: '[T]o pass as a woman for any length of time requires understanding how gender inflects speech, manner, the interpretation of experience. Women attempting to pass as men face the same challenge.' This is something Paul Brady recognises as he explains below why he would not try to pass as female on-line. Paul's reluctance to play with his gender identity also reflects the low regard in which he holds the girls in his class. Although his disdain was reciprocated by many of the girls (see Chapter 3) who regard boys of their own age as immature (Holloway *et al.* 2000; Valentine and Holloway 2002).

INTERVIEWER: What about your age or your sex – would you pretend to be a girl?

PAUL: No [laughs]. No I couldn't pretend to be a girl 'cos I'd . . .

INTERVIEWER: Talk about fashion [laughter, interviewer referring back to a previous comment he had made about girls' preoccupation with fashion].

PAUL: No, I wouldn't know what to talk about because half the girls talk about rubbish anyway . . . (Station Road).

Aspects of the 'real' world are also incorporated into virtual worlds through the way off-line social relations, such as gender and class differences, are reproduced in on-line spaces. Paul Brady, for example, tailors his on-line conversation topics according to whether the person he is interacting with claims to be male or female: talking about sport or fashion respectively. While the disembodied nature of on-line contact is often argued to remove power and inequality (Herring 1992; Yates 1997: 282), the evidence of this research is that this is a naïve representation. Many of the practices and structures (organisation and regulation of space, time and movement) that shape off-line lives also shape on-line interactions (Kitchin 1998a). While women have a significant input in cyberspace and there is a strong feminist and lesbian on-line culture, Herring (1992, 1993) suggests that cyberspace is still the domain of white males. Women's messages are shorter and gain fewer replies than men and they are subject to on-line abuse, harassment and even rape. The gendered nature of ICT was notably evident among the children interviewed. Only boys talked about how they enjoyed 'flaming', 'dissing' and 'nuking' other participants on-line.

Finally, children's 'real' and virtual worlds are connected by the material realities of the technology and the economic and temporal realities of everyday life, all of which constrain the nature and length of children's on-line activities. Several children reported technical difficulties on-line. Others described how their parents restrict their access to the Internet at home because it is expensive to use (UK local calls are not free), or limit their use to particular times that fit in with school and domestic routines. Off-line time differences also hamper children's ability to communicate with people in other countries or to find those whom they have met on-line again. In other words, despite utopian discourses about disembodiment which promote virtual spaces as spaces of freedom and liberation, these still have to be accessed from bodies located in off-line worlds with all the constraints this involves.

INTERVIEWER: And do you talk to the same people regularly?

ALISTAIR NEAL: Yeah, a bit. Apart from the time difference is a bit of a pain at times, 'cos like I go on sometimes and it's like, say, seven o'clock here and it's like three in the morning there so it's a bit of a problem.

[Edit]

ALISTAIR NEAL: It's just whenever we go on because with all the different time zones you may say, like, this time and, like, people say, half of the people will say, like, 'What time zone is that?' and then I'll say, like, 'Yes, see you' or whatever and somebody'll go 'What's BST?' [British Summer Time] and it just ends up being confusing so people just go on whenever (Station Road).

COLIN BOWNESS: It's [use of the Internet] fairly controlled 'cos it is quite expensive still to use the Internet other than on a Sunday when it only costs a penny a minute. But if you're on there for like two or three hours at a time, which I usually am sometimes for three hours off, you know it adds up . . . Dad's paying the bill, so you know, he gets a bit restricting on it, like usually only three times a week [he is allowed to go on-line] something like that (Westport).

In this section we have argued that the extensibility afforded by ICT enables children to reconfigure their social relationships and identities in on-line spaces. Notably, the premises of virtuality and anonymity, which often underpin adults' characterisations of ICT, are valued by many children for producing on-line spaces as spaces of separation from their off-line worlds. At the same time, however, we have used a number of examples to show that despite the fact that some children think of on-line spaces in this way, their virtual activities are not completely disconnected from their off-line identities and relationships. Rather, our empirical data shows that children's off-line worlds and on-line worlds are mutually constituted in a number of different ways. In this section, for example, we have shown that: on-line activities maintain and develop both local and distant off-line relationships; that information gathered on-line is incorporated into off-line activities and used to enhance children's identities within their local peer group networks; that children's on-line identities can be direct (re)presentations of their off-line identities and activities; that when children construct alternative identities on-line these are often situated or contingent upon their off-line identities and peer group cultures in that they are constructed to enhance their off-line identities or to compensate for perceived off-line inadequacies; that children's on-line worlds reproduce off-line class and gender relations; and that the limitations of the technology children use and the economic and temporal realities of their everyday lives affect the nature and extent of their on-line activities. In the next section we go on to consider how such uses of ICT shape children's understandings of their place in the world.

A world as small as a hard-drive?: children's sense of place in the digital age

Writing about the social and spatial consequences of communication technologies, McLuhan (1964: 5) suggested that the world is now bound so closely together that the 'global is no more than a village'. His thesis was based on the premises that: oral forms of communication are set to replace the dominance of the printed word; that electronic media are facilitating distant social interactions and that previously remote or self-contained places are becoming more enmeshed into the global system. As such, ICT are being attributed by some not only with increasing our scope of information acquisition and changing our patterns of social interactions, but also with re-scaling our horizons such that we think about, identify and take on responsibilities as global citizens. These children describe how the Internet is altering their sense of place in the world. While they all agree that ICT make them feel as if the world is getting smaller, Sebastian Baker points out that at the same time the opportunities that the Internet offers to connect with distant others also means that it makes Westport, a small rural town, feel like a bigger place.

ANNIE WRIGHT: It [the Internet] makes you feel more involved with . . .
GREGOR OTTERBURN: Yeah, you could sort of go to a school in Australia's webpage and sort of feel you're actually part of that school.
INTERVIEWER: So I mean . . .
SARAH GODDARD: It [the Internet] makes the world smaller.
GREGOR OTTERBURN: As small as a hard drive (Westport).

SEBASTIAN BAKER: Using emails and these chat lines as well, it can make you feel as if the world is a smaller place, because talking to someone in America or as far away as you can get, you know, it makes you feel as if they're sort of in the same place.
INTERVIEWER: Have you felt that personally yourself when you've talked to someone a long way away?
SEBASTIAN BAKER: Well, Mum's got a friend that lives in America that is in touch with us [by email] and it's, it can be the same when you go to an American website or something and you, you can get addresses from it.
INTERVIEWER: Sure.
SEBASTIAN BAKER: Most of them are American but if feels as if it's, America's, coming closer really.
INTERVIEWER: Do you feel that's particularly the case with somewhere like Westport which is kind of cut off and is some way from a big city or railway station or an airport?
SEBASTIAN BAKER: Yes. Most, most of the stuff on the Internet I think is American so it's not, there's no real links to the nearest cities or anything but it can make you feel as if you're [living] in a bigger place (Westport).

The Head and IT teachers in our three schools all embrace this vision of using technology to bring the world closer together. Unlike broadcast media that only provide a glimpse of the wider world, ICT enable children to participate in it by allowing them to represent themselves and the place where they live directly to people in other parts of the world (e.g. through web-pages, email or Internet relay chat). Such on-line exchanges also have the advantage of being cheaper and safer than traditional off-line international exchanges, in which English and European children spend brief periods of time visiting each other's schools and living with each other's families, as well as enabling children to range much further afield.

BILL JONES, Head Teacher: I think we don't recognise, um, properly enough how quickly and rapidly the world has changed, the world is now talked about as a global village and I think that is really true . . . the Internet is just gonna add to all of that. And . . . I actually think it will broaden understanding. I think it will break down barriers between countries. I mean, we're all guilty of it, aren't we, to some level of racism, for example, you know, 'oh, the French', 'oh, the Germans' or oh, you know we all do it, we've all been guilty, we've all said it, let's be honest about it. But I actually think that once you get into this business of people communicating with other countries and finding out 'Hey d'you know, the Germans, the average German kid's just like the average English kid?' And how are you gonna do all that? You can't do it by visits all the time. Something in terms of accessing a communication medium which is visual and verbal and written has got to improve all of that and it's got to understand other people's cultures. So I think, I see it is a force for good (Highfields).

PETER THOMAS, IT teacher: I think what we would want to do is promote global links which alter the way that pupils, young people look at the world and look at people from other countries and perhaps even look at how in future years, because we're moving towards a global . . . there is a globalisation which is being fed by a social globalisation, if you like, that's being fed by the Internet . . . and I think that is gonna be major advancement in terms of social globalisation and how pupils will develop, you know, in the very near future and I think that can be extended out into the community 'cos I don't think we've got to forget that schools are an integral part of the community (Station Road).

JAMES PUNT, IT teacher: You know if we're, if we are to take seriously the concept of producing the citizen of the future, you know, in schools. I think we have to do these things [use ICT]. We've got to break down the barriers between different cultures. [Later he returned to the same theme] I think the more they can understand other cultures in a very non-threatening way, in other words, they don't necessarily have to go there, but they can talk to somebody who's of a similar age and find out how things happen in their, in their particular institution (Westport).

To these ends Westport School has actively participated in the *Interlink* project. The aim of this project – which was founded by the British Council but developed and managed by Copeland Wilson and Associates Ltd, a specialist producer of educational learning materials in New Zealand – was to use ICT to bring children from UK and New Zealand schools together. Westport was one of twelve UK schools (including those from the state and independent sectors) to be partnered with a school from New Zealand. The children were asked to undertake a range of educational activities and to share the results of these with those in their partner institution by using email and webpages. These activities included emailing their counterparts with first impressions (i.e. prior to doing any research into the subject) of what they thought the country and people were like and what a typical week and weekend day would be like for the children who lived there. The children were then asked to respond to their counterparts' first impressions either by agreeing that these provided an accurate reflection of their nation or by challenging suppositions and ill-informed accounts. The link this project established between these two nations is particularly interesting because of their long historical and changing contemporary relationship. New Zealand is a former British colony but the two countries are actively reworking their relationship in a post-colonial world.

The imaginative geographies that were uncovered through this exercise revealed that both UK and New Zealand children's perceptions of each other were a complex mix of stereotypical understandings of difference, as well as assumptions of sameness across boundaries (see Holloway and Valentine 2000c). Perceptions of difference were notably evident in terms of place, with many children imagining the other nation in terms of stereotypical differences. As the extracts below, which are taken from email exchanges illustrate, the Westport children imagine New Zealand to be hot because it is in the south. In turn, the New Zealand children draw on references to a British soap opera *Coronation Street*, which is set in urban Manchester, to characterise Britain as an industrial landscape. Such 'othering' of another nation is, according to Said (1985), a universal part of the construction of an imagined geography.

British children's perceptions of New Zealand
New Zealand is South and close to the equator. Therefore it is hot. It is very near to Australia.

We presume that the climate is warmer and dryer than ours, because you are in the Southern Hemisphere.

New Zealand children's perceptions of the UK
The towns are all made up of funny old buildings and cobblestone streets. People go around in dark clothes talking in funny accents about

the soccer game yesterday or what happened in *Coronation Street* last night.

The houses are old and of an older style than seen in New Zealand. They often have two storeys and no front or back gardens like *Coronation Street*.

Enabling the children from each nation to contest their counterparts' imaginative geographies through email exchanges proved, however, to be an important way of challenging these stereotypical differences. For example, as Lorna Thyme and Matthew Parks explain in the extract below, the New Zealand children strongly contested the Westport children's conflation of New Zealand with their more powerful neighbour, Australia. The on-line activities also challenged Lorna's and Matthew's ideas about what New Zealanders look like. Their first impressions were largely predicated on stereotypes derived from sport and television soap operas (though here Lorna again slips into the trap of culturally assimilating Australia and New Zealand when she refers to the Australian TV show *Neighbours* as if it was set in New Zealand).

LORNA THYME: They didn't like us referring to them as Australia, did they [to Matthew]? They were, like, 'We're not Australia, we're New Zealand'. And I'd always thought the two was one really. I didn't know, I mean New Zealand and Australia I'd just always assumed all was Australia. So that was – and they didn't like us calling them Australian.

INTERVIEWER: So that was something you kind of assumed to start with and that made you think differently about that. What about the kids there? What did, what did you expect them to be like . . .?

LORNA THYME: We saw a picture of them, didn't we?

MATTHEW PARKS: Yeah, there was a load of pictures put on them [webpages]. I mean we were expecting them to be, like, 'cos of big rugby, we expected them to be big bruising, you know, surfers, totally the opposite. Generally they were totally different [to their expectations], [they] were just like us here.

LORNA THYME: They were just like us really, weren't they? Just saying you could imagine seeing them, a picture of, like, say, and you wouldn't think they were from Australia or New Zealand if you saw a picture of them and it said they were from Manchester. Just the same really.

[Edit]

LORNA THYME: Our cultures are not that different. I mean, I think I presume they just dress like we do. But in some cultures they have special robes and everything and that's different – not bad or anything – just different. So they were like, you know, they just dress in shorts and T shirts or whatever, so they are to me, 'cos you see them on *Neighbours* [an

Australian TV soap opera] and they're the same, they're not diff- you see them on *Neighbours* and that's how you assume them to be. The same sort of (Westport).

As the last comment from Lorna implies, the children did not just think of their international partners in terms of differences. Understandings of sameness were also evident in the children's imaginative geographies, particularly in relation to the ways the children thought about each other's daily lives. Despite their somewhat different cultural contexts, children from both Britain and New Zealand imagined children from the other nation to have a broadly similar way of life to their own (Holloway and Valentine 2000c) as these email extracts demonstrate:

British children on New Zealand children's daily life
What I think you do on Saturday is go to town and eat out with friends or family and go to the cinema sometimes. What I think you wear is short sleeve tee shirts, shorts and baseball caps because of the hot weather.

New Zealand children on British children's daily life
We think on an average Saturday that you would probably be listening to music, playing sport, going to the movies, shopping or meeting your friends, if you were at home you would most probably be watching television.

This emphasis on sameness rather than difference appears to support Hengst's (1997) argument that children from high status nations might imagine commonalities across boundaries, perhaps in this case because many children assumed a shared ethnicity or whiteness between the two nations. At the same time, however, the danger is that children from advanced nations are defining each other as 'us' against more technologically disadvantaged 'others' (Hengst 1997).

While television is a global phenomenon – in terms of its institutions and reach – with over 750 million TV sets being watched by 2.5 billion people a day in 160 countries (Kellner 1990) – as we argued in Chapter 2 ICT is not yet this global. Hess (1995: 16) comments: 'Cyberspace is an elite space, a playground for the privileged . . . There is a global glass ceiling, and for many in the world a large part of . . . technoculture lies well above it.' Furthermore, while a British Telecom advertisement for the Internet recently claimed that 'geography is history', cyberspace is not as placeless as some commentators would have us believe. Rather, on-line spaces reflect the off-line socio-spatial context through which they are partially constituted. For example, a web-page is placeless in the sense that it is accessible from many different parts of the globe, but the information its words, sounds and pictures contain are likely to articulate the place-routed culture of its author.[1] Likewise, email, chat environments and bulletin boards enable users from around the world to communicate with one another, but their interactions are as likely as a webpage to reflect their place-routed interests, cultures and concerns (Holloway and Valentine 2001b). Given that the Internet is thoroughly Western, or more specifically American in its origins, development and usage, with English its first language (Sardar 1995; Kitchin 1998a, 1998b; Dodge and Kitchin 2001), there is obviously a limit to how far on-line exercises such as the Interlink project might extend children's global horizons and encourage them to question their place in the wider world. James Punt observes:

JAMES PUNT, IT teacher: I fear that all we'll really see is a fairly Western view of, you know, because of the nature, you know, the high tech countries, even Japan is technologically Western.

We found in our study that children's on-line experiences are often, though not always, Americanised because many of their off-line interests are already shaped by American culture. Television shows such as *Star Trek* and *Friends*, film and music stars such as Leonardo DiCaprio and the Back Street Boys, and sports such as basketball and surfing are all popular off-line interests for British children. Not surprisingly, then, they often actively seek out on-line spaces that are shaped by Americanised cultures as some of the quotes used earlier in this chapter imply.

The Americanisation of the on-line spaces used by these children is not simply a matter of choice, however, the numerical domination of US Internet hosts and users is also important (Holloway and Valentine 2001b). Alex Newton, for example, mainly talks to Americans in chatrooms: this is not intentional but rather a product of the number of US citizens that are on-line:

ALEX NEWTON: Well, I tend to go in, like, a few certain rooms and they are like often there, 'cos, I mean, it's free local calls in America, so they're like always on-line, so I just end up talking to them.

The interests and language American users bring with them in turn shape the cyberspaces that they create. Patrick Redwood, for example, would like to talk about football on-line; however, he tend to avoids sports chatrooms because they are overwhelmingly focused on American sports, and it requires effort on his part to discuss football in ways culturally intelligible to Americans. He explains:

PATRICK REDWOOD: I go on general chat, or you can do sports, but the sports tend to be all American and they talk about football and it's American football so you've gotta put soccer (Highfields).

In these ways both the actions and interests of children, and the domination of America in terms of hosts and users, combine to produce much of the on-line space used by these British children as an Americanised place (Holloway and Valentine 2001b).

The importance of American culture in shaping on-line space, as well as children's off-line interests, is explicable given America's position as a world hegemon (Taylor 1999). Although the children we interviewed are experiencing Americanised life on-line at a period when this hegemonic power has gone into partial decline, they clearly still construct modern America as a cultural leader as these quotes demonstrate:

DAVE MATTHEWS, IT teacher: If they know it's [an email] from America then they're giddy (Highfields).

LORNA THYME: America is the biggest place because . . . so much is happening there and everything and you talk to people that are amongst it all every day (Westport).

STEPHANIE PRICE: They've just got different things, they're more up to date aren't they? [She continues later] America is like one up from Britain, isn't it? (Station Road).

The consumption of this culture on-line is not only desirable in its own terms but also because of the way that it can be used in off-line life, further reinforcing our argument in the previous section about the mutual constitution of children's 'real' and 'virtual' worlds. As Todd Garrett points out below, knowledge gained on-line about new films, games, etc. that have been released in America but not yet in Britain can be used as social currency in off-line relationships. There is also the possibility that on-line friendships with American children might be cemented by a visit to the USA to meet face-to-face. As such, as sisters Rachel and Helen Oats point out, they would rather communicate with someone living in California, USA, than Birmingham, UK.

TODD GARRETT: Sort of, you could use them as sort of a way of finding out stuff. Whereas if you're with your normal friends you probably, say you went from that [Internet] to your normal friends, you'd say, 'Oh, do you know what's happening in America?' [tape is unclear] you know some amazing sort of fact or something (Highfields).

INTERVIEWER: What particular area, particular places or that you'd like to sort of have friends?
RACHEL OATS: America.
HELEN OATS: America, yeah.

INTERVIEWER: Why's that?

RACHEL OATS: So we can go and visit them [laughs].

HELEN OATS: Yeah, you like to talk to them and one night on the Net you say, 'Oh can I just come and visit you?'

RACHEL OATS: Say, 'Yeah, come over any time'. Show up on the doorstep. But in hot places.

INTERVIEWER: [laughs] Yeah.

HELEN OATS: Yeah. Somewhere really good . . . California?

[Edit]

HELEN OATS: Yeah, it's not really worth talking to someone who lives in Birmingham . . . (Highfields).

Most children's response to the American culture of the Internet echo those found by Bryman (1999) in his study of visitors to Disney theme parks. While some of the visitors he interviewed were aware of the processes of Americanisation on-going in these amusement sites, most opted for a ludic reading of these and chose to embrace them as part of the Disney experience. Similarly, in our study, most children are clearly aware that much on-line space is Americanised (Holloway and Valentine 2001b). Indeed, access to this Americanised culture, which they actively seek out and desire to consume, is what contributes to making the Internet 'cool' in their eyes (see also Chapter 3). One child for example, Charles Stevenson, is so enamoured with Americanised culture that he actively promotes this on-line. He has produced his own webpage about the American cartoon characters *The Simpsons* from material that is available to him on- and off-line. Though his site does not attract many visitors, his practices raise interesting questions about the nature of Americanisation of on-line space. In particular, they point to the fact that children are not simple passive dupes of Americanisation but may be both complicit with, and active in, the (re)circulation of 'American' culture. In so doing, they also raise questions about the degree to which American culture is exclusively American (cf. Cresswell and Hoskin 1999). While *The Simpsons* is undoubtedly a product of American culture, its consumption by British children makes it more than that, as it becomes part of a hybrid American culture in Britain (Taylor 1999).

We do not, however, want to over-emphasise the degree to which the on-line space used by these children is Americanised. Doel (1999) makes clear in his discussion of world cinema that it is too easy to generalise and overestimate the power of Americanisation. Rather, he suggests that we need to pay due attention to detail, and include an analysis of the formation and maintenance of dominant processes as well as counter-currents. Todd Garrett, for example, observes somewhat perceptively, that finding information about US culture on the Internet is not the same as knowing about the realities of American children's everyday lives.

TODD GARRETT: You're not told [about everyday USA], they don't interview somebody, say, in how they feel about like a normal, normal average person who goes to school and anything.

INTERVIEWER: Right.

TODD GARRETT: They don't tell you about how they live and how they feel and everything (Highfields).

Likewise, one counter-current evident in the accounts of the children we interviewed is the desire to search for information about, and communicate with, people who share their place-routed culture (Holloway and Valentine 2001c). In terms of information, this can be seen in the activities of children who searched for their local football team, as well as American sport and pop stars on the web. In terms of communication, it is clearly articulated by Francesca Leighton who, despite having a number of on-line friends based both in America and other countries, still values the connections with those in her own nation because they understand the place-routed culture she wants to discuss:

FRANCESCA LEIGHTON: I mean, obviously, I like sort of the people from Britain because there is a British thing that you know, you can't explain to foreigners, there's the whole stiff upper lip and all that kind of stuff . . . I mean, you can't, you can't explain the way Britain's arranged and the classes and all that kind of thing to someone else, so it's good to be able to talk – and also, you know, British culture like TV and music and magazines and books and what have you. You know it's easy if you

Figure 6.1 The Internet provides children with a window on the wider world. Reproduced by kind permission of *The Sheffield Telegraph.*

want to talk about that kind of stuff to someone who's living here rather than try to introduce it all to a foreigner (Highfields).

What Francesca's experience demonstrates is that American culture has not simply saturated British children's on-line and off-line experiences to such a degree that they enjoy the same cultural background as young people in America. Rather, as we argued above, American culture merges with existing British culture to produce a hybrid form (Taylor 1999; Cresswell and Hoskin 1999). As such, there is still a desire among some British children to talk to people from their home regions who can more fully understand their cultural background. While sometimes enjoying America on-line, these children also seek non-Americanised spaces on the Internet which are shaped by their own place-routed cultures.

A second, and less evident, counter-current was the desire of some children to stretch beyond Americanised on-line places and find out about other less familiar cultures. Sarah Gould, for example, does not share most children's fascination with America, arguing that their way of life is already something she understands from the media. Instead, she would like to use on-line space to learn about other places with which she is less familiar. Her desire, shared by David Phelps, to seek out 'other' places and to evaluate the extent to which the experiences of children living there are the same as, or different from, her own everyday life interestingly reflects the aims of the Interlink project described above:

SARAH GOULD: You sort of know how Americans live don't you? . . . It's sort of hamburgers, and guns in pockets and handbags, and big houses. [Edit] I mean, the lifestyle is different but, like, it's not that different from here. I mean, the climate and everything [is], but it's, I don't think like the living, the actual style of living's any different. They go to school and they live in a house and [edit] it is different, but in a way it's like the same if you know what I mean . . . and you're told about how Americans live though, aren't you, on the news and everything . . . and it doesn't tell you anything about Iceland. [Later she goes on to reflect on what she would like to know about Iceland] . . . how they do things I think. And what like the basic stuff, like that we do, like playing football. I mean, do they play football or do they play ice hockey and ice skating all the time and things like that? (Highfields).

DAVID PHELPS: I'd like to talk to people in America and Australia, that sort of thing but same interests.
INTERVIEWER: Why those sorts of countries . . .?
DAVID PHELPS: Because I'd like to visit America and I'm just interested in Australia because it's completely different and it would be nice to find out what it's like over there (Highfields).

The importance of these counter-currents should not, however, be over-estimated. Sarah Gould was still to learn about Iceland, while her knowledge of American TV programmes and pop music was firmly established through both her on-line and off-line activities. Moreover, the desire to consume American culture on-line is an integral feature of most children's ICT usage and thus on-line space is often, though not always, experienced as an American place (Holloway and Valentine 2001b).

In the conclusion to this chapter we draw out, and reflect upon, the different aspects of children's on- and off-line geographies that have been implicit in our discussions in this, and the preceding two sections.

Reflections on children's cyber-geographies

In this chapter we have provided primary empirical evidence to show how young people use, interpret and encounter on-line spaces within the context of their off-line everyday lives. Our material demonstrates that the extensibility afforded by ICT enables children to reconfigure their social relationships and identities in on-line spaces. While some of the children represented ICT to us as a space of separation from their off-line worlds, their 'virtual' activities are not in practice oppositional to, or disconnected from, their off-line identities and relationships. Rather, we have identified a number of different processes through which children's off-line worlds and on-line worlds are mutually constituted: through the way on-line activities maintain and develop both distant and local off-line relationships; through the way information gathered on-line is incorporated into off-line activities; through direct (re)presentations of their off-line identities and activities; through the production of alternative identities which are contingent upon their off-line identities; through the reproduction on-line of off-line class and gender inequalities; through the way everyday material realities limit the scope of their on-line activities. In other words, children's use of ICT is embedded into their everyday lives. Their on-line identities, relationships and spaces are no less 'real' than those encountered 'off-line' (Valentine and Holloway 2002).

As such, on-line connections can implicitly reconfigure children's off-line geographies. By enabling children to extend themselves beyond the bounds of their locality and the limitations of their own lack of personal mobility, ICT allow children to glean knowledge from, and about, other parts of the world and to meet distant 'others'. The information and ideas gathered in this way can then be incorporated into their off-line peer group networks and relationships thus contributing to the production of globalized local cultures (Holloway and Valentine 2000b).

Adults (both parents and teachers) imagine that by extending their knowledge terrain and horizons beyond the boundaries of the place where they live, children's educational, and implicitly therefore, children's employment opportunities (see also Chapter 2) will be enhanced. Further, they also imagine that by facilitating children's ability to communicate with people in different countries these technologies will also encourage their children to participate in, and take responsibility for, the wider world: in other words, to become global citizens.

In contrast to this adultist, macro and future-orientated vision of ICT, as we also demonstrated in the context of the school in Chapter 3, these technologies actually appear to emerge for children in practice in more mundane ways. Some children are interested in connecting with, and finding out about, the wider world, and there is some evidence that on-line communication can help break down stereotypes and misunderstandings that children hold about other countries (Holloway and Valentine 2000c). However, young people's peer groups still provide a more important frame of reference for their activities than wider concerns, and rather than thinking globally children tend to take their cultural bearings from the USA. As such, contrary to popular representations of cyberspace as a placeless social space, somewhere that is both everywhere and nowhere, the children's on-line and off-line activities suggest that on-line space is often an Americanised place, as it is in part constituted through the off-line place-routed cultures in which it is produced (Holloway and Valentine 2001b).

When ICT is used in different times/places it also constitutes varying forms of 'private' and 'public' space. As some of the quotations used in the second section of this chapter imply, on-line activities can constitute a 'private' space. This is because 'virtual' space can seem like a space of separation and therefore escape from everyday off-line social relations. The anonymity afforded by disembodied interactions can also offer on-line participants some measure of 'privacy' in the confidential sense of the meaning of this word. However, as we pointed out in Chapter 5, children frequently go on-line together, as indeed they often did as part of the Interlink project. They also meet strangers in open forums (spaces for the dissemination of information, ideas and opinions) such as chat rooms. These examples further support our argument in Chapter 5 that using ICT is not necessarily an anti-social activity and can in itself constitute a form of 'public' space.

While the findings of this chapter do not support some of the grander claims made by adults about the ability of ICT to change children's sense of place in the world, they do demonstrate the growing importance of ICT within the local context of children's everyday lives. This significance is captured in the words of one boy, who, when asked how he would feel if he no longer had access to ICT, replied: 'Gutted'.

In the following chapter we draw together the empirical evidence presented in this and the preceding chapters to evaluate some of the theoretical understandings and popular fears of ICT.

Chapter 7

Bringing children and technology together

This book has focused on what happens when children and technology come together in practice. While many popular and academic commentaries on the Information Age have told 'big' dramatic stories about the alleged impact of ICT (either positively or negatively) on our economic, social and political worlds (see Chapter 1 for an overview), this book has looked instead at mundane stories of children's everyday use of technology. The accounts we have uncovered are important because they are at odds with both popular/policy understandings of technology, and academic theories of its use, and as such shed new light on both.

As outlined in Chapter 2, schools are being mobilised by the UK Government (there are obvious parallels in the USA and elsewhere) as key sites for the propagation of the sort of technical skills that it is imagined will be crucial for labour markets of the future. The Government's commitment to deliver this training through schools is underpinned by an aim to provide access to IT for all. It is a strategy that is motivated not only by a need to safeguard the wealth-generating capacities of the nation by maximising the technological literacy of the future workforce, but also by the need to guard against aggravating existing, or opening up new, social divisions. Although, figures for home computer ownership do not map exactly onto 'traditional' patterns of social inequalities (based on class, gender, 'race', etc.), our work in households shows that it is certainly true that these divisions are evident in shaping young people's opportunities to develop ICT skills. As more and more everyday practices, from shopping and banking to voting, are transferred on-line, those who are technologically disenfranchised may find themselves increasingly excluded from these 'normal' activities.

While noble in its rhetorical intention, we have found little evidence that the Government's IT for all policy is working in practice. Our research has identified a highly uneven pattern of ICT provision between schools. This is a product of a number of different factors, most notably, the processes through which resources are allocated. This occurs at a local level. Some local authorities place more importance on ICT than others. Likewise, individual schools also respond differently to the difficult choices that they have to make about the amount of their budgets to invest in hardware and software compared to other priorities, such as staff numbers or the maintenance and improvement of the infrastructure. Although a significant amount of additional resources are made available through various technology initiatives, schools must bid for these against each other. This is a process that inevitably creates winners and losers. Finally, the success of particular schools' IT strategies depends upon the motivation, skills and commitment of the key individuals (most notably the IT teacher) who must put them into practice.

Yet, access to ICT in the classroom is not just a case of the large-scale allocation and distribution of resources, it is also about usage policies. Different schools' management philosophies encourage or discourage different types of use according to their own interpretations of central Government policy and their vision of the role of ICT in the life of the school and the community in which it is located. These differences are also shaped by informal teacher practices.

Finally, even schools' differential access policies do not completely account for how ICT is used in practice by children. Notably, the Government's IT for all policy fails to take account of the fact that some children will not take up the opportunities that they are offered to develop their technical skills. Chapters 3 and 5 touch upon the technophobia that is evident among some children and some adults. In other words, while computer hardware and software are obviously essential in developing children's computer literacy, so too is the social context in which the technology is used. As Chapter 3 clearly demonstrates, children's technophobias rarely represent a fear of the machines *per se* but, rather, fears about their performance in the classroom and how the technology might transform their social identities and relationships in the context of their highly gendered and heterosexed peer group cultures. The 'communities of practice' that have emerged in two of our case-study schools work to marginalise girls' use of computers, though this is being (inadvertently) challenged in the third school through a focus on the communicative aspects of ICT. In other words, social exclusion is not just a product of macro-scale forces, it is also an everyday practice.

Here our focus on children's diverse peer group cultures demonstrates that in order to encourage young people to use ICT, rather than to resist it, adults need to promote these technologies in ways that relate to the social context of children's everyday lives. Notably, the emphases that adults place on the educational and future employment uses of ICT contribute to the technology emerging as a 'boring' tool that has little relevance to children's everyday off-line lives. Instead it emerges as the preserve of 'boffins' and 'geeks'. In contrast, by encouraging children to use email and the Internet – on-line activities that children understand as connected to their off-line lives and activities – adults can contribute to helping ICT emerge as a 'cool' tool in more children's eyes. In sum, our study of children's use of ICT in schools suggests that policy-makers at the national level need to take into account: different schools' visions of the role of technology in education; teachers' classroom practices and pupil cultures; as well as the provision of hardware and software if they are serious about advancing ICT skills in a way that promotes social inclusion.

Chapters 4 and 5 focused on the site of the home. It is apparent that both parents and children regard a home PC as an educational asset, and moreover, that computers are also highly valued as a leisure/entertainment tool by many children. The purchase of a home computer does not, however, have any inevitable impact on household relations. Rather, computers are domesticated in different ways depending on: parenting styles, parents' and children's differential interpretations of what the machine is for, the time–spaces within which the home PC is located and used, and so on. As such the home PC emerges as a different tool in different domestic 'communities of practice'.

A key point of interest is that traditional adult–child relations appear to be reversed in many households because children are more technologically competent than their parents. They perform this competency in a variety of different ways, for example, teasing parents, or training them with the skills that they need to improve their position in the labour market. Despite many children's technological competencies, some parents fear that their children will be put at risk of 'virtual' dangers through their use of ICT because they do not consider their children to have a level of emotional competence to match their technical skills. This is something commonly disputed by children who regard themselves as able to manage their own lifeworlds, often drawing on peer rather than family relations for support. Other parents however, reject moral panics about children's on-line activities, regarding the PC as a protective tool because it keeps children indoors and therefore out of both 'danger' (Apollonian child) and 'trouble' (Dionysian child) in public space. Only a minority of parents, but the majority of children, recognise that the 'real' and the 'virtual' are mutually constituted rather than oppositional spaces, and consequently regard on-line and off-line dangers as related rather than oppositional issues.

Finally, our research demonstrates that other popular fears about children's use of computers in general, and the Internet in particular, are also unfounded. Children are not spending excessive amounts of time indoors in front of the computer screen instead of playing outdoors, and ICT use does not encourage social isolation or the breakdown of family relations and friendships. Rather, young people appear to use technology in balanced and sophisticated ways to develop and enhance both on- and off-line social relationships which can open their minds to a wider, if Americanised, world.

It is important that we do not let unfounded fears dominate contemporary debates because they deflect attention from more real concerns. Of greater importance is the need to challenge the new social exclusions currently being established through the uneven provision of, and access to, PCs that we outline above.

What does this all mean in practice?

The findings summarised here clearly challenge the technologically determinist framework within which much Government thinking and policy-making is constituted. Our findings show that ICT do not have any inevitable, or fixed outcomes – either positive or negative ones – rather, they emerge in practice as different tools for different 'communities of practice'.

Popular speculations about the potential negative impacts of ICT (addictive, dangerous, isolating, home-centred), also commonly fall into the trap of assuming that children are less knowledgeable, competent and able to manage their own lifeworlds than adults. Yet, as we have shown throughout this book, children are competent social actors in their own right. They are no more, or less, capable than adults at: managing their time and activities in a sensible and balanced way; identifying potential dangers and taking action to avoid them; and using their skills in ways to enhance their off-line social identities and relationships at home, school and in the local community. While some children may occasionally behave irresponsibly, or make misjudgements, the same, as the children themselves point out, is also the case for many adults. Indeed, children have shown themselves to be capable of using their ICT skills to re-negotiate the boundaries of childhood and adulthood at home and school, while some parents have shown themselves to be ill-informed in their attitudes to, and use of, Internet-connected PCs.

Most significantly, however, teachers and parents are oblivious to the extent to which their attitudes to ICT are adultist. Adults have different temporal and spatial horizons from children. For adults the home PC is not only a 'knowledge machine', that Morley (1992: 214) has likened to a set of encyclopedias, but it is also an object that symbolises the future. Adults stress to children the importance of using this technology in a constructive and productive way in order to maximise their potentials (i.e. the accent is on using educational software and on not 'wasting time' playing computer games or surfing the Net for pleasure). Their outlook is also global, focusing on the possibilities ICT offer children to access information from a wider terrain and to understand their place in the world, rather than being locally focused on children's peer cultures.

In contrast, children's horizons are oriented more towards the present than the future, and local interpretations of their activities on the WWW provide a more important frame of reference than notions of their global rights and responsibilities. They are more concerned about the way computers (re)produce their social identities at school, and the way that these are read by their peers, than they are about their future employment prospects. Most children prefer to use ICT as a social and leisure tool, rather than as an educational tool, and to take their cultural bearings from the USA. In the process, their on-line and off-line activities are used to mutually inform and constitute each other. Contrary to popular representations of cyberspace as a placeless social space, children's on-line activities and spaces are constituted through the off-line place-routed cultures in which they are located. As we observe above, because Governments, schools and parents present ICT to children through an adult lens, they can therefore unwittingly discourage rather than stimulate their use.

What this all adds up to is the need for adults to listen to children's voices and to incorporate these into policy frameworks from the national scale down to the local environs of the classroom.

What does this mean in theory?

This book highlights the need for academics studying children, notably within the fields of the social studies of childhood and children's geographies, to recognise the importance not only of relations between children and adults, and between different individuals/groups of children, but also their relations with the objects that surround them.

Children's identities, most notably here in terms of gender and the extent to which young people are defined as 'adult' or 'child', are negotiated, accepted, and (re)produced as part of the organisation, materialisation and use of ICT. It is a process in which both social and technical elements are simultaneously brought into being in a complex and continuous way, such that each is transforming of, and transformed by, the other (Ormrod 1994). This is evident in Chapter 3, where we show how the PC can contribute to the definition of some children as 'geeks' or 'nerds' and therefore to their social exclusion from peer group relations. At the same time, the way that the Internet-connected PC emerges differently in our three case-study schools demonstrates the way that humans can also change the properties attributed to, and meanings of, the computer (e.g from work tool to leisure tool). In Chapter Four, our empirical material illustrates the ways that children can use their technological competence to help them re-negotiate understandings of their 'adultness' in the eyes of their parents, and the way that the PC could also define the parenting roles of particular mothers and fathers. Again, however, the way that the PC emerges differently in these different domestic communities of practice can once again define whether it is an educational tool, a leisure tool and so on. In Chapter 5 the same process of mutual con-stitution is also evident in relation to the social and the meanings of time–spaces. Here, the PC can play different roles either binding household members together, or fragmenting them into different domestic time–spaces. The way that the PC is domesticated within the time–spaces of the home by different families can influence, for example, whether it is read as a 'private', individualised tool or a 'public', shared tool. Without the PC, social relations and time–spaces in both our case-study schools and homes might look very different. In other words, the tools, people and the time–spaces they inhabit co-develop in ways that cannot be read off from presumed states of the tools, the people or the contexts individually.

The mention of time–space also bring us to the question of the different spatialities that are evident in children's use of ICT. First, throughout this book we have built upon existing interests in the ways in which children's identities and lives are made and (re)made through the sites of everyday life. In particular, we argue that schools and homes need to be thought of not as bounded spaces, but as porous ones produced through their webs of connections with wider societies which inform socio-spatial practices within those spaces.

Second, we have also demonstrated how ideas about childhood inform our understanding of particular spaces. For example, showing how the idea that children's place is in the home, and that they are either at risk, or need to be considered risky, within public space is dependent upon ideas of children as 'angels', or less often as 'devils'. These spatial discourses are important because they inform socio-spatial practices in these sites. These socio-spatial practices then reinforce, or occasionally challenge, our understandings of childhood. The material and ideological consequences of this dialectical relation between our spatialised ideas of childhood and the socio-spatial practices surrounding childhood warrant further academic attention.

Third, in Chapter 6 we employ what Massey (1994) has referred to as a 'progressive sense of place', in which global and local are understood to be embedded within one another, rather than as dichotomous categories, in order to show how children's on-line cultures are both global in their reach and local in their interpretation. This approach provides an implicit critique of work within the social studies of childhood that has tended to separate out the 'global' from the 'local' (see James *et al.* 1998) for a summary of these dichotomous positions). In doing so we illustrate the ways that thinking spatially in these terms might produce more fully contextualised studies of childhood.

Although, here, we have focused on these three spatial dimensions we do not want to suggest that these are distinct and different ways in which we might think about the spatiality of childhood. Rather, we are suggesting that all three of these takes on spatiality are part of inter-related processes (Holloway and Valentine 2000b). The ICT use among the children we studied was at once shaped by global/local processes, experienced within particular sites, which were themselves shaped by our understanding of childhood. As Massey (1998: 124–5) argues:

> the social relations which constitute space are not organised into scales so much as into *constellations of temporary coherences* . . . set within a social space which is the product of relations and interconnections from the very local to the intercontinental.

It is these interconnections that we think could be fruitfully explored in an interdisciplinary approach to the new social studies of childhood that takes spatiality seriously.

In Chapter 1 we pointed out the tendency of research within social studies of technology and cyber-geographies to focus on the theorisation of technology to the detriment of empirical understandings of how ICT are used in practice. In particular, we observed the way that where empirical evidence is presented, it is often taken from studies of cyber-enthusiasts, and as such has focused on extreme users and utopian visions of virtual life. We have addressed this bias here through our interest in children's use of ICT in everyday life. By focusing on the routine, mundane and the banal we have provided detailed empirical evidence that clearly demonstrates the complex mutual constitution of children's on-line and off-line lives. The different 'communities of practice' that we identify and the diverse ways that ICT emerge for the schools, households and children in our study also further bolster critiques of technological determinism. This remains stubbornly evident within the social sciences despite the sophistication and repetition of the challenges to it. Likewise, our findings also dismiss popular commentaries on children's use of cyberspace (as outlined above) by providing clear-cut evidence for children's actual everyday practices that refute the grand claims of both 'boosters' and 'debunkers'.

Finally, in highlighting children's agency, in terms of: their ability to resist adults' control at school, at home and on-line; to negotiate understandings of their own and adults' competence; their potential to make strategic alliances with adults to avoid domination by other children; and in their ability to shape the meanings of technology and domestic time–spaces, we have advanced the study of children as social actors. We hope not only to reinforce this approach within sub-disciplinary areas where the focus is already on children (such as within the social studies of childhood and children's geographies) but also to promote it within the social studies of technology, and more generally within the social sciences.

After all, as we have demonstrated throughout this book – to paraphrase Bruce (1997) – understanding children's activities *in situ*, more or less mediated by computers, provides a clearer understanding of the meanings of the activities, the computers and the context, than that provided through a focus on the technological features alone.

Notes

1 Cyberworlds: children in the Information Age

1 This was produced in 1995 when the the Party was still in opposition.
2 The names of the places, schools and the informants have been changed in an effort to protect individuals' anonymity and confidentiality.
3 The interviews were carried out by Gill Valentine, Sarah Holloway and Nick Bingham (who was employed on the project as a research assistant).

2 The digital divide?: Children, ICT and social exclusion

1 According to the Family Expenditure Survey conducted between October–December 2000, approximately 8.6 million UK households had access to the Internet at home. This figure represented a four-fold increase on the figure for the Family Expenditure Survey of 1998. This survey, published by the Office for National Statistics (ONS), involves interviewing a nationally representative sample of households. About 7000 provided information for the 1999–2000 survey (URL 5).
2 This is a multi-purpose questionnaire survey covering a variety of topics which is carried out eight times per year. It has been developed by the Office of National Statistics (ONS) for use by government departments, public bodies, charities and academics (URL 5).
3 This difference is significant at the $p = 0.001$ level.
4 Published in 1996.

3 Peer pressure: ICT in the classroom

1 In households where parents are in professional or managerial employment (classes I and II), 87 per cent of boys had access to a home PC compared with 86 per cent of girls. In households where parents were in skilled non-manual or all grades of manual work (classes IIIN, IIIM, IV and V), the gender differences are larger (51 per cent of boys have access, cf. 44 per cent of girls) but not statistically significant at the $p = 0.05$ level.

4 On-line dangers: questions of competence and risk

1 Although it later published a partial retraction after concerns were raised about the methodology, ethics and even the true authorship of the report (http://TFRN.pgh.pa.us/guest/mrtext.html) on which the article was based (see

Cate 1996 and McMurdo 1997) for a detailed discussion of the report and its aftermath).

5 Life around the screen: the place of ICT in the 'family' home

1 In a small number of households the PC was located in the parents' bedroom, either because of a lack of space elsewhere or, in one instance, to protect the machine from heavy-handed use by the young children of visiting relatives.

6 Cybergeographies: children's on-line worlds

1 We use the term 'placed-routed' here to signify that cultures are not authentically rooted in particular places but are made through the connections of that place to others at a variety of different scales (Massey, 1994).

References

Abiodun, A.A. (1994) '21st century technologies: opportunities or threats for Africa?', *Futures*, 26, 944–63.

Acker, S. (1994) *Gendered Education*. Buckingham, Open University Press.

Ackrich, M. (1997) 'The de-scription of technical objects', in W. Bijker and J. Law, (eds) *Shaping Technology/Building Society*. Cambridge, MA, MIT Press.

Adam, B. (1990) *Time and Social Theory*. Cambridge, Polity Press.

Adam, B. (1994) 'Perceptions of time'. *Companion Encyclopedia of Anthropology*. London, Routledge.

Adam, B. (1995) *Timewatch: The Social Analysis of Time*. Cambridge, Polity Press.

Aitken, S. (1994) *Putting Children in Their Place*. Washington, DC, Association of American Geographers.

Alanen, L. (1990) 'Rethinking socialisation, the family and childhood', *Sociological Studies of Child Development*, 3, 13–28.

Alderson, P. (1995) *Listening to Children: Children, Ethics and Social Research*. Ilford, Barnardos.

Ambert, A. (1986) 'Sociology of sociology: the place of children in North American sociology', in P. Alder and P. Alder (eds) *Sociological Studies of Childhood Development*, vol. 1. Greenwich, CT, JAI Press.

Argyle, K. and Shields, R. (1996) 'Is there a body in the net?', in R. Shields (ed.) *Cultures of Internet: Virtual Spaces, Real Histories, Living Bodies*. London, Sage.

Ariès, P. (1962) *Centuries of Childhood*. New York, Vintage Press.

Baranshamaje, E., Boostrom, E., Brajovic, V., Cader, M., Clement-Jones, R., accessed: Hawkins, R., Knight, P., Schware, R. and Sloan, H. (1995) *Increasing Internet Connectivity in Sub-Saharan Africa: Issues, Options and World Bank Group Role*. Washington, DC, World Bank. http://www.worldbank.org/html/emc/documents/africa0395.html

Barry, B. (1998) *Social Exclusion, Social Isolation and the Distribution of Income*. Centre for Analysis and Social Exclusion discussion paper. Available at: http://www.sticerd.lse.ac.uk/case.html.

Beamish, A. (1996) *Communities On-Line: Community-Based Computer Networks*. accessed: anneb@mit.edu

Beck, U. and Beck-Gernsheim, E. (1995) *The Normal Chaos of Love*. Cambridge,

Polity Press.

Beck-Gernsheim, E. (1996) 'Life as a planning project', in S. Lash, B. Szerszynski and B. Wynne (eds) *Risk, Environment and Modernity: Towards a New Ecology*. London, Sage.

Benedikt, M. (1991) 'Cyberspace: some proposals', in M. Benedikt (ed.) *Cyberspace: First Steps*. London, MIT Press.

Bigum, C. (1997) 'Teachers and computers: in control or being controlled?' *Australian Journal of Education*, 41, 247–61.

Bingham, N. (1996) 'Object-ions: from technological determinism towards geographies of relations', *Environment and Planning D: Society and Space*, 14, 635–57.

Bingham, N., Holloway, S.L. and Valentine, G. (1999) 'Where do you want to go tomorrow? Connecting children and the Internet', *Environment and Planning D: Society and Space*, 17, 655–72.

Bingham, N., Holloway, S. L. and Valentine, G. (2001) 'Bodies in the midst of things: relocating children's use of the Internet', in N. Watson (ed.) *Reformulating Bodies*. London, Macmillan.

Blaut, J.M. (1991) 'Natural mapping', *Transactions of the Institute of British Geographers*, 16, 55–74.

Blaut, J. and Stea, D. (1971) 'Studies of geographic learning', *Annals of the Association of American Geographers*, 61, 387–93.

Brannen, J. and O'Brien, M. (1995) 'Childhood and the sociological gaze: paradigms and paradoxes', *Sociology*, 29, 729–37.

Breitbart, M. (1998) 'Dana's mystical tunnel: young people's designs for survival and change in the city', in T. Skelton and G. Valentine (eds) *Geographies of Youth Cultures*. London, Routledge.

Bromley, H. (1997) 'The social chicken and the technological egg: education, computing and the technology/society divide', *Educational Theory*, 47, 51–65.

Brosnan, M. (1998) *Technophobia: The Psychological Impact of Information Technology*. London, Routledge.

Bruce, B. (1998) 'Literacy technologies: what stance should we take?', *Journal of Literacy Research*, 29, 289–309.

Bruckman. A. (1992) 'Identity workshop: emergent social and psychological phenomena in text-based virtual reality', unpublished manuscript, MIT Media Laboratory Cambridge, MA. Available at: media.mit.edu, pub/MediaMOO/Papers/identity-workshop.

Bryman, A. (1999) 'Global Disney', in D. Slater and P.J. Taylor (eds) *The American Century*. Oxford, Blackwell.

Bryson, M. and de Castell, S. (1994) 'Telling tales out of school: modernist, critical and postmodern "true stories" about educational computing', *Journal of Educational Computing Research*, 10, 199–221.

Buckingham, D. (1998) 'Children of the electronic age?: Digital media and the new generational rhetoric', *European Journal of Communication*, 13, 557–65.

Bunge, W.W. (1973) 'The geography', *Professional Geographer*, 25, 331–7.

Byrne, D. (1999) *Social Exclusion*. Buckingham, Open University Press.

Callon, M. (1987) 'Society in the making: the study of technology as a tool for social analysis', in W. Bikker, P. Hughes and T. Pinch. (eds) *The Social Construction of Technological Systems*. Cambridge, MA, MIT Press.

Callon, M. (1991) 'Techno-economic networks and irreversibility', in J. Law (ed.) *A*

Sociology of Monsters: Essays on Power, Technology and Domination. London, Routledge.

Callon, M. and Latour, B. (1981) 'Unscrewing the big leviathan', in K. Knorr-Cetina and A. Cicourel (eds) *Advances in Social Theory and Methodology: Toward an Integration of Micro and Macro Sociologies.* New York, Routledge.

Callon, M. and Law, J. (1995) 'Agency and the hybrid collectif', *South Atlantic Quarterly*, 94, 481–507.

Campbell, C. (1995) 'The sociology of consumption', in D. Miller (ed.) *Acknowledging Consumption.* London, Routledge.

Cate, F. (1996) 'Cybersex: regulating sexually explicit expression on the Internet', *Behavioural Sciences and the Law*, 14, 145–66.

Chaiklin, S. and Lewis, M. W. (1988) 'Will there be teachers in the classroom of the future? . . . But we don't think about that', *Teachers College Record*, 89, 431–40.

Charles, N. and Kerr, M. (1988) *Women, Food and Families.* Manchester, Manchester University Press.

Christensen, P., James, A. and Jenks, C. (2001) 'Home and movement: children constructing "family time",' in S.L. Holloway and G. Valentine (eds) *Children's Geographies: Playing, Living, Learning.* London, Routledge.

Clark, A. and Millard, E. (1998) *Gender in the Secondary Curriculum: Balancing the Books.* London, Routledge.

Cohen, A. (1967) *Folk Devils and Moral Panics.* London, Paladin.

Collis, B. (1985) 'Psychological implications of sex differences in attitudes towards computers: results of a survey', *International Journal of Women's Studies*, 8, 207–13.

Comber, C., Colley, S., Hargreaves, D.J. and Dorn, L. (1997) 'The effects of age, gender and computer experiences upon computer attitudes', *Educational Research*, 39 123–33.

Connell, R.W. (1987) *Gender and Power: Society, the Person and Sexual Politics.* Cambridge, Polity Press.

Correll, S. (1995) 'The ethnography of an electronic bar: The lesbian café,' *Journal of Contemporary Ethnography*, 24, 270–98.

Corrigan, P. (1979) *Schooling the Smash Street Kids.* London, Macmillan.

Crang, M., Crang, P. and May, J. (eds) (1999) *Virtual Geographies: Bodies, Space and Relations.* London, Routledge.

Cresswell, T. and Hoskin, B. (1999) '"The kind of beat which is currently popular": American popular music in Britain', in D. Slater and P. J. Taylor (eds) *The American Century.* Oxford, Blackwell.

Curtis, P. (1992) 'Mudding: social phenomena in text-based virtual realities', *Intertek*, 3, 26–34.

Dant. T. (1999) *Material Culture in the Social World.* Buckingham, Open University Press.

Davidson, G. V. and Ritchie, S. D. (1994) 'Attitudes toward integrating computers into the classroom: what parents, teachers and students report', *Journal of Computing in Childhood Education*, 5, 3–27.

Department of Employment and Education (1998) *Excellence in Schools.* London, HMSO.

Dixon, C. (1997) 'Pete's tool: identity and sex-play in the design and technology classroom', *Gender and Education*, 9, 89–104.

Dixon, C. and Allatt, P. (2001) 'The colonisation of domestic space in transforming economies', paper available from the authors: Dept. of Landscape and Politics, University of Teeside.

Dodge, M. and Kitchin, R. (2001) *Atlas of Cyberspace*. Harlow, Addison-Wesley.

Doel, M. (1999) 'Occult Hollywood: unfolding the Americanization of world cinema', in D. Slater and P.J. Taylor, (eds) *The American Century*. Oxford, Blackwell.

Doel, M. and Clarke, D. (1999) 'Virtual worlds: simulation, suppletion, s(ed)uction and simulacra', in M. Crang, P. Crang and J. May (eds) *Virtual Geographies: Bodies, Space and Relations*. London, Routledge.

Doheny-Farina, S. (1996) *The Wired Neighbourhood*. New Haven, CT, Yale University Press.

Durkin, K. and Bryant, C. (1995) 'Log onto sex: some notes on the carnal computer and the erotic cyberspace as an emerging research frontier', *Deviant Behaviour*, 16, 179–200.

Durndell, A. and Thomson, K. (1997) 'Gender and computing: a decade of change?', *Computers in Education*, 28, 1–9.

Dyck, I. (1990) 'Space, time and renegotiating motherhood: an exploration of the domestic workplace', *Environment and Planning D: Society and Space*, 8, 459–83.

Dyrkton, J. (1996) 'Cool runnings: the coming of cybereality in Jamaica', in R. Shields (ed.) *Cultures of Internet: Virtual Spaces, Real Histories and Living Bodies*. London, Sage.

Eckert, P., Goldman, S. and Wenger, E. (1996) *The School as a Community of Engaged Learners*. Institute for Research on Learning Report no. 17.101, Menlo Park, CA.

Elmer-DeWitt, P. (1995) 'Welcome to cyberspace', *Time*, 145, 4–11.

England, K. (1996) (ed.) *Who Will Mind the Baby? Geographies of Childcare and Working Mothers*. London, Routledge.

Epstein, D. (1993) 'Practising heterosexuality', *Curriculum Studies*, 1, 275–86.

Epstein, D. (1997) '"Boyz" own stories: masculinities and sexualities in schools', *Gender and Education*, 9, 105–15.

Evans, M. and Butkus, C. (1997) 'Regulating the emergent: cyberporn and the traditional media', *Media International Australia*, 85, 62–9.

Failla, A. and Bagnara, S. (1992) 'Information Technology, decision time', *Social Science Information*, 31, 669–81.

Fenton, N., (1998) 'Media youth and technological futures', *European Journal of Communication*, 13, 566–71.

Fernback, J. and Thompson, B. (1995) 'Virtual communities: abort, retry, failure?', http://www.well.com/user/hlr/texts/VCcivil.html (accessed: 28 July 1998).

Fielding, S. (2000) 'Walk on the left!: Children's geographies and the primary school', in S.L. Holloway (ed.) *Children's Geographies: Playing, Living, Learning*. London, Routledge.

Fischer, C. (1994) *America Calling: A Social History of the Telephone to 1940*. Berkeley, CA, University of California Press.

Froehling, O. (1999) 'Internauts and guerrilleros: the Zapatista rebellion in Chiapas, Mexico and its extension into cyberspace', in M. Crang, P. Crang and J. May (eds) *Virtual Geographies: Bodies, Space and Relations*. London: Routledge.

Giacquinta, J., Bauer, J. and Levin, J. (1993) *Beyond Technology's Promise: An*

Examination of Children's Educational Computing at Home. Cambridge, Cambridge University Press.

Gillis, J. (1996) 'Making time for family: the invention of family time(s) and the reinvention of family history', *Journal of Family History*, 21, 4–21.

Glucksman, M.A. (1998) 'What a difference a day makes: a theoretical and historical exploration of temporality and gender', *Sociology*, 32, 239–58.

Golding, P. (1990) 'Political communication and citizenship: the media and democracy in an egalitarian social order', in M. Ferguson (ed.) *Public Communication: The New Imperatives*. London, Sage.

Graham, S. and Marvin, S. (1996) *Telecommunications and the City: Electronic Spaces, Urban Places*. London, Routledge.

Green, N. (1997) 'Beyond being digital: representation and virtual corporeality', in D. Holmes (ed.) *Virtual Politics: Identity and Community in Cyberspace*. London, Sage.

Gumpert, G. and Drucker, S.J. (1998) 'The mediated home in the global village', *Communications Research*, 25, 422–38.

Haddon, L. (1992) 'Explaining ICT consumption: the case of the home computer', in R. Silverstone and E. Hirsch (eds) *Consuming Technologies: Media and Information in Domestic Space*. London, Routledge.

Hanson, S. and Pratt, G., (1988) 'Reconceptualising the links between home and work in urban geography', *Economic Geography*, 43, 299–321.

Hapnes, T. (1996) 'Not in their machines: how hackers transform computers into sub-cultural artefacts', in M. Lie and K.H. Sorensen (eds) *Making Technology Our Own?*, Oslo, Scandinavian University Press.

Haraway, D. (1991) *Symians, Cyborgs and Women: The Reinvention of Nature*. London, Free Association Books.

Haraway, D. (1997) *Modest_Witness@Second_Millennium.FemaleMan©_Meets_OnceoMouse™*. London, Routledge.

Hart, R. (1979) *Children's Experience of Place*. New York, Irvington.

Haywood, T. (1998) 'Global networks and the myth of equality: trickle down or trickle away,' in B. Loader (ed.) *Cyberspace Divide: Equality, Agency and Policy in the Information Society*. London, Routledge.

Heim, M. (1991) 'The erotic ontology of cyberspace', in M. Benedikt (ed.) *Cyberspace*. Cambridge, MA, MIT Press.

Heim, M. (1993) *The Metaphysics of Virtual Reality*. New York, Oxford University Press.

Hendrick, H. (1990) 'Constructions and reconstructions of British childhood: an interpretive survey, 1800 to present', in A. Prout and A. James (eds) *Constructing and Reconstructing Childhood*, Basingstoke, Falmer Press.

Hengst, H. (1997) 'Negotiating "us" and "them": children's constructions of collective identity', *Childhood*, 4, 43–62.

Herring, S. (1992) 'Gender and democracy in computer mediated communication', *Electronic Journal of Communication*, 3, 1–17.

Hess, D.J. (1995) *Science and Technology in a Multicultural World: The Cultural Politics of Facts and Artifacts*. New York, Columbia University Press.

Hickling-Hudson, A. (1992) 'Rich schools, poor schools, boys and girls: computer education in Australian secondary schools', *Journal of Education Policy*, 7, 1–21.

Holderness, M. (1993) 'Greetings from the twilight zone', *Times Higher Education*

Supplement, 12 February, 15.(http://www.poptel.org.uk).

Holderness, M. (1998) 'Who are the world's information poor', in B. Loader (ed.) *Cyberspace Divide: Equality, Agency and Policy in the Information Society*. London, Routledge.

Holloway, S.L. (1998) 'Local childcare cultures: moral geographies of mothering and the social organisation of pre-school childcare', *Gender, Place and Culture*, 5, 29–53.

Holloway, S.L. and Valentine, G. (eds) (2000a) 'Children's geographies and the new social studies of childhood', in *Children's Geographies*. London, Routledge.

Holloway, S.L. and Valentine, G. (2000b) 'Spatiality and the new social studies of childhood', *Sociology*, 34, 763–83.

Holloway, S.L. and Valentine, G. (2000c) 'Corked hats and *Coronation Street*: British and New Zealand children's imaginative geographies of the other', *Childhood*, 7, 335–57.

Holloway, S.L. and Valentine, G. (2001a) '"It's only as stupid as you are": children's and adults' negotiation of ICT competence at home and at school', *Social and Cultural Geography*, 2, 25–42.

Holloway, S.L. and Valentine, G. (2001b) 'Placing cyberspace: processes of Americanization in British children's use of the Internet', *Area*, 33, 153–60

Holloway, S.L. and Valentine, G. (2001c) 'Children at home in the wired world: reshaping and rethinking the home in urban geography', *Urban Geography*, 22, 562–83.

Holloway, S.L., Valentine, G. and Bingham, N. (2000) 'Institutionalising technologies: masculinities, femininities and the heterosexual economy of the IT classroom', *Environment and Planning A*, 32, 617–33.

Horning, K.H., Ahrens, D. and Gerhard, A. (1999) 'Do technologies have time? New practices of time and the transformation of communication technologies', *Time and Society*, 8, 293–308.

Hyams, M. (2000) '"Pay attention in class . . . [and] don't get pregnant": a discourse of academic success amongst adolescent Latinas', *Environment and Planning A* 32, 635–54.

INSINC (1997) *The Net Result: Social Inclusion in an Information Society*. London, IBM UK.

IT for All, Dept of Trade and Industry, 151 Buckingham Palace Road, London SW1W 9SS, http://www.itforall.gov.uk (accessed: 18 July 1998).

Jackson, S. and Scott, S. (1999) 'Risk anxiety and the social construction of childhood,' in D. Lupton (ed.) *Risk and Socio-Cultural Theory: New Directions and Perspectives*. Cambridge, Cambridge University Press.

James, A. (1986) 'Learning to belong: the boundaries of adolescence', in A.P. Cohen (ed.) *Symbolising Boundaries: Identity and Diversity in British Cultures*, Manchester, Manchester University Press.

James, A. (1993) *Childhood Identities*. Edinburgh, Edinburgh University Press.

James, A. and Prout, A. (1990) (eds) *Constructing and Reconstructing Childhood: Contemporary Issues in the Sociological Study of Childhood*. Basingstoke, Falmer Press.

James, A. and Prout, A. (1995) 'Hierarchy, boundary and agency: towards a theoretical perspective on childhood', in A. Ambert (ed.) *Sociological Studies of Children*. Greenwich, CT, JAI Press.

James, A., Jenks, C. and Prout, A. (1998) *Theorizing Childhood*. Cambridge, Polity Press.

James, S. (1990) 'Is there a "place" for children in geography?', *Area*, 22, 278–83.

Janelle, D.G. (1969) 'Spatial reorganization: a model and concept', *Annals of the Association of American Geographers* 59, 348–64.

Janelle, D.G. (1973) 'Measuring human extensibility in a shrinking world', *The Journal of Geography*, 72, 8–15.

Jenks, C. (1996) *Childhood*. London, Routledge.

Johnsson-Smaragdi, U., d'Haenens, L., Krotz, F. and Hasebrink, U., (1998) 'Patterns of old and new media use among young people in Flanders, Germany and Sweden', *European Journal of Communication*, 13, 479–501.

Jones, O. (1997) 'Little figures, big shadows: country childhood stories', in P. Cloke, and J. Little (eds) *Contested Countryside Cultures: Otherness, Marginalisation and Rurality*. London, Routledge.

Katz, C. (1991) 'Sow what you know: the struggle for social reproduction in rural Sudan', *Annals of the Association of American Geographers*, 8, 488–514.

Katz, C. (1993) 'Growing girls/closing circles: limits on the spaces of knowing in rural Sudan and US cities', in C. Katz and J. Monk (eds) *Full Circles: Geographies of Women over the Life Course*. London, Routledge.

Katz, J. (1998) 'The rights of kids in the digital age', http://www.wired.com/wired/4.07/features/kids.html (accessed: 29 June 1999).

Katz, J. and Aspden, J. (2000) *IT and the Citizen*. National Science Board, Science and Engineering Indicators, Arlington, National Science Foundation.

Kellner, D. (1990) *Television and the Crisis of Democracy*. Boulder, CO, Westview Press.

Kenway, J. (1996) 'The information superhighway and post-modernity: the social promise and the social price', *Comparative Education* 32, 217–31.

Kitchin, R. (1998a) *Cyberspace: The World in the Wires*. Chichester, John Wiley.

Kitchin, R. (1998b) 'Towards geographies of cyberspace', *Progress in Human Geography*, 22, 385–406.

Knobel, M. and Lankshear, C., (1998) 'Ways with Windows: what different people do with the same equipment', http://www.schools.ash.org.au/litweb/ways.html (accessed: 29 June 1999).

Kopytoff, I. (1986) 'The cultural biography of things: commoditization as process', in A. Appadurai (ed.) *The Social Life of Things: Commodities in Cultural Perspective*. Cambridge, Cambridge University Press.

Kornblum, J. (1998) 'Girls part of children's market, too', http://www.news.com/News/Item/0,4,11275,00.html (accessed: 29 June 1999).

Kroker, A. and Weinstein, M. (1994) *Datatrash: The Theory of Virtual Class*. New York, St. Martin's Press.

Labour Party (1995) *Communicating Britain's Future*. London, HMSO.

Lamb, M. (1998) 'Cybersex: research notes on the characteristics of the visitors to online chat rooms', *Deviant Behaviour: An Interdisciplinary Journal*, 19, 121–35.

Latour, B. (1988) 'Visualisation and reproduction', in G. Fyfe and J. Law (eds) *Picturing Power: Visual Depiction and Social Relations*. Oxford, Basil Blackwell.

Latour, B. (1993) *We Have Never Been Modern*. London, Harvester Wheatsheaf.

Laurel, B. (1990) 'On dramatic interaction', in R. Hattinger, C. Morgan and G. Schopf (eds) *Ars Electronica 1990, volume 2, Virtuelle Welten*. Linz, Veritas-Verlag.

Laurie, N., Dwyer, C., Holloway, S. L. and Smith, F. M. (1999) *Geographies of New Femininities*. Harlow, Addison-Wesley Longman.

Law, J. (1994) *Organising Modernity*. Oxford, Blackwell.

Leccardi, C. (1996) 'Rethinking social time: feminist perspectives', *Time and Society* 5, 169–86.

Lee, H. and Liebenau, J. (2000) 'Time and the Internet at the turn of the millenium', *Time and Society*, 9, 43–56.

Levendosky, C. (1997) 'Internet wowsers under siege', *Australia*, 1 April, 1.

Light, J. (1997) 'From city space to cyberspace', in M. Crang, P. Crang and J. May, (eds) *Virtual Geographies: Bodies, Space and Relations*. London, Routledge.

Little, J. and Austin, P. (1996) 'Women and the rural idyll', *Journal of Rural Studies* 12, 101–11.

Livingstone, S. (1998) 'Mediated childhoods: a comparative approach to young people's changing media environment in Europe', *European Journal of Communication*, 13, 435–56.

Livingstone, S., Gaskell, G. and Bovill, M., (1997) 'Europäische Fernseh-Kinder in veränderten Medienwelten', *Television*, 10, 4–12.

Loader, B. (1998) 'Cyberspace divide: equality, agency and policy in the information society', in B. Loader (ed.) *Cyberspace Divide: Equality, Agency and Policy in the Information Society*. London, Routledge.

Lumby, C. (1997) 'Panic attacks: old fears in a new media era', *Media International Australia*, 85, 40–6.

Lupton, D. (1995) 'the embodied computer/user', in M. Featherstone and R. Burrows (eds) *Cyberspace, Cyberbodies, Cyberpunk: Cultures of Technological Embodiment*. London, Sage.

Lupton, D. (1998) *The Emotional Self*. London, Sage.

McCellan, J. (1994) 'Netsurfers', *The Observer*, 13 February, 10.

McKinsey and Company (1998) *The Future of Information Technology in UK Schools*. London, McKinsey.

McLaughlin, M., Osbourne, K., and Smith, C. (1995) 'Standards of conduct on the Usenet', in S. Jones (ed.) *Cybersociety: Computer-Mediated Communication and Community*. London, Sage.

McLuhan, M. (1964) *Understanding the Media: Extensions of Man*. London, Routledge & Kegan Paul.

McMurdo, G. (1997) 'Cyberporn and communication decency', *Journal of Information Science*, 23, 81–90.

Mac an Ghaill, M. (1996) 'Deconstructing heterosexualities within school arenas', *Curriculum Studies*, 4, 191–209.

Maney, K. (1997) 'New generation gap: computer chasm', http://www.usatoday. com/life/cyber/tech/ctb557.htm (accessed: 5 May 1998).

Marshall, D. (1997) 'Technophobia: video games, computer hacks and cybernetics', *Media International Australia*, 85, 700–78.

Massey, D. (1994) *Space, Place and Gender*. Cambridge, Polity Press.

Massey, D. (1996) 'Politicising space and place', *Scottish Geographical Magazine*, 112, 117–23.

Massey, D. (1998) 'The spatial constructions of youth cultures', in T. Skelton and G. Valentine (eds) *Cool Places: Geographies of Youth Cultures*. London, Routledge.

Massey, D. and Jess, P. (1995) 'Places and cultures in an uneven world', in D. Massey and P. Jess (eds) *A Place in the World? Places, Cultures and Globalization*. Milton Keynes, Open University Press.

Matthews, M.H. (1987) 'Gender, home range and environmental cognition', *Transactions of the Institute of British Geographers*, 12, 32–56.

May, J. and Thrift, N. (2001) (eds) *Timespace: Geographies of Temporality*. London, Routledge.

Mayall, B. (1994) (ed.) *Children's Childhoods: Observed and Experienced*. London, Falmer Press.

Mellman, M., Lazarus, E. and Rivlin, A. (1990) 'Family time, family values', in D. Blankenhorn, S. Bayme and J. Bethke Elshtain (eds) *Rebuilding the Nest: A Commitment to the American Family*. Milwaukee, Family Service America.

Mitchell, D. (1995) *City of Bits*. Cambridge, MA, MIT Press.

Moore, N. (1998) 'Confucius or capitalism? Policies for an information society', in B. Loader (ed.) *Cyberspace Divide: Equality, Agency and Policy in the Information Society*. London, Routledge.

Morgan, D.H.J. (1999) 'Risk and family practices: accounting for change and the fluidity in family life', in E.B. Silva and C. Smart (eds) *The New Family*. London, Sage.

Morley, D. (1992) *Television, Audiences and Cultural Studies*. London, Routledge.

Moss, P. (1997) 'Negotiating spaces in home environments: older women living with arthritis', *Social Science and Medicine*, 45, 23–33.

Motorola (1998) *The British and Technology*. London, Motorola.

Murdock, G. (1989) 'Critical inquiry and audience activity', in B. Deruin, L. Grossberg, B. O'Ceefe and E. Wartella (eds) *Rethinking Communication*, vol. 2. London, Sage.

Murdock, G., Hartman, P. and Gray, P., (1992) 'Contextualising home computing: resources and practices', in R. Silverstone and E. Hirsch (eds) *Consuming Technologies: Media and Information in Domestic Space*. London, Routledge.

Myers, D. (1987) 'Anonymity is part of the magic: individual manipulation of computer-mediated communication contexts', *Qualitative Sociology*, 10, 251–66.

Nelson, L.J. and Cooper, J. (1997) 'Gender differences in children's reactions to success and failure with computers', *Computers in Human Behaviour*, 13, 247–67.

Nippert-Eng, C. (1996) *Home and Work*. Chicago, University of Chicago Press.

Nixon, H. (1998) 'Fun and games are serious business', in J. Sefton-Green (ed.) *Digital Diversions: Youth Culture in the Age of Multi-Media*. London, UCL Press.

O'Connor, J. and Brie, J. (1994) 'The effects of technology infusion on the mathematics and science classroom', *Journal of Computing in Teacher Education*, 10, 15–18

Opie, C. (1998) 'Whose turn next?: Gender issues in information technology', in A. Clark and E. Millard (eds) *Gender in the Secondary Curriculum: Balancing the Books*. London, Routledge.

Ormrod, S. (1994) 'Let's nuke dinner', in C. Cockburn and R. Furst Dilic (eds) *Bringing Home Technology: Gender and Technology in a Changing Europe*. Milton Keynes, Open University Press.

Oswell, D. (1998) 'The place of "childhood" in Internet content regulation: a case study of policy in the UK', *International Journal of Cultural Studies*, 1, 131–51.

Paechter, C.F. (1998) *Educating the Other: Gender, Power and Schooling*. London, Falmer Press.

Papert, S. (1997) *The Connected Family: Bridging the Digital Generation Gap*. Georgia, Longstreet Press.

Parks, M.R. and Floyd, K. (1996) 'Making friends in cyberspace', *Journal of Computer Mediated Communications*, 46, 5–21

Perloff, L. (1983) 'Perceptions of vulnerability to victimisation', *Journal of Social Issues* 39, 41–61.

Philo, C. (1995) 'Journey to asylum – a medical-geographical idea in historical context', *Journal of Historical Geography*, 21, 148–68.

Philo, C. and Parr, H. (2000) 'Institutional geographies: introductory remarks', *Geoforum*, 31, 513–21.

Plant, S. (1993) 'Beyond the screens: film, cyberpunk and cyberfeminism', *Variant*, 14, 12–17.

Plant, S. (1996) 'On the matrix: cyberfeminist simulations', in R. Shields (ed.) *Cultures of Internet: Virtual Spaces, Real Histories, Living Bodies*. London, Sage.

Ploszajska, T. (1994) 'Moral landscapes and manipulated spaces: gender, class, and space in Victorian reformatory schools', *Journal of Historical Geography*, 20, 413–29.

Pringle, R. (1989) *Secretaries Talk: Sexuality, Power and Work*. London, Verso.

Prout, A. and James, A. (1990) 'A new paradigm for the sociology of childhood? Provenance, promise and problems', in A. James and A. Prout (eds) *Constructing and Reconstructing Childhood: Contemporary Issues in the Sociolgical Study of Childhood*. Basingstoke, Falmer Press.

Qvortrup, J., Bardy, M., Sgritta, G. and Wintersberger, H. (eds) (1994) *Childhood Matters: Social Theory, Practice and Politics*. Aldershot, Avebury.

Reinen, I.J. and Plomp, T. (1997) 'Information technology and gender equality: a contradiction in terminis?', *Computers in Education*, 28, 65–78.

Rheingold, H. (1993) *The Virtual Community: Finding Connection in a Computerised World*. London, Secker and Walbury.

Riccobono, J.A. (1986) *Use of Electronic Information Technologies for Non-School Learning in American Households: Report of Findings from the 1985 Home Information Technology Study (HITS)*. Washington, DC, US, Department for Education Center for Statistics.

Riddell, S. (1989) 'Pupils, resistance and gender codes: a study of classroom encounters', *Gender and Education*, 1, 183–97.

Robinson, P., Barth, C. and Kohut, G. (1997) 'Personal computers, mass media and use of time,' *Social Science Computer Review*, 15, 65–82. http://www.nsf.gov/sbe/srs/seind00/c9/c9s5.htm (accessed: 18 April 2001)

Ross, A. (1991) *Strange Weather: Culture, Science and Technology in the Age of Limits*. London, Verso.

Rubins, G. (1992) 'Thinking Sex: notes for a radical theory of the politics of sexuality', in C. Vance (ed.) *Pleasure and Danger: Exploring Female Sexuality*. London, Pandora Press.

Rutherford, J. (ed.) (1990) *Identity: Community, Culture, Difference*. London, Lawrence and Wishart.

Said, E. (1978) *Orientalism: Western Conceptions of the Orient*. Harmondsworth, Penguin.

Sardar, Z. (1995) 'alt.civilisations.faq: cyberspace as the darker side of the West', *Futures*, 27, 777–94.

Schofield, J.W. (1995) *Computers and Classroom Culture*. Cambridge, Cambridge University Press.

Schofield, J.W. (1997) 'Computers and classroom social processes – a review of the literature', *Social Science Computer Review*, 15, 27–39.

Schor, J. (1991) *The Overworked American: The Unexpected Decline of Leisure*. New York, Basic Books.

Schuler, D. (1995) 'Public space in cyberspace'. *Internet World*, 6, 88–95.

Sefton-Green, J. and Buckingham, D. (1998) 'Digital visions: children's creative uses of multi-media technologies', in J. Sefton-Green (ed.) *Digital Diversions: Youth Culture in the Age of Multimedia*. London, UCL Press.

Shashaani, L. (1993) 'Gender-based differences in attitudes towards computers', *Computers in Education*, 20, 169–81.

Shaw, J. (2001) 'Winning territory: changing place to pace', in J. May and N. Thrift (2001) (eds) *Timespace: Geographies of Temporality*. London, Routledge.

Sheehy, G. (1995) *New Passages: Mapping Your Life Across Time*. New York, Random House.

Shilling, C. (1991) 'Social space, gender inequalities and educational differentiation', *British Journal of Sociology of Education*, 12, 23–44.

Sibley, D. (1995) 'Families and domestic routines: constructing the boundaries of childhood', in S. Pile and N. Thrift (eds) *Mapping the Subject: Geographies of Cultural Transformation*. London, Routledge.

Silverstone, R., Hirsch, E. and Morley, D. (1992) 'Information and communication technologies and the moral economy of the household', in R. Silverstone and E. Hirsch (eds) *Consuming Technologies: Media and Information in Domestic Space*. London, Routledge.

Skeggs, B. (1991) 'Challenging masculinity and using sexuality', *British Journal of Sociology of Education*, 12, 127–39.

Skelton, C. (1998) 'Feminism and research into masculinities and schooling', *Gender and Education*, 10, 217–27.

Smith, F.M. and Barker, J. (2000) '"Out of school", in school: a social geography of out of school childcare', in S.L. Holloway and G. Valentine (eds) *Children's Geographies*. London, Routledge.

Smith, K. and Ferri, E. (1996) *Parenting in the 1990s: Family and Parenthood, Policies and Practice*. London, Family Policy Studies Unit.

Smith, M. (1992) 'Voices from the WELL: the logic of virtual commons', http://www.sscnet.ucla.edu/soc/csoc (accessed: 10 January 1997).

Smithers, R. (1999) 'Parents told how to police internet', *The Guardian*, 11 October, 7.

Sobchack, V. (1995) 'Beating the meat/surviving the text, or how to get out of this century alive', in M. Featherstone and R. Burrows (eds) *Cyberspace, Cyberbodies, Cyberpunk: Cultures of Technological Embodiment*. London, Sage.

Solberg, A. (1990) 'Negotiating childhood: changing constructions of age for Norwegian children', in A. James and A. Prout (eds) *Constructing and Reconstructing Childhood: Contemporary Issues in the Sociological Study of Childhood*. Basingstoke, Falmer Press.

Spender, D. (1995) *Nattering on the Net*. London, Spinfax Press.

Spender, D. (1997) 'The position of women in information technology – or who got there first and with what consequences?', *Current Sociology*, 45, 135–47.

Spiegel, L. (1992) *Make Room For TV: Television and the Family Ideal in Postwar America*. Chicago, University of Chicago Press.

Springer, C. (1991) 'The pleasure of the interface', *Screen*, 32, 303–23.

Squire, S. (1996) 'Re-territorialising knowledge(s): electronic spaces and virtual geographies', *Area*, 28, 101–3.

Stacey, J. (1990) *Brave New Families: Stories of Domestic Upheaval in the Late Twentieth Century America*, New York, Basic Books.

Stainton-Rogers, .R. and Stainton-Rogers, W. (1992) *Stories of Childhood: Shifting Agendas of Childhood*, Hemel Hempstead, Harvester Wheatsheaf.

Star, S. (ed.) (1995) *Cultures of Computing*. Oxford, Blackwell.

Star, S.L. and Ruhleder, K. (1996) 'Steps towards an ecology of infrastructure: design and access for large information spaces', *Information Systems Research*, 7, 111–34.

Steedman, C. (1990) *Childhood, Culture and Class in Britain*. London, Virago.

Steele, J. (1998) 'Information and citizenship in Europe', in B. Loader (ed.) *Cyberspace Divide: Equality, Agency and Policy in the Information Society*. London, Routledge.

Steward, B. (2000) 'Changing times: the meaning, measurement and use of time in teleworking', *Time and Society*, 9, 57–74.

Stone, R.A. (1992) 'Will the real body please stand up? Boundary stories about virtual cultures', in M. Benedikt (ed.) *Cyberspace: First Steps*. Cambridge, MA, MIT Press.

Suss, D., Suoninen, A., Garitaonandia, C., Juaristi, P., Koikkalainen, R. and Oleaga, J.A. (2001) 'Media use and the relationships of children and teenagers with their peer groups: a study of Finnish, Spanish and Swiss cases', *European Journal of Communication*, 13, 521–38.

Tang, P. (1998) 'Managing the cyberspace divide: government investment in electronic information services', in B. Loader (ed.) *Cyberspace Divide: Equality, Agency and Policy in the Information Society*. London, Routledge.

Tapscott, D. (1998) *Growing Up Digital: The Rise of the Net Generation*. London, McGraw-Hill.

Taylor, P.J. (1999) 'Locating the American century: a world-systems analysis', in D. Slater and P.J. Taylor (eds) *The American Century*. Oxford, Blackwell.

Thompson, J.B. (1995) *The Media and Modernity: A Social Theory of the Media*. Cambridge, Polity Press.

Thrift, N. (1996) 'New urban eras and old technological fears: reconfiguring the goodwill of electronic things', *Urban Studies*, 33, 1463–93.

Thu Nguyen, D. and Alexander, J. (1996) 'The coming of cyberspacetime and the end of polity', in R. Shields (ed.) *Cultures of Internet: Virtual Spaces, Real Histories, Living Bodies*. London, Sage.

Turkle, S. (1995) *Life on the Screen: Identity in the Age of the Internet*. London, Weidenfeld & Nicolson.

Turkle, S. (1997) 'Constructions and reconstructions of self in virtual reality: playing in the MUDS', in S. Kiesler (ed.) *The Culture of the Internet*. New Jersey, Lawrence Erlbaum Associates.

URL 1: 'IT and the citizen' (National Science Foundation), http://www.nsf.gov/sbe/srs/seind00/c9/c9s5.htm (accessed: 19 April 2001).

URL 2: 'Worldwide Internet population' (CommerceNet), http://www.commerce.net/

research/stats/wwstats.htm (accessed: 19 April 2001).

URL 3: 'NetValue reveals latest European Internet statistics and first ever panel results in Spain' (NetValue), http://www.netvalue.com/corp/presse/cp0016.htm (accessed: 19 April 2001).

URL 4: IT FOR ALL, http://www.itforall.gov.uk/it/survey/3.html (accessed: 28 July 1999).

URL 5: 'Internet Access' (National Statistics) http://.statistics.gov.uk/statbase/product.asp?vlnk=5672 (accessed: 18 April 2001).

URL 6: 'Falling Through the Net: Defining the Digital Divide' (National Technologies Information Administration), http://www.ntia.doc.gov/ntiahome/digitaldivide/ (accessed: 19 April 2001).

URL 7: http://theatlantic.com/issues/97/jul/computer.html (accessed: 29 June 1998).

URL 8: http://www.bbc.co.uk/the_net/5/2/howells.html (accessed: 29 June 1998).

Valentine, G. (1996a) 'Angels and devils: moral landscapes of childhood', *Environment and Planning D: Society and Space*, 14, 581–99.

Valentine, G. (1996b) 'Children should be seen and not heard: the production and transgression of adults' public space', *Urban Geography*, 17, 205–20.

Valentine, G. (1997a) ' "My son's a bit dizzy." "My wife's a bit soft": gender, children and cultures of parenting', *Gender, Place and Culture*, 4, 37–62.

Valentine, G. (1997b) ' "Oh yes I can." "Oh no you can't." Children and parents' understandings of kids' competence to negotiate public space safely', *Antipode*, 29, 65–89.

Valentine, G. (1997c) 'A safe place to grow up? Parenting, perceptions of children's safety and the rural idyll', *Journal of Rural Studies*, 13, 137–48.

Valentine, G. (1999a) 'Eating in: home, consumption and identity', *Sociological Review*, 47, 491–54.

Valentine, G. (1999b) 'Being seen and heard? The ethical complexities of working with children and young people at home and at school', *Ethics, Place and Environment*, 2, 141–55.

Valentine, G. (1999c) ' "Oh please Mum. Oh please dad": negotiating children's spatial boundaries; in L. McKie, S. Bowlby and S. Gregory (eds) *Gender, Power and the Household*. Basingstoke, Macmillan Press.

Valentine, G. (1999d) 'Exploring children and young people's narratives of identity', *Geoforum*, 31, 257–67.

Valentine, G. and Holloway, S.L. (1999) ' "The vision thing": schools and information and communication technology', *Convergence: The Journal of Research into New Media Technologies*, 5, 63–79.

Valentine, G. and Holloway, S.L. (2001a) 'On-line dangers?: Geographies of parents' fears for children's safety in cyberspace', *The Professional Geographer*, 53, 71–83.

Valentine, G. and Holloway, S. L. (2001b) 'Technophobia: parents and children's fears about information and communication technologies and the transformation of culture', in I. Hutchby and J. Moran-Ellis (eds) *Children, Technology and Culture: The Impact of Technologies in Children's Everyday Lives*. London, Routledge.

Valentine, G. and Holloway, S.L. (2001c) 'A window on the wider world: rural children's use of information and communication technologies', *Journal of Rural Studies*, 17, 383–94.

Valentine, G. and Holloway, S.L. (2002) 'Cyberkids? Exploring children's identities and social networks in on-line and off-line Worlds', *Annals of the Association of American Geographers*, 92, 302–19.

Valentine, G. and McKendrick, J. (1997) 'Children's outdoor play: exploring parental concerns about children's safety and the changing nature of childhood', *Geoforum*, 28, 219–35.

Valentine, G. and Skelton, T.L. (2001) 'Finding a place in the world: the use of the Internet by vulnerable young people', paper available from the author: Dept. of Geography, University of Sheffield, Winter Street, Sheffield, S10 2TN, UK.

Valentine, G., Holloway, S.L. and Bingham, N. (2000) 'Transforming cyberspace: children's intervention in the new public sphere', in S.L. Holloway and G. Valentine (eds) *Children's Geographies: Playing, Living, Learning*. Routledge, London.

Valentine, G., Holloway, S.L. and Bingham, N. (2002) 'The digital generation? Children, ICT and the everyday nature of social exclusion', *Antipode*, 34, 296–315.

van der Voort, T. H. A., Beentjes, J. W. J., Bovill, M., Gaskell, G., Koolstra, C. M., Livingstone, S. and Marseille, N., (1998) 'Young people's ownership and uses of new and old forms of media in Britain and the Netherlands', *European Journal of Communication*, 13, 457–77.

Van Gelder, L. (1996) 'The strange case of the electronic lover', in R. Kling (ed.) *Computerization and Controversy: Value Conflicts and Social Changes*. San Diego, Academic Press, pp. 533–46.

Wajcman, J. (1991) *Feminism Confronts Technology*. Cambridge, Polity Press.

Wakeford, N. (1999) 'Gender and the landscapes of computing in an Internet café', in M. Crang, P. Crang and J. May (eds) *Virtual Geographies: Bodies, Space and Relations*. London, Routledge.

Waksler, F.C. (ed.) (1991) *Studying the Social Worlds of Children: Sociological Readings*. London, Falmer Press.

Walker , A. and Walker C (eds) (1997) *Britain Divided: The Growth of Social Exclusion in the 1980s and 1990s*. London, Child Poverty Action Group.

Wark, M. (1994) *Virtual Geography: Living with Global Media Events*. Bloomington, IN, Indiana University Press.

Wellman, B. and Gulia, M. (1996) 'Net surfers don't ride alone: virtual communities as communities', http://www.acm.org/ccp/references/wellman/wellman.html (accessed: 2 March 1999).

Wenger, E. (1998) *Communities of Practice*. Cambridge, Cambridge University Press.

W.G.S.G. (1997) *Feminist Geographies*. Harlow, Longman.

Wilkinson, H. (1995) 'Take care in cyberspace', *The Independent,* 1 December.

Willis, P.E. (1977) *Learning to Labour: How Working Class Kids Get Working Class Jobs*. Farnborough, Hants, Saxon House.

Willson, M. (1997) 'Community in the abstract: a political and ethical dilemma?', in D. Holmes (ed.) *Virtual Politics: Identity and Community in Cyberspace*. London, Sage.

Winston, B. (1995) 'Tyrrel's owl: the limits of the technological imagination in an epoch of hyberbolic discourse', in B. Adams and S. Allan (eds) *Theorising Culture*. London, University College London Press.

Wood, D. and Beck, R. (1990) 'Dos and don'ts: family rules, rooms and their relationships', *Children's Environments Quarterly*, 7, 2–14.

Wynn, E. and Katz, J. (1998) 'Hyperbole over cyberspace: self presentation and social boundaries in Internet home pages and discourse', *The Information Society: an International Journal*, 13, 297–328, http://www.slis.lib.indiana.edu/TIS/hyperbole.html.

Yates, S. (1997) 'Gender, identity and ICT', *Journal of Computer Assisted Learning*, 13, 281–90.

Zeldin, T. (1994) *An Intimate History of Mankind*. New York, HarperCollins.

Index

abuse 2, 13, 21, 56, 75, 82, 89, 138–9
access 1, 6–7, 11, 16–19, 20–41, 42, 44–6, 50, 61–2, 64, 67–8, 70–1, 75–6, 82–4, 88–9, 93, 94–5, 103, 105, 110, 116–18, 121, 124–5, 127, 131, 139, 145, 148, 152–6
actor network theory 13
addiction 18, 99, 108
adulthood 74, 95, 156
Afro-Caribbean 55
Americanisation 19, 22, 146–51, 155
artifactual 12
Asian 50, 58

Black 25
bodies 1, 3, 10–11, 13, 19, 21, 54, 63, 107, 133, 138–9
body 10, 13, 74, 76, 84, 133–4
booster 9, 11, 14–15, 18, 72–4, 76–7, 95, 159

childhood 2–9, 18–19, 48–9, 72–3, 74–7, 94–6, 98, 120, 124, 128, 156–9
children: angels 4, 75–6, 87, 158; Apollonian 4, 6, 18, 87, 155; as biological category 3, 4, 67; biology 57, 67; devils 4, 75, 87, 158; Dionysian 4, 7, 18, 87, 155; neglect of by academics 2, 5, 43; as social actors 3, 5, 7–8, 18, 29, 41–2, 60, 72, 76, 98, 128, 156, 159; voices 6, 8, 102, 157
citizenship 1, 25, 39–40
class 5, 7, 17, 22–7, 29–30, 36, 43–5, 61, 76, 81–2, 103–5, 116, 139–40, 149, 151, 153

communicate 1, 19, 21, 29, 37, 67, 113, 119–20, 127, 130–1, 139, 146–7, 149, 151
communication 1, 10, 12, 19, 24, 26, 30–1, 37, 40, 59, 68, 101, 127, 130–4, 140, 142, 149, 151
communities of practice 14–15, 17–18, 40–2, 69–70, 78, 82, 87, 96–8, 119, 124–5, 154–7, 159
community 1, 7–8, 11, 14, 21, 24, 30, 35–6, 38–41, 118–20, 123–4, 128, 142, 154, 156
competence: adults 159; children's 33, 159; emotional 18, 71, 155; general 8, 9, 16, 72–98; social actors 29; teacher 32; technical 18, 27, 30, 33, 35, 55–6, 59–60, 62, 64, 68–72, 100, 107, 157
computer-mediated communication 44, 133
corruption 2, 82, 94
cyberspace 1, 3, 7, 9–11, 14–15, 19, 22, 24, 74, 76, 87–8, 93–4, 96–7, 120, 127, 133, 139, 145, 151, 157, 159

danger 1, 4, 6–7, 72–98, 105, 115, 126, 145, 155–6
debunker 9–11, 14–15, 18, 72, 74–7, 95–9, 159
domestication 12, 18, 71, 98, 100–3, 108, 125, 155, 157
democracy 1, 21
dichotomy 6, 11, 125, 158
digital divide 11, 20–41
disadvantage 1, 15, 21, 23–5, 28, 35, 61, 64, 128, 145
discipline 4, 7, 75, 90–1, 109

employment 20, 24, 26, 29, 102, 128, 151, 154, 156
Enlightenment 4, 87
escape: body 133, 146; family 109, 120; inequalities 10; local friends 136; off-line social relations 137, 152; surroundings 10
essentialism 4, 18, 57, 59, 72–3, 76–8, 96–7
ethnicity 17, 24, 44, 74, 145

father: fears 27; good father 8; helped by children 79–1; IT literacy 35, 79; IT use 113, 116, 127; parenting role 89–91, 157; purchases 29; respect for children 81; rules 83, 85–6, 90–1; technophobia 64; work 105
femininities 7, 59–70, 138
future 1, 3, 18–19, 21, 25–8, 30, 35, 39, 42, 44–6, 62, 68, 70–3, 76, 77, 81–2, 96–7, 102, 114–5, 142, 151, 153–4, 156

gender 5, 7, 9–10, 17, 53–72, 76, 90, 93, 95, 98, 117, 133, 136, 138–40, 151, 153–4, 157
global 1, 6, 9, 16, 19–23, 26, 39–40, 42, 48, 72, 109, 129–30, 140–2, 145–6, 151, 156, 158

heterosexuality 7, 17, 44, 53–6, 61, 63, 68–70, 93, 138
home: adult–child relations 7, 98, 102, 108, 117, 156; children's ICT use/skill 15, 24, 30, 60–1, 64, 96; English not 1st language 15; environment 16, 96; fear and safety 84–5, 88, 102; feminist geography 7; the home 9, 11, 14, 18, 25, 40, 61, 71–2, 78, 98, 99, 145, 155–6, 158; imagine impact of PC 18, 100, 105; incorporating technology 90, 96; Internet access 23, 115, 139; links to neighbourhood 18, 99, 103, 119–21, 123–5, 158; ownership/access to PC 24–9, 34–5, 38, 44–5, 59, 61, 64, 96, 97, 153; parents use of ICT 89; PC 8, 16, 23, 29, 30, 71, 98–100, 155; place of ICT 99–126; pollution by ICT 82, 87, 94, 104; region 150; rules 8, 88, 92; spatial discourses 8, 94, 98, 158; support for ICT 77, 82,

96, 98; time 104–7, 109, 114; time-spaces 18, 99, 102, 117, 126, 157
homework 28, 38, 88, 102, 105–7, 108, 113, 117, 121, 123, 125
homosexuality 53
identity: children 6, 8–9, 43, 60, 63, 67, 76, 99, 151, 157–8; embodied/disembodied 10, 21, 55, 63, 127, 130–40; gender 7, 44, 50–70, 138, 154, 157; general 1, 5, 8, 14, 33, 43, 48, 63, 74, 77, 107, 115; online/offline 10, 25, 130–40, 151, 156; politics 43–6; sexual 7, 50–70; social 4, 7–8, 43, 67, 71, 76–7, 154, 156

immaturity 3, 38, 54–5, 85, 93, 95, 138
indoors 85, 100, 115, 119–25, 155
individualisation 8
Information Age 1, 7, 18, 20–3, 26, 39, 41, 71, 100, 137–40, 153
isolate 15, 21, 36, 40, 52, 83, 105, 109, 124–5, 127, 136, 155–6

job 25–8, 33–4, 43, 62, 80, 82

local 1, 6–9, 15–16, 18–19, 21, 26, 31–2, 35–6, 39–40, 71, 82, 85, 89, 99, 108, 119–21, 123–7, 129–30, 132, 136–7, 139–40, 146, 149, 151–3, 156–8

masculinities 7, 48, 50–9, 68–9, 93, 138
maturity 69, 76, 81, 83, 93, 95
media 2, 24, 73, 74–5, 82–3, 85, 102, 104, 122, 130, 132, 141, 150
mind-to-mind 84, 133
moral panic 18, 71, 76, 96, 99, 108, 114, 155
mother: good mother 8; fear 27; helped by children 80; lack of IT skill 89; parenting role 90–1, 157; rules 90–1, 117; purchases 103; hostility to IT 107; IT use 112–13

national 6–7, 9, 15–16, 20–4, 26, 29–30, 33, 44–5, 67, 97, 129, 132, 135, 142, 145, 155, 157

neighbourhood 18, 92, 99, 119, 121, 123
net generation 1, 73, 77–82

obsess 2
offspring 8, 18, 27, 73, 83–4, 85
outdoor play 2, 120

parenting cultures 8
patriarchal 48
peers 2, 19, 37, 42–71, 82, 93, 94–5, 97–8, 99, 109, 124, 127–9, 134, 137, 140, 151, 154–7
place 6, 12, 19, 30, 38, 40, 49, 70, 94, 97, 102, 108, 110, 119, 127–30, 134, 140–52, 156–8, 161
placeless 19, 127, 136, 145, 151, 157
policy: general 18, 42, 44, 45, 67, 71–3, 75, 95–7, 153; government 19, 39–40, 42, 80, 153–7; makers 67, 155; school 17, 37, 41–3, 46–9
popular concerns 2, 18, 99

race 7, 43, 48, 58, 76, 153
real 9–12, 82, 84, 94, 109, 120–1, 137, 139, 147, 151, 155
responsibility: children 3, 83; individual citizens 1, 21, 25, 141, 151, 156; IT users 10, 66; parents 8, 90, 96; school 34–5; teachers 38
revolution 1, 17, 124
rights 1, 21, 25, 39–40, 156
risk 1, 2, 7–9, 24–5, 72, 75–7, 823, 86, 93–4, 95, 97, 115, 155, 158
role reversal 78–82
rules: familial 8; parental 83, 88–92; social 91, 98
rural 15, 22, 24–5, 36, 127–8, 141

scale 1, 2, 6, 16, 20–1, 23, 39, 154, 157–8
school 5, 7, 9, 11, 14–20, 24, 28–72, 74, 80, 82, 845, 90, 93–100, 101, 104–8, 109, 112, 115–17, 120, 123–4, 127–9, 131, 133, 139, 141–3, 149–51, 153–9
schoolwork 16, 28–9, 34, 37, 49, 50, 51–3, 55–6, 61, 64–6, 105–8, 117, 127
screen 54, 73, 79, 85, 87, 99, 107, 113, 125, 127, 155
skill 1, 8, 16, 24–8, 30, 34–6, 38, 40,

42, 45–6, 49, 51–2, 60–2, 64–5, 68, 70, 73, 76–8, 80–2, 85–7, 96–8, 107, 153–6
social exclusion 17–18, 20–41, 67–71, 154–5, 157
space: classroom 43, 48–50, 54, 57; fantasy 10; general 6, 8–9, 11, 18, 45, 57, 59, 62, 70, 74, 75, 91, 94, 97–8, 128, 136, 157; home 7–8, 18, 27, 78, 87, 95, 97, 99, 101–2, 102–26, 157–9; institutional 7, 43, 48, 67, 69; off-line 9, 11, 14, 19, 63, 82, 85, 93–8, 126, 130, 133–4, 151; on-line 2, 10–12, 14, 19, 63, 82, 85, 93–4, 96–8, 124, 127–52; outdoor 10, 18, 71, 85, 87–8, 96, 99–100, 119–28; public 2, 6–7, 10, 18, 71, 85, 87–8, 91, 96, 99–100, 115, 119–20, 152, 155, 158; school 47–8, 61, 72, 97, 158; social 19, 127, 151, 157, 158; time–space 8, 16, 18, 47–8, 61, 67, 71, 88, 99, 102–19, 125–6, 130, 155, 157–9; virtual 9–11, 76, 94, 134–5, 139, 152
spatial discourses 8, 158
speed 10, 21, 65
stranger 2, 74–5, 82, 84, 93, 152
street 6, 85–6, 115, 120, 143

technological determinism 12, 14, 95–6, 159
technological literacy 2, 3, 68, 153
telecommunications 21–3
threat: adult control and status 7, 8, 33; childhood 2–4, 7, 63–4, 71, 75, 83, 96; cities 11; general 57; home and family 83, 104, 107–9, 126; people 12; 'real' world 10, 94; relationships 136; values 22

unemployment 15, 32
urban 11, 15, 22, 91, 127–8, 141
utopia 3, 139, 159

virtual: activities 87, 137, 140, 151; class 25; communities 119, 124; dangers 155; environment 3; friends 19, 133, 135–6; geography 11; life 3, 75, 159; nightmare 74; relationships 10; sex 135; space 9–10, 76, 94, 134, 139, 152; the virtual 9–12, 137, 155; worlds 11, 139, 147

white 15, 22, 25, 50–1, 58, 139, 145
work 1, 20, 2–5, 27, 59, 78–82,
    89–91, 103–7, 108–10, 112, 114,
    117, 118, 131
workforce 40, 42–3, 153
workplace 12